MAYFIELD GIRL
A WOMAN'S SEARCH FOR A MOTHER'S LOVE

Iris Wheatley and Jean Sharp (right) shopping in Inverell, early 1950s.

MAYFIELD GIRL

A WOMAN'S SEARCH FOR A MOTHER'S LOVE

A MEMOIR OF NEWCASTLE AND COUNTRY NSW

JEAN SHARP
With additional material and edited by Stephen Wallace

HUNTER PRESS

First published 2019 by:
Hunter Press
PO Box 671
Hamilton NSW 2303
Email: publisher@hunterpress.com.au
Web: www.hunterpress.com.au (online shop: www.hunterpress.bigcartel.com)

© Stephen Wallace 2019

ISBN (print): 978-0-9945863-3-9
ISBN (ebook): 978-0-9945863-4-6

 A catalogue record for this book is available from the National Library of Australia

Cover photograph of Jean Sharp (left) and friend Gwen Brown at Moree, 1949.
Photographs are property of Stephen Wallace, unless otherwise credited.
Book design: Christine Bruderlin

Copyright and permissions
The editors and publisher gratefully acknowledge the permission granted to reproduce the copyright material in this book. Every effort has been made to trace copyright holders and to obtain their permission for the use of copyright material. The publisher apologises for any errors or omissions and would be grateful if notified of any corrections that should be incorporated in future reprints or editions of this book.

Contents

Editor's note vii
Prologue 1
1 · Crybaby 3
2 · Horses, buggies and steam trains 6
3 · Please give me a penny, sir 8
4 · A King George V childhood 12
5 · No more flowers 18
6 · More tears 25
7 · "How is the little boy?" 29
8 · No time for kisses and cuddles 30
9 · Boots, beards and braces 38
10 · Messages to the terminus 42
11 · Roast lamb, jam, baths and Methodist Sundays 48
12 · My father the bushie 51
13 · Simple pleasures 57
14 · An intrepid ten-year-old 58
15 · The Pommy invasion 62
16 · Cynthia, school and me 65
17 · The big lie 68
18 · Wilhelmina, the lost love 74
19 · Whatever happened to Cynthia? 81
20 · Tom, my starstruck brother 87
21 · The prettiest girl in Mayfield 90
22 · "I suppose you must all love babies?" 100
23 · Bedbugs and breech births 108
24 · First love 112
25 · No one left to be proud of me 117
26 · A second-class railway ticket to a new life 121
27 · Who's in charge here, you, me or Doctor Wheatley? 125

28 · Getting to be part of the "in" crowd 131
29 · The doctor, his wife, the chemist, the dentist, the
     hospital sister and me 137
30 · Married life in the "place of wild honey" 143
31 · "Tall, healthy and with their own teeth . . . " 150
32 · Messerschmitts, Spitfires, Dunkirk and childbirth 153
33 · The terror of the Japanese.....................................159
34 · A barbershop, two rooms and a bathtub........................162
35 · Babies and the Battle of the Coral Sea.........................166
36 · The end of the War and soldier settlers.........................173
37 · After the surrender — civil war at home 175
38 · Strains in the family...181
39 · Forbidden romance 185
40 · Living and partly living — a hard-won partial happiness 189
41 · Movement, turmoil and misery................................199
42 · The tarot reader 213
43 · Return to Bull Street 218
44 · So..222
Epilogue 225
Index...227

Editor's note

This autobiography was created from the handwritten notes of my mother, Jean Wallace (née Sharp). They were written in dribs and drabs over a period of twenty years, between 1974 and 1994. She started making the notes at her home in Collaroy in Sydney, at my suggestion, to understand better her difficult childhood in Newcastle. I said, "It might make a good story for the family too" and I promised I'd put it all together later. She asked, "Where do I start?" I said, "What you first remember", having no real idea what she was going to write.

There was no order in the way she wrote, just when the mood took her. She wrote on old pads, slips of paper, the back of envelopes, in exercise books, on mini pads and loose pages and gave them to me to put away. She wrote very honestly, knowing some things weren't complimentary to her. She kept writing because I kept asking for more.

It's taken some years to put her whole story together. I've added to her writing from my own knowledge and from that of my brothers and sister, cousins Cheryl Small (her sister Winnie's daughter), Carol Ray (her brother Bill's daughter) and Dale Worth (her brother Tom's daughter). I've left in as much of what she wrote as possible, including some language of the day that may jar with modern readers. This is done in the interests of authenticity — my mother loved the truth and lived by what truth she could.

I've organised her notes chronologically, as much as possible, shaped a narrative structure, created bridging texts and added photographs from family members. I do not pretend to know the whole truth about my mother (or anyone else) just what can be gleaned from what she wrote or said to my siblings and relations, and to me.

I am grateful to my wife Fiona, without whose patience, assistance and intelligence this memoir would not have been possible. Thanks go also to cousins Carol, Cheryl and Dale for supplying family photographs, to my siblings Dianne, Geoff and Bill (Wallace) for supplying family stories and photos, to Richard Lever for his copyediting and to Christine Bruderlin of Hunter Press for her tireless work on the manuscript. Also, posthumous thanks to my mother's sister, Winnie, and her younger brother, Gilbert, who twenty years ago talked to me about Jean and what they remembered.

Stephen Wallace

Prologue

One hot day in 1921, when I was eleven years old, my mother took my siblings and me to Newcastle Beach. As we played in the sand, I overheard my mother talking with an old friend that she had bumped into. She said something that shocked me. In the tram on the way home, I asked her bluntly why she had lied to her friend about me. She didn't answer but remained silent, as was her way. When we arrived home, I ran to one of our neighbours to ask her about what I had heard. What she told me was to haunt me for the rest of my life.

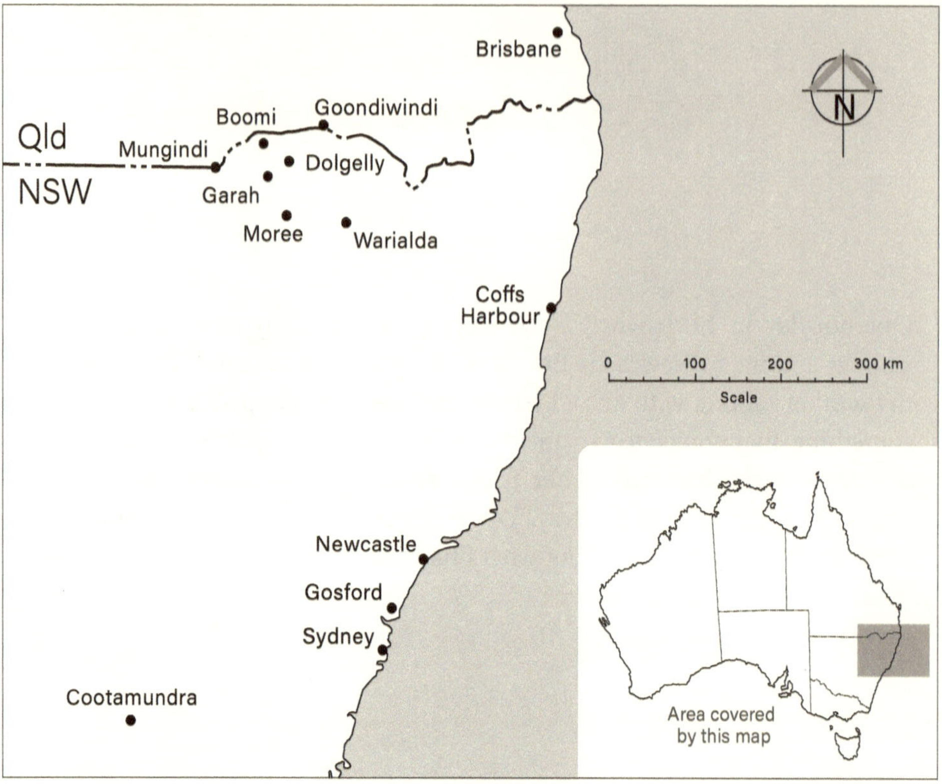
Brisbane
Goondiwindi
Boomi
Qld
NSW
Mungindi
Dolgelly
Garah
Moree
Warialda
Coffs Harbour
N
0 100 200 300 km
Scale
Newcastle
Gosford
Sydney
Cootamundra
Area covered by this map

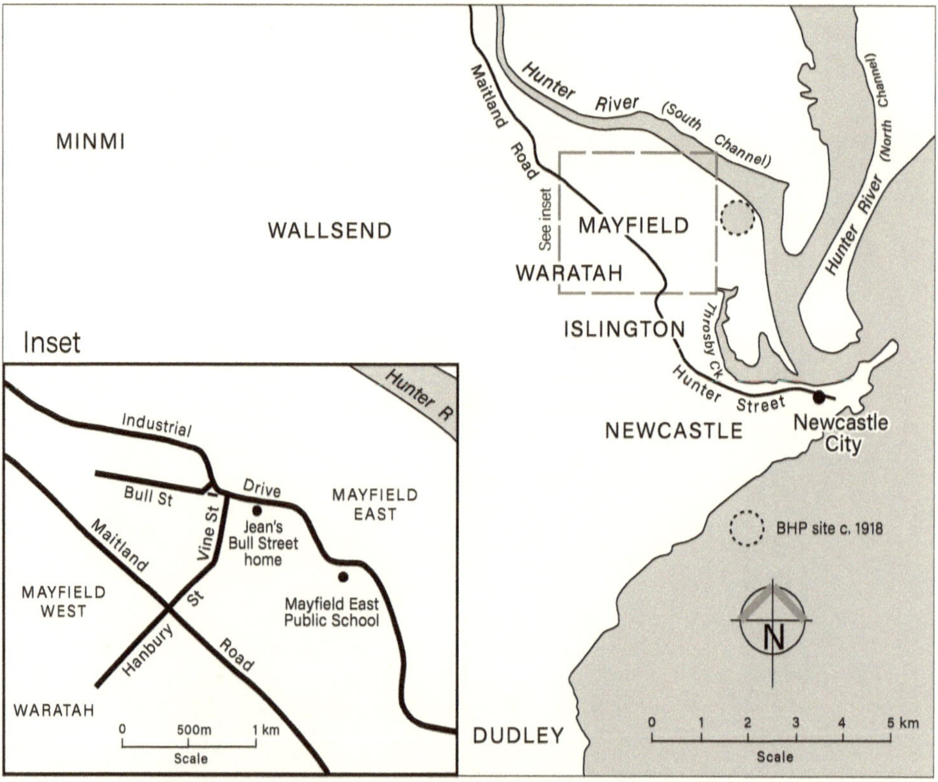
MINMI
WALLSEND
Maitland Road
Hunter River (South Channel)
Hunter River (North Channel)
See inset
MAYFIELD
WARATAH
ISLINGTON
Throsby Ck
Hunter Street
NEWCASTLE
Newcastle City
BHP site c. 1918
N
DUDLEY
0 1 2 3 4 5 km
Scale
Inset
Hunter R
Industrial Drive
Bull St
Vine St
Jean's Bull Street home
MAYFIELD EAST
Maitland Road
MAYFIELD WEST
Hanbury St
Mayfield East Public School
WARATAH
0 500m 1 km
Scale

1 · Crybaby

I was two years old. The adults were absent and Cynthia, my six-year-old sister, had me at her mercy. I don't remember her face, just a feeling. I was a crybaby and I knew she delighted in making me cry. Tom, my brother, aged four, was her henchman. He was just a feeling too. They set to work.

I had a small toy dog, a tan-and-white cloth dog with a bell tied under its jaw. It stood upright on stiff little legs. Cynthia and Tom decided to "slaughter" it, like they'd seen men in the country slaughter a calf or a steer. I closed my eyes and screamed. They skinned it, ripped it apart and placed the hide out to dry on the fence, just as they'd seen the men do. I was aghast. My little dog, slaughtered and his skin hung out to dry on the fence. I was inconsolable. Poor fool that I was, I always gave my affection to inanimate objects. It was the beginning of years of torment from Cynthia.

I know now that this happened in the autumn of 1912 in remote, north-western New South Wales. Our family was living in an isolated place called Dolgelly. We lived in the Dolgelly "hotel" (or what was then called a "half-way house") — an overnight stop for coaches and buggies travelling between Moree and Goondiwindi or Garah and Mungindi on the Dolgelly Road.

I remember, from a later time, the battered hotel stone and wood building on the desolate Dolgelly road, the massive backyard, the stench of the stables, the horses and buggies, the never-ending wooden post-and-rail fences, and the surrounding flat, almost treeless countryside.

I sat on the hotel verandah and cried. Ah Fong, the hotel's Chinese cook, came out and sat beside me. I can still remember his round, kindly, smiling face. He put his arm around me and said, "Don't cry. I'm the one who should cry. I have no wife and no children and no one to love me."

"But I love you," I said and I kissed him on the cheek. He was very affected my father told me years afterwards. He had watched us from the hotel doorway.

I met Ah Fong years later when I had grown up and he was a vegetable dealer in Moree. He told me, "Oh you were a cranky baby. You cried and

Jean's father, Tom Sharp, as a young man; probably dressed for his wedding in 1905.

cried and cried." He made no mention of the kiss.

My father, Tom Sharp, had become the teacher at a public one-teacher school in a nearby town called Boomi in 1903 and I was born there. The family move to Dolgelly came late in 1910 when the halfway house or hotel became available. I don't know why my parents moved from Boomi. Most likely my Dad just wanted a change from teaching.

Boomi was then a very small, isolated town in the outback. It had a few houses, a school for the district sheep-station and wheat-farm families, a pub or two and very few shops. It was a shire centre for sheep graziers and wheat growers with a population of less than 150. I didn't go back for eighty years and I didn't recognise it when I did, but my birth certificate says: "Born in Boomi in 1910."

Life felt strange and cruel for me in those days at Dolgelly. I cried a lot. I knew something was wrong in our family but I didn't know what. As I grew older I was to find out just how cruel life could be.

Tom Sharp, right, with his one-teacher class at Boomi, 1908. Cynthia Sharp, aged two, is in the front row, seventh from the right. (Photo: NSW State Archives)

2 · Horses, buggies and steam trains

We lived another two years at the hotel at Dolgelly before leaving for good. I was four when we left. The whole family set off in a two-horse buggy. Mum was pregnant again. We had many suitcases with us. It was a long trip (roughly thirty-five miles) to a big town, which I know now was Moree. We fought and argued the whole trip and it took such a long time I was sick. We were heading for Gosford, near Sydney. Why we were going to Gosford was a mystery to me, just one more mysterious decision that adults made.

The flat featureless country that surrounds Boomi, the Dolgelly road, the desolate, long, straight Boggabilla and Carnarvon roads into Moree, the sweeping treeless plains, the rich black soil and occasional sparse rivers that flood mercilessly, the relentless Australian heat of summer and blanket frosts of winter were embedded in my psyche from that time, even if my memory of them is hazy.

All I remember of Moree is that it was busy and there were motorcars, which I'd never seen before, as well as horses and carts and buggies. We were there for a day. We went to the bore baths, which were opposite the railway station, and there was a big hailstorm afterwards. The hailstones were as big as cricket balls and we huddled under the awning of the hotel near the pool and watched them smashing into the ground. It was terrifying.

It was exciting when our steam train finally pulled out with lots of smoke and steam hissing and we got grit in our eyes and noses when we leaned out the window. We probably weren't easy to travel with, Cynthia, Tom and me, with Mum pregnant. Dad told me later the train trip took thirteen hours to get from Moree to Gosford, which was to be our home for the next two years.

Gosford was where that I first became aware that I wasn't the centre of the universe, that my family had bigger priorities than myself.

Moree railway station, c. 1911. (Photo: NSW State Archives)

Moree c. 1890-1910, when Tom Sharp first arrived in the area. (Photo: courtesy Royal Australian Historical Society)

3 · Please give me a penny, sir

In Gosford we lived in a furnished house owned by a Mrs White, who was very old and who lived in the house as well. We were boarders. Mrs White was an old friend of my father's from when he was a miner in Minmi, near Newcastle. Years later I realised Dad must have been desperate to get away from Dolgelly and this was the best option.

I don't remember where the house was in Gosford or much about it but my father obtained a job as a commercial traveller selling Corona kerosene pressure lamps around the country, and we saw very little of him. My sister Cynthia and brother Tom went to primary school, and I started kindergarten. My sister, Winifred, was born there in July 1914.

Gosford is where I became more aware of Cynthia's hidden resentment towards me. I'm not sure whether it was her anger at me for being a crybaby or jealousy that I'd been born at all. She made a huge fuss over baby Winifred when she was born at the house. She was forever fondling and cuddling it. I didn't look at the baby myself but I do remember wondering secretly why she made *such* a fuss over the silly thing. I was very timid and forever clutching a doll or a picture book, and spent a lot of time in tears. I began to be aware that along with indifference I wasn't getting much paren-

Gosford, date unknown. (Photo: source unknown)

tal love. Not only Cynthia, but Mum gave all her affection to the baby. I was just as much a part of the family as the baby. Why did I feel like an outcast? What did I do wrong? Why was Cynthia so awful to me? I must have had some feeling for Cynthia though because I remember being terrified of storms and I once shut myself in the toilet and prayed it wouldn't rain until Cynthia and my brother arrived home from school.

Despite this there were happy times in Gosford. Mum's family were always big on concerts. Mum (or "Annie" as Dad called her) taught Cynthia to sing and perform on stage and in a school concert at Gosford she sang a pathetic old English song, *Please give me a penny, sir.*

> *Please give me a penny, sir?*
> Please give me a penny, sir?
> My mother dear is dead,
> And, oh, I am so hungry, sir,
> A penny please, for bread?
> All day I have been asking.
> But no one heeds my cry,
> Will you not give me something?
> Or surely I must die.
>
> *Chorus*
> Please give me a penny, sir?
> My mother dear is dead,
> And, oh, I am so hungry, sir,
> A penny please, for bread?
>
> Please give me a penny, sir?
> You won't say no, to me,
> Because I'm poor and ragged, sir.
> And, oh, so cold you see.
> We were not always begging,
> We once were rich like you,
> But father died a drunkard,
> And mother she died, too.
>
> Please give me a penny, sir?
> Is heard on every side,
> Lisped by little trembling lips,
> And singing on life's tide.
> Oh, listen to their pleadings,

And pity these, the poor,
Then blessings brought from heaven,
Will shine on thee the more.

People showered the stage with pennies when Cynthia sang this song. I'm not surprised. Cynthia, a forthright little girl of eight, looked like a waif with her homemade ragged clothes, delicate face and a shock of well-brushed hair, singing her song so sincerely.

She was in another item with some little girls dressed as bathing belles and singing "Splashing in the briny, splashing in the sea. Molly and me, Polly and me. What better fun can there be?" That was also very popular and naturally all the girls looked adorable in their homemade bathing-belle outfits.

I clutched my doll and chewed my handkerchief and watched her, tongue-tied and inarticulate. I was in awe of her; she was so much bolder than me, so much more confident, so dismissive of any fear. Adults were impressed by her. I was proud she was my sister even if she was horrible to me.

I had a special doll, a rag doll with an old metal head on it with the mouth perpetually open. With my deep and growing maternal instinct, I stuffed pieces of food in its mouth. Any old thing would do — porridge or pieces of meat and potato. Nothing was too good for my child. However, as time went by the food began to go bad and people noticed a bad smell about the place and soon traced it to my doll. It was dispatched to the rubbish tip followed by me howling.

I was puzzled that I was ignored. I thought maybe some of us got less attention because we were older and were expected to look after ourselves. I believe Cynthia also felt some lack of attention and fussed over Winnie partly to please Mum and win more motherly affection, but then took out her frustration on me when she didn't get it. Cynthia liked attention as much as me though she never admitted it. We were made to keep quiet about our feelings.

Suffering hurts in silence was the beginning of me learning to hide everything, not just keeping quiet, but not telling the truth about anything. It never got you anywhere. You were expected to hold your tongue on all personal matters and speaking the "truth" was not held in high regard. Nor was telling lies — only silence was acceptable. I never agreed with this and it would get me into trouble later.

Australia Day parade, Donnison Street, Gosford, July 1915. (Photo: R. Hazlewood; Gosford Library)

4 · A King George V childhood

We lived uneasily at Mrs White's in Gosford for two years until the early winter of 1916 when we moved to my grandparents' farm in Boundary Road, Wallsend, just outside Newcastle. I wasn't aware that they were my grandparents till later but I loved being with Grandma Sharp. Mum was pregnant again and Dad tried to go back to teaching. It was to be a temporary six to eight month move before we moved to a house in Mayfield.

Our grandparents' house was a picturesque weather-beaten, grey-slab house in the then rural Plattsburg part of Wallsend. My grandmother must have done quite a lot of arranging to fit us all in: my father, mother, Cynthia, Tom, myself and baby Winnie. It was here I discovered I had *another* brother called Bill (Wilhelm) who was four years old and had been looked after by Grandma Sharp all his life.

I was confused. Why hadn't anyone ever mentioned him? Why was Grandma caring for him? Mum explained that Grandma looked after him because she could not manage so many children on her own in the country. I supposed that's what Grandmas had to do but she already had our grandfather to look after as well as her other eight grown-up children — two of whom were under twenty (the youngest, Bertram, was only seventeen) — who kept dropping in and staying over, often with their children. That this new brother of ours, Bill, was living there was a surprise. I didn't know who was whom with my aunts or uncles, I just knew the house was always full of grown-ups and children. I thought Grandma was brave, being so old, to look after our young brother as well as us.

There was a large garden, fowls, cows and horses and an abundance of grapes, which I wrongly thought was a vineyard, for my grandparents to look after. Some months after we burst in on my grandmother, Mum had another baby, a son whom she and Dad named Stuart Granville. Suddenly, I had *another* brother, which made three.

My poor hard-working grandmother, Janet. I knew even then what a burden we were on her but families were different then . . . everyone depended on their extended family in some way. Even so, she was extraordinarily generous in taking our whole family for six months.

My grandparents became a big force in my early life, especially Grandma Sharp. I became very close to her and loved her dearly. She treated me as if I was her favourite grandchild, even when I knew she had twenty-eight others. She was quite short but had a friendly face and a warm smile — she had been very pretty when she was young — and that smile meant everything to me. She seemed both a grandmother *and* a mother to me.

My grandfather had married her when she was sixteen and he was twenty. She wasn't even a bride; they married in a registrar's office in Newcastle in 1876. Janet was born in Edinburgh, and emigrated with her parents in the 1860s. Thomas was the grandson of convict Thomas Sharpe, who was sent to Australia from Birmingham in 1833. They settled in Wallsend, then a coal-mining satellite of Newcastle, where my grandfather grew up and became a miner, like his father before him.

My father, Tom (the eldest boy in the family was always named Tom), was born in 1877 followed by five daughters (Janet; Mary, whom we always called Aunty Mollie; Anne; Maude; and Bertha) then three more sons (Ernest, Oliver and Bertram). It was a big family but my grandfather managed it well on his coal-miner's salary. He somehow managed to save enough to buy the small farm and later on other properties in Mayfield, including a boatshed on the Hunter River near Hexham. He was hard working and industrious all his life.

Grandma's house in Boundary Road, three miles from the Wallsend town centre, not only had an abundance of grapevines, but also mandarin and orange trees and the first flower garden I had seen, which was full of Grandma's sweet-scented stocks. She had red, purple, pink and white stocks with petals that were soft and reassuring. These were the first flowers I recognised and could name.

I learned through my grandmother's garden how you could make a house beautiful with garden flowers. My family had lived in houses without flowers. Flowers were my first conscious pleasure in nature for its own sake; the mysterious beauty and scent of flowers was a liberating force for me. I took joy in them even as a five- and six-year-old. The love for those scented stocks never left me. I always associate them with my grandmother.

It was here, too, in Grandma's garden, that I tasted my first mandarins and passionfruit. When I peel a mandarin, even now, the tangy smell of the rind reminds me of stealing them and lying to Grandma about it. What a conniver I was, even at five. This is my first memory of deliberately hiding the truth from my elders for fear of reprisal and reprimand. The lies increased as I grew older until I became a teenager, when I finally started to confront my parents.

The taste of watermelon and grapes was also special. I said to my friend Maizie Parks that the best tastes in the whole world were mandarins, grapes and watermelons. The world and its sensations were beginning to be known to me. I thought watermelon was the most beautiful taste on earth, except sweet black grapes. I said victoriously to another friend, "I think grapes are the best and second is watermelon." I could not articulate it then but I meant "for sheer and utter sensual pleasure in eating them." It was the sugar, but I was a deeply senses-driven child, be it food, physical comfort, flowers or affection.

Wallsend in those days was a place quite unlike today, a thriving mining community with a large population, many houses and churches, a hospital, pubs, a rail connection to Newcastle and, would you believe, a racecourse. It was dominated by, and profited from, the rich coalmines in Wallsend and nearby Plattsburg and Minmi. Wallsend was named after the coal-mining township of Wallsend outside Newcastle-upon-Tyne in the north of England. The English Wallsend was built at the end of Hadrian's Wall, hence the name.

Wallsend, c. 1906. (Photo: Josiah Cocking collection, Cultural Collections, University of Newcastle, NSW)

The sunken, barren landscape where Jean's grandmother's house and farm once stood in Boundary Road, Plattsburg, photographed in 1955 when she visited the site.

Although I started kindergarten at Gosford, my strongest early memory of school is first class at Wallsend–Plattsburg Primary School. This was my father's old school. I remember the slightly faded pale-yellow two-storey building with the corrugated tin roof and big playing area and my first tearful days at the school, not knowing anybody in my class and everyone staring at me.

We wore long white dresses up to our necks and over our knees, pinafores in summer, dark dresses and pinafores in winter and lace-up boots. We always had a ribbon in our hair.

Every Monday morning in school we assembled around a flagpole and solemnly declared we would "honour our God and serve our King (George V) and salute our flag" and then the flag went up. That's how we became little patriots and it was responsible for my later warm feelings for the royal family and for Britain, whom I felt personally related to.

I had no idea who King George V was or what Britain was or why we had a flag but I soon realised I was going to have a King George V childhood and there was more of this to come. It mysteriously made me feel safe and reassured and increased my awareness of an outside world and a life that had responsibilities. At this time, World War I was in full swing, there

Girls' class 4, Plattsburg public school, 1916. Cynthia may be in the photograph. (Photo: NSW State Archives)

Plattsburg high school in 1922. This is the same group of girls that Jean attended Plattsburg public school with. Alice Moss is in the second row, fifth from the right. (Photo: NSW State Archives)

were soldiers everywhere, going off to fight in France and patriotism was rampant.

My main preoccupation was not being late for school. We had to walk two miles from my grandparents' farm in Boundary Road (surrounded by bushland and empty fields), up and down a long hill, then past the racecourse and the Racecourse Hotel, up the Minmi dirt road and down another hill to the school which was beside a huge bushland park. It took the best part of an hour to get there and to get home. I was six years old and I walked there with my sister and brother but I usually walked home by myself. I thank God for my friend Maizie Parks who lived near us and was a strong soul who protected me and took my part against other children on the walk home. I was unusually timid in those days.

My worst day at school was when another so-called friend called Alice Moss, also aged six and who had cropped hair, told me when I spilled a drop of sheep dip on my desk (we were given a dab of this antiseptic to wash our slates on Friday so they would be antiseptic on Monday) that when I came to school on Monday the desk would be rotted through and I would suffer dire perils. What a weekend I spent in despair and agonies of mind only to find out on Monday the desk was the same as ever.

These perils lasted another six months until our family packed up yet again and moved to a suburb in the centre of Newcastle, Mayfield, which was to be my home for the next fifteen years.

5 · No more flowers

The house we moved to in Mayfield was owned, like the farmhouse in Wallsend–Plattsburg, by my grandfather. The most notable thing about the house was that it was in Bull Street, directly opposite the recently completed Newcastle steelworks.

The whole family, including my newborn brother Stuart Granville — but *not* the mysterious newfound brother Bill who remained with Grandma Sharp — travelled to Mayfield in a spring cart and horse in October 1916. It was a hot day and our horse had to pull the cart up and down so many hills (people forget how hilly Wallsend is) that it had to stop for a rest every half hour. It took many hours to travel the ten miles to Mayfield.

I vividly remember our arrival. It was a terrible disappointment. Even at six years of age I thought the house looked dismal — that is, the front garden did. It was a green-painted wooden one-storey house fenced off with an old fishing net, dirty grey-and-black sandy loam soil instead of a lawn, with a few onions, beetroot and tomato plants growing. Two scraggy-looking kangaroo greyhound dogs were tied up to a peach tree.

I felt so desolate I didn't want to get out of the cart. After the pretty, sweet-smelling cottage garden at my grandmother's this was a big letdown.

I burst into tears. My uncle Ernie, Dad's younger brother, who had been living in the house with his wife Mabel, tried to comfort me and introduced the dogs as Spring and Sarah, but he didn't understand why I was crying.

"Don't cry, pet, you'll be happy here. This is a lovely house and, you know, there's a big backyard and a cow and a place for the horse. And lots of fruit trees. These dogs are my friends. Don't cry, love. I hate to see you cry. I've got to go away to the war you know."

Ernie had separated from Mabel, who had been unfaithful, and enlisted in the army to fight in the War. He was leaving for France in a month and was wearing his army uniform. He was very generous to give us the house, even though it actually belonged to my grandfather. I loved him calling me "pet" and "love", even though I didn't know what "pet" meant. I had never been called "pet" or "love". He fought in Europe and,

Mayfield butcher with horse and spring cart, similar to Jean's transport from Plattsburg to Mayfield, early 1900s. (Photo: John Turner collection, Cultural Collections, University of Newcastle, NSW)

although I longed to, I didn't see him again till late 1918. I cried because there was no flower garden and I was ashamed we would be living in a house that looked like this. Even though I was only six, shame was a strong emotion. I felt ashamed we never had enough money and that we lived in other people's houses. This house wasn't ours although we had possession of it. I don't know whether we paid rent or not, but I suspect not.

We did grow a few white arum lilies down the side later on but everyone had those. I had left my beloved grandmother and her magical garden and I had a foreboding of what life would be like here with my mother who wasn't interested in flowers. Children often can feel the future even if they can't articulate it and somehow as a child I guessed, correctly, what my life was going to be like.

I had no idea that this was a historic moment in Mayfield's history: the BHP steelworks was just beginning and I would actually live to see it begin to close down. Mayfield had been for years the beautiful suburb in Newcastle, situated by the Hunter River, with sweeping hills and Chinese garden flats by the river and a serene landscape. The best families in Newcastle lived there. No one foresaw what the steelworks would do to the place, what enormous changes it would bring.

Such transitory experiences of life happen just when you think everything is stationary and permanent.

BHP had started building the steelworks in 1912 with government approval and it became operational in 1915.[1] It was a huge presence over Mayfield and Newcastle, belching smoke into the air and covering Newcastle and Mayfield in black grit. Grit covered the clothes on the line and smog curled all about Newcastle with the wind. No one thought anything of this at the time. I thought it had always been like this.

It was always a huge, dark, dirty and squealing presence across the road. Everyone referred to it with reverence but I thought it was a dashed nuisance. I had no idea why it was there or what happened there. It just was a part of life, a part of the mysterious outside world, full of more steelworks and more "soldiers departing for wars" for all I knew. I had no idea how it would come to dominate my life. I was more interested in getting into our new house and trying to find a space for myself.

My mother, always practical, hard-working and energetic, wasted no time in setting up house in the late afternoon. My tears, as usual, were ignored. Cynthia was her main little helper with Tom. I was in the way so I explored the house and backyard. Later, Dad went out in the spring cart and came back with some iron double beds and kapok mattresses. The rest of the family worked to make the empty house look more like a home. Uncle Ernie took away the offending racing dogs.

It was a sturdy four-roomed weatherboard with front and back verandahs of diminutive proportions. It had little or no furniture when we arrived except for four chairs that my uncle Ernie had left. He was only twenty-two when we arrived and had never had any children, so there was not much furniture. His marriage had been short-lived and it was never spoken of in our house. There was no bathroom, no laundry, no electricity or gas or sewerage. Our water came from corrugated water tanks and a hand pump in the backyard where there was a well. The toilet was far down into the backyard. The backyard itself was huge, over two blocks (all owned by my grandfather) and there was a cow called Nellie tethered with a cow-bail[2], which Uncle Ernie left us.

---

1. The Broken Hill Proprietary Company Limited acquired land on the Hunter River near present day Mayfield East in 1896 to build an iron ore smelter. In 1910, the government approved the construction of a major steelworks and foundries, a blast furnace, open hearth steel furnaces, bloom mill, heavy rail mill, and coke ovens. The site had rail and shipping transport and was close to the Newcastle and South Maitland coalfields.
2. Two pieces of wood joined to keep a cow's head in position while milking.

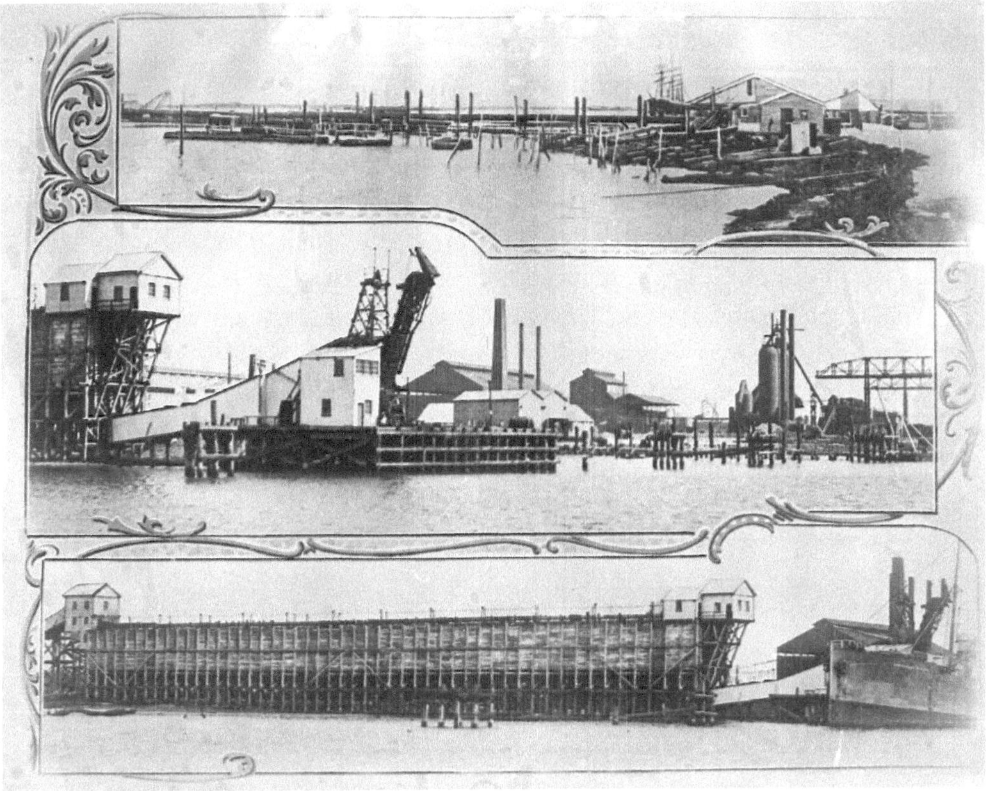

A page from the souvenir booklet of the opening of Newcastle steelworks, 2 June 1915. (Photo: Bert Lovett collection, Norm Barney Photographic collection, Cultural Collections, University of Newcastle, NSW)

Newcastle steelworkers leaving work (date unknown). (Photographer unknown)

By the next day, three of the rooms were proper bedrooms. Mum and Dad had one of the front rooms with an iron brass bed with a kapok mattress and a white Marcella bedspread, and a few shelves with Dad's good books: *The Decameron*, not to be touched or read for fear of a "good hiding"; I remember a book of Australian birds, *Webster's Dictionary* and *An Outline of History* by H. G. Wells. A curtain under a rail that acted as a wardrobe, a dressing table and The Old Tin Trunk in which were kept any valuables . . . of which there were very few.

The other front bedroom — with a black iron double bedstead (no brass) with a wire base and frame that often became dislodged and a kapok mattress, and a single iron bedstead with a horsehair mattress — was for Cynthia, Winnie and me, and later on, another sister. My mother's bed was

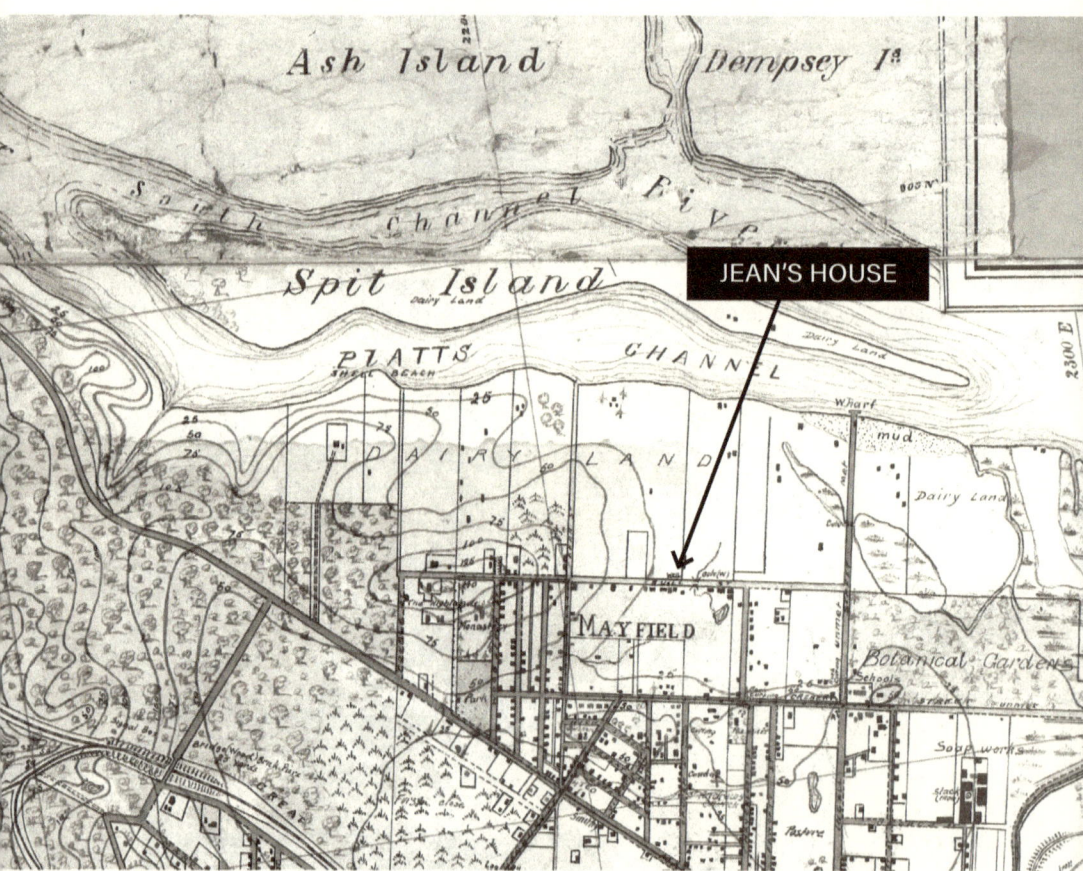

Map of Newcastle (detail) showing Mayfield, 1910. (Image courtesy Cultural Collections, University of Newcastle, NSW)

much more comfortable than ours.

The back bedroom for Tom also had a black iron double bedstead. It would also house Bill when he returned from Grandma's late in 1917 and another new baby in 1918. Baby Stuart, for the moment, slept between Mum and Dad. The boys' bedroom would eventually hold all three brothers but with another single bed in there.

The other room was the combined kitchen, sitting room and dining room. All scrupulously clean but poorly furnished with oddments left over from Uncle Ernie's broken marriage. There were only four chairs, so some of us had to sit on wooden kerosene boxes. Three kerosene boxes also made a good dressing table in our bedroom with two uprights with a horizontal across the top painted white and hung in front with voile (a soft cotton fabric) or cretonne and a pink bow.

The back verandah was half glassed in and we used it as a scullery to keep our dishes in and wash up. There was a big old tin dish where we put the hot water.

All the floors in the house were covered in brown linoleum which we kept polished. The front and back verandahs were plain boards which were scrubbed on Saturdays and swept with a straw broom on other days.

The laundry was washed in zinc tubs on the back verandah or a kerosene tin of boiling water on a wood and coal fire enclosed in bricks in the backyard. Kerosene was used for lighting because we had no gas or electricity. It came in four-gallon tins in a wooden case. A hole was made in the corner of the top tin and a kerosene pump inserted and Tom's job was to fill the lamps every day. Cynthia's job was to trim the wicks and clean the globes so we were ready for the dark. On days they forgot, there were ructions.

We used coal for heating and it became Tom's job to get the kindling ready to start the fire in the mornings in the stove. Sometimes the fire wouldn't catch and we'd sprinkle it with sugar. If that didn't work we'd use a drop of kerosene and if we put too much on it would flare with a big "whoosh" and frighten us.

Mayfield is where my problems with my mother grew worse. She had doted on Winnie as a baby and now she doted on Stuart *and* Winnie. I felt as though I didn't exist and it upset me. Cynthia and Tom didn't get much attention either but they seemed to cope. Our mother became stricter than ever. She rarely smiled, she started to smack me whenever I did the slightest thing wrong and never so much as put her arm around me. There wasn't much motherly empathy for us as she set the pattern for our household chores that continued until we were much older. She had two more children and made us older children the "helper/slaves". Cynthia, who was always good at needlework and crochet, became the house cleaner who helped Mum around the house and with the mending, dressmaking and cooking. I was the baby-minder, nurse and message-goer, and Tom did the heavy chores, handled the coal and wood and milked the cow. Tom also helped Dad in the garden where he grew vegetables and fruit.

This was the house that sheltered us for five years (we moved around the corner to Vine Street later) and where I first became aware of the outside world. My experiences here with the family overshadowed my later life experiences, powerful though some of them were. We were very poor and my mother asserted her stoic Methodist doctrine mercilessly.

It was an intense, emotional time for me. My days were overwhelmed with mother, father, endless looking after babies, running messages, dealing with my siblings, hair curlers, baths, clothes, the hilly streets in Mayfield, the vast Hunter River and its surrounds, the Methodist church and Sunday school, primary school, the imposing steelworks, endless soldiers everywhere and the War. I felt trapped in a world I didn't understand, which always seemed unfair and loveless, and from which, at an early age, I silently longed to escape.

6 · More tears

Daylight saving was introduced on 1 January 1917. That year I was in second class at Mayfield Public School (formerly Waratah Public School, later Mayfield East Public School). Cynthia was in sixth class and Tom in fourth class. Winnie was only three and Stuart was a baby.

My father had a teaching job at Dudley Public School, a distant southern suburb of Newcastle. He rode a bicycle to school there every day, ten miles (sixteen kilometres), mostly up hill. He was paid three pounds ten shillings a week. It was barely enough to keep us fed but it was regular.

Mayfield Public School was a trial at first. Being a shy new girl was hard and I cried so much in the first few days that one boy in my class said to me, "Haven't you cried enough yet?" as if I'd filled my allowable crying quota. Another classmate, who I met years later on a train, told me that I was so quiet at school she didn't think I could actually speak.

The school was on the corner of Ingall and Crebert streets and had started as a slab hut in 1874 on a two-acre block of land. It was first named Folly School, North Waratah. The headmaster, while I was there, was Mr Robertson.

The buildings when I first attended were old and rambling. They consisted of three or four wooden rooms and two portable classrooms although a new two-storey brick building with four classrooms was under construction. There was also part of an old derelict house in the grounds, in one room of which Mrs Higgins taught sewing. The back room was reserved for bad boys who went there for caning by Mr Bob Stove, whose youngest son, David, later became an associate professor of philosophy at Sydney University (and incidentally taught my own son at university in 1961). Bob Stove was hated for his canings at Mayfield but he was a good teacher. I was taught in an old wooden shelter shed by Mrs Henry.

Whatever the trials of school I quickly learnt to read and write. We had primers in those days up to sixth class and later the school magazine came into being. I was good at sums as well as reading and writing. Our whole family was bright at school, a source of great pride to us.

Waratah Public School in 1905. The school's name was changed to Mayfield East Public School in 1923. By 1916 this building was used as a sewing and caning room. (Photo: Cultural Collections, University of Newcastle, NSW)

In my first year at school, Cynthia was very much the older sister. Being four years older she never associated with me or recognised me at school.

She was head of a group of big girls in sixth class, all aged ten and eleven, who did things like have mock weddings at lunchtime. Someone would bring a piece of mosquito netting and some flowers for her head to be the bride, and another girl would be the groom in a boy's coat. Both wore old buttoned-up black boots. They would stage the "wedding" and pool their lunches and have a "wedding breakfast". They ignored us little kids peeping around the corner of the school.

On the way home one afternoon after one of these weddings Cynthia said to me, "Keep away from me at school. You're embarrassing. You're so ugly I can't stand the sight of you. And it's a real deep ugliness, too, not just on the surface. You're repulsive."

When I said, "Am I really that awful?" she simply replied, "You're too horrible to speak to."

This was hardly unexpected as Cynthia did all she could to make me feel unwanted at home. She was particularly insistent on my ugliness. I began to believe I was the ugliest, most unnatural child in the world. I'm so ugly, I thought, and lucky to have a sister as pretty as Cynthia. I insisted to myself that, no matter what, she was my sister and therefore to be endured. After all, she was only telling me the truth.

It was hard not to be impressed by Cynthia as a young girl. She had lovely thick hair with a natural wave that was never plaited. Mine was thick and straight and always in plaits, if it wasn't cut short by Dad. She was very intelligent and always did wonderfully at school. She was also well versed in the reciting world. I can still see her standing on the verandah of the old school and reciting *Oxford to London, 1884* by Lewis Carroll:

> Against the crimson arm-rest leaned a girl.
> Often. Holding a muff, twisting a curl,
> Drumming her heels in boredom on the floor.
>
> Until a white haired gentleman who saw
> She hated travelling, produced a case
> Of puzzles: "Seven Germans run a race . . .
> Unwind this maze, escape the lion's paw . . .
> The princess must be lowered by her hair . . .
>
> The train entered a tunnel, shrieking, all
> The lights went out and when he took her hand
> She was the princess in the tower and
> A lion faced her on the moonlit wall
> Who roared and reaches and caught her there.

I didn't cringe so she must have been good, otherwise I would have cried and nibbled at my hankie again. Or just said "yukkie" and pretended she was a cousin.

Her recitals elevated her beyond being my sister. When she recited she became another being, a noble soul, as if she and she alone understood the magic words of the poet and the past. Years later she would recite lines from poems to me when she thought no one else was listening. It was even more poignant then.

"Oh what can ail thee knight-at-arms, alone and palely loitering? The sedge has withered from the lake and no birds sing . . . " she would recite to me self-consciously in her tiny kitchen at the back of a barber shop where she then lived. Keats was a favourite.

Tom could never match her in any of these things. He was quiet and in the background. He had a brain, too, but he never matched us girls in cleverness and boldness. I think the girls in the family overwhelmed him.

Cynthia crocheted, knitted dolls' clothes and scrubbed the kitchen table with sand soap and made it white as snow. She taught Winnie to dance, sing and act. Winnie was no threat to her. Cynthia was sent on important messages into town on the tram, to change library books at Newcastle Council lending library, which had a carpeted entrance hallway, a ladies' room and a quietness that was holy. She was never sent down to the tram terminus like me to buy food and pay bills.

When I was quite small I wondered, why does my grandfather think that boys are better than girls? He never paid much attention to any of us girls. He fussed over the boys, any boys, as though they were the only worthwhile human beings. I thought he was way off the mark but my father had the same idea, too, which gave me something to ponder on. I didn't think they were right but I never gave tongue to my thinking. Private thoughts were something to keep to oneself and not to go noising abroad. It was best to keep your mouth shut and merge into the background. I knew that the girls in the family were brighter than the boys. Winnie later won scholarships and Cynthia should have gone to university.

Tom could not compete. I liked him but he had different interests to us. He never said much but went about his own business making a few shillings here and there, caddying at the golf links, going on messages for other people or milking cows. He spent his money on himself; he had a hoard of Nelson Lee and Sexton Blake paperbacks and one book, a prized possession, *The Last of the Mohicans* by James Fenimore Cooper. He never answered Mum or Dad back, even when older. I didn't have much conversation with him even though we were together a lot.

I was the only one who rebelled when I was older, when I was a teenager. I yearned for something different. I was bright at school in sums or English, but careless in my writing. A watcher and noticer of other children's clothing and possessions and envious of lovingly dressed little girls, especially ones with curly hair.

Just when our family was settling down in Mayfield, with dad's teaching job and our pattern of life falling into place, something tragic unfolded.

7 · "How is the little boy?"

We came home from school one day in mid-winter of 1917 to find the house deserted. No mother or father, no dinner. Later, Dad and Mum came home on the tram and Dad told us that our baby brother, Stuart, was in Newcastle hospital. On Thursday 5 July, Harry Gane, a near neighbour, lent Dad his horse and sulky to take Mum to the hospital. When they came home that night Mrs Lempke, who lived next door, came to the door and asked, "How is the little boy?" and Dad said, "He's dead." Dad hadn't told us.

Cynthia started to cry. It's a date that stuck in Tom's mind because it was the day boxer Les Darcy was buried in Maitland (not far away) with a crowd of thousands: 5 July 1917.

Stuart was only six months old and had been sickly from birth. He got worse as the year went on. Our parents were unable to tell us truthfully what was wrong. He was always covered in bruises. I think it was some sort of blood disorder.

There was gloom in our house. Miss Russell, who lived nearby, brought down a wreath of jonquils. Tom told me he heard the words "rheumatoid purpura" when Dad was telling people about it. It was an inherited blood disease, and that's why Mum and Dad kept it quiet. They were devastated it might have come from them.

We were told nothing. People would ask, what did your brother die of? We were told to say, "I don't know", which was embarrassing. How could we not know how our own brother died? One day, when asked, Tom said "a family complaint" and Mum roused on him. We felt there was something to hide but it was also our family's tradition of saying nothing about anything upsetting. It didn't stop Mum and Dad from having more babies.

To this day I can't be sure what Stuart contracted . . . the truth died with Mum and Dad. But it was something inherited and something to do with his blood. It would have been better for the family to talk about it.

We had a tearful funeral at the Methodist church in Mayfield. Stuart was so young and we never got to know him, but he was never forgotten. Every child is important to one's family, even those who die young. I often think about Stuart and what we missed.

8 · No time for kisses and cuddles

After the painful death of Stuart, the pattern of our household life slowly resumed. My education was set for the next four years when I moved from second class to sixth class at Mayfield Public School.

I felt, as a child in that first year after Stuart died, that I didn't love anyone and no one loved me. Dad was too busy to pay attention to us. I felt he didn't notice me round the place. I can't remember a word of love spoken to me by either parent, though Dad did sometimes call me "his little Miss Sunshine." I thought, then, that I would be better off in an orphanage.

I remember thinking I must be unnatural because I didn't love my mother like other children loved theirs. Anything I did wrong I was now beaten for, especially when Dad wasn't there. The beatings from my mother were meant to weaken my resolve but they only made me strong and resentful. I never understood them.

The effect this was having on me was long range. I was an unpaid slave/worker in my own home. I didn't feel loved for myself. I felt I was worth nothing. No time for kisses and cuddles for me. Six years old with a sister who tormented me and told me how ugly and bad I was and a younger sister and brother (before he died) to mind as nursemaid, a preoccupied father and a mother who was strict, unemotional and zealous. I felt alone, isolated and without any sense of a future.

As I grew older these feelings were hard to deal with, especially as I couldn't talk about them. When I was young I suppressed them because I thought I was abnormal. When older they took over my life. No one else in the family seemed to have these feelings. I was beaten more than the others because I resisted more than they did.

Cynthia left primary school in 1918 and went to Cooks Hill Intermediate High School and began to learn French and Latin, widening the gap between us. I kept very quiet when she practised her French lessons and silently registered the sounds she made. "*Robert est grand, Charles est petit*", "*Robert a le chapeau*" etc. It sounded exciting. She was still aggressive to, and dismissive of, me but I always remained impressed by her.

Grandma returned five-year-old baby Bill to the family at the end of 1917. She couldn't face him starting school in Wallsend and continuing to look after him. Dear Grandma, with so many other worries it had taken a toll on her to take him for as long as she did. Bill slept with Tom, in the same bed. I still shared the front bedroom with Cynthia and Winnie.

My memory of those years is not linear. It's a jumbled assembly of random memories of school, home life, the Great War, my grandmother and grandfather, and other close relations who looked down on us as the poor unfortunates of the family.

The Great War dominated our lives. We had the *Newcastle Morning Herald and Miner's Advocate* delivered every morning for one penny. I saw drawings of Belgian babies impaled on brutal Hun bayonets in the paper. I saw drawings of Belgian children (who were stupid enough to hold out their hands for German bread) with their hands chopped off. To us, any clap of thunder was the thunder of German guns and the loud furnace noises from the steelworks terrified us in our beds because we thought it was Kaiser Wilhelm's men out to get us.

At school, we were given a "silver" medal from the king in commemoration of the Australian cruiser *Sydney* sinking the German cruiser *Emden* at the Cocos Islands in 1914. I thought at the time that the king had given it to me personally but every school child in Australia received one.

Empire Day was 24 May and we only had to make a token appearance at school. We were allowed to wear our Sunday clothes and Thora Wiseman, whose hair was usually just a wild frizz, had it neatly curled. We could bring our younger siblings to school on this day and we delighted in dolling them up and showing off our classrooms to them.

Everyone was seated on every form and seat imaginable and a flag was draped across the stage where a table with a large picture of the king and queen stood along with chairs for the ministers of the various churches. These men talked to us about Empire and inspired us with British might and power. We were made to feel very British and grateful to Britain. We believed that no matter where we were in the world, if we were in trouble, Britain would send a gunboat to save us.

Everywhere we went *God save the King* was played: at church, at concerts, at the movies and when they did we had to stand and sing sternly. I found it hard to sing that song then and it was even harder later in life.

There must have been pictures of King George V in the *Newcastle*

The Australian Army's 35th Battalion formed in Newcastle in 1915. (Photo: National Collection, Australian War Memorial)

Morning Herald and Miner's Advocate because I remember him in a dark naval uniform and overcoat. Never in casual wear. No scandal and never an ankle or leg showing. He was always grave and courteous, never sour but never openly smiling — our "friend", caring for us, looking after us. And we believed all this.

I felt both dismissed by and afraid of the men in army uniforms who sat in our house at the kitchen table, talking grimly. These were perhaps my uncles and their mates or Dad's friends. My memory is of "boots, beards and braces" and deep, serious voices . . . nothing joyous; it was male company from which girls were excluded.

I know now that these men had either been or were going to war. I never felt comfortable with them. I didn't know where "war" was or what it meant. To me they were an unwelcome intrusion into our home. It made me fearful of soldiers.

Later on I remember seeing a headline, "German Losses at Verdun 40,000". When it was explained this meant 40,000 men were dead, war and the idea of war horrified me. Why would people kill each other and treat each other so badly when life was so difficult anyway? I started to believe that grown-ups were stupid.

I remember seeing women knitting socks for soldiers on trams and at the tram stop at the Mayfield Terminus. Women seemed to be knitting everywhere, even Cynthia and Mum knitted at home. There was a poem in the paper that advertised Patons' Wool and Brooks' designs.

Knitting
On the trams and on the ships
With diligence befitting
They are knitting
Some with a smile upon their lips
Some with manners debonair
Some with earnest looking air
But each heart its own fashion
Heaves with pity and compassion
In their knitting, knitting, knitting
For the soldiers over there

Patons 4 ply 6½ skein
K. Brooks good designs 1d
65 Bone 9" long
All sized 8½d pkt of 4

Although I had learned to read at Mayfield primary the only books I read were about English children. You could say I was mentally brought up in London instead of dull old Mayfield with the steelworks forever blowing its whistle. I didn't know that its loud and angry hooting was telling men to go to work and to stop work.

There were whistles at 8am, 4pm, and 12pm indicating the different eight-hour shifts. If the whistles came loud and painfully long it meant that someone had been killed. To me, they were just annoying, piercing sounds that were part of the incomprehensible adult world.

The 8am whistle meant that I had to hurry through my oatmeal breakfast, which had been put in a big black cast-iron pot on the stove to soak overnight. As soon as the old black Metters stove was lit in the morning, it was heated up and cooked. We had Golden Syrup on our oatmeal and the first "big" words I learned to spell were "The Colonial Sugar Refinery Company Ltd."

Eight am found me spooning up the sometimes lumpy oatmeal with a reminder from my mother to put Bill's boots on, wash my face and hands,

The Newcastle steelworks, c. 1920. (Photo: John Turner collection, Cultural Collections, University of Newcastle, NSW)

Aerial view of the BHP steelworks, Mayfield, 1940s. (Photo courtesy Greg and Sylvia Ray)

comb my hair ready for her to plait it and/or mind the baby while she cut our lunches.

The 4pm whistle meant I was to be home from school to mind the baby or go on messages. "No, you can't play with Nellie!" Little sisters and brothers had to be minded. My school friend who I walked home with was a small inoffensive girl called Nellie Norgard, who lived a few doors down. She owned a big celluloid doll that she would let me hold, so I was always desperate to go to her place after school.

Her father worked at the steelworks. Most of my friends' fathers worked at the steelworks. Some were accountants, clerks, inspectors, foremen or just plain labourers, but they all worked at the steelworks.

Ours didn't. My father was a misfit. As a schoolteacher, he made us think we were better than the manual labourer and steelworker families with whom we mixed. I didn't know why: they were much better off than we were. The girls of those families had big celluloid dolls and Nellie Stewart gold bangles that cost two pounds two shillings. They went to the Church of England whilst we were unkempt and went to Mayfield Methodist (although old families like Winns, Goninans, Morrisons and Trewarthas also attended). This troubled me all my early childhood, especially as Nellie Norgard had a celluloid doll and I didn't.

Dad's younger brothers were, as he was, strong, dark-looking men, always dressed in dark clothes with heavy beards or five o'clock shadows, very much men's men. Good honest decent men, uneducated but loyal, hard-working, well behaved, humble. Good with money and what it took to survive. "Poor and honest" they said of themselves. They'd learnt a lot from their father, my grandfather; he'd made them all property ambitious. Every one, except Dad, joined the army during the War and fought overseas.

Every night after we'd eaten, Cynthia did the washing up on the back verandah in the tin dish. One night in 1918 I was carrying our plates from the kitchen after dinner and I fell over and broke a lot of them. There was so much agitation that I went outside and hid in the bushes till everything settled down. We had so little, we could scarcely afford to buy new plates. Mum replaced them with tin plates, which I thought wasn't all that bad. I said to everyone, "All the soldiers overseas get is a tin plate and a tin mug, so I think we should have the same as them."

This didn't go down well with my siblings, especially Cynthia who said, "You did that deliberately, to spite us, you selfish girl. No one cares what you think." It was a long time before we had china plates again and a long time that Cynthia held that grudge.

The Great War continued in full swing though 1918. I was in dread of the Germans catching me off guard. Mr Durham drove standing up in his dray and the rattle of his cart going over the nearby wooden bridge always made me think the Germans were coming to get us.

Our clocks at home were set by the steelworks' whistles . . . "Has the eight o'clock whistle gone yet?" "No? Well, the clock is fast." The steelworks' whistle was right on time; it was so loud and shrill it could be heard all over Newcastle. We had no radios or telephones to rely on then, so the steelworks kept time for us. It wasn't called BHP in those days, just "the steelworks".

The men arrived at the steelworks walking or on bicycles as no one owned cars. At each shift change, hundreds of bicycles covered the road like an army, with hordes of men walking beside them. All of them were in working clothes, clean when they came, filthy as they left, all with cheerful, robust faces. It's a powerful image imprinted in my mind. It was a forty-eight-hour, six-day week for those men. They seemed to be permanently entrenched in the belching monster, like disconsolate prisoners, with just Sundays to recover.

We had the poorest clothing. One of my dearest wishes was for a pink silk dress. We had a rich aunt Maggie on my mother's side, in Suva, who would infrequently send a trunk full of cast-off clothing which gave us the greatest delight.

Around this time Tom awakened my interest in movies and was the first in our family to discover their pleasure. When he was ten he discovered they were playing in Waratah and they became his escape. They were shown at the Waratah Council Chambers, an old red-brick building on the edge of Waratah Park. It was the town hall, a building that looked less like a theatre can't be imagined.

He took me to my first movie when I was eight in 1918. It was quite a long walk, about two miles. It became my escape too even though we rarely talked. Every Saturday he would take my hand and walk me to our little bit of paradise. For threepence we had a couple of hours of fantasy.

One film I remember well was a serial, *The Perils of Pauline* with Pearl White. Also Mary Pickford in *Daddy Long Legs* and an adventure serial called *The Lure of the Circus* starring Eddie Polo and Eileen Sedgwick. They may not have been the first movies I saw but they were my most remembered.

Waratah town hall in Turton Road, Waratah, in 1898. This is where Jean and her brother Tom went to the movies. (Photo: Ralph Snowball, Newcastle Region Library)

Tom was quiet but always entertaining. One of his acts was to put a hat on back-to-front and imitate a child who had lost his mum in Winn's department store and say, in imitation of the movies, "I don't belong here, I'm going back to ma people."

He loved the actresses Clara Bow, Bebe Daniels, Barbara Marr, Olga Petrov, Billie Burke, Barbara Marr, Anne Q. Nilsson, Wanda Hawley, Constance Talmadge, Agnes Ayres, Bissie Love, Mary Pickford, Theda Bara and his greatest love, Greta Garbo. He liked actors Warren Baxter, Antonio Moreno, William S. Hart, Charlie Chaplin (who I didn't like as he was too sad and reminded me of my home life), Tom Mix, Fatty Arbuckle, Charles Farrell, Harold Lloyd, Tom Mix and his horse Tony and his dog Duke, Buster Keaton, Richard Dix, Edmund Lowe, Buck Jones, Hoot Gibson, Thomas Meighan, Wallace Beery and Raymond Hatton. We both loved the *Our Gang* silent comedies.

He said he would have liked to have John Gilbert's looks. I wished he had them too. I went along with his likes and dislikes like a devotee because it was so nice to be taken to the movies. In later life, I was always flattered if someone asked me out.

9 · Boots, beards and braces

My uncle Ernie returned from France in September 1918. He had been wounded in action in France and had recovered in an English hospital. I was so happy to see him. He was still in the army but at least he was home.

His wounds, whatever they had been, had healed pretty well while he was in England. He seemed normal. He never talked about the War or his wounds or what he saw in France but he was never the same as he was before he left. He was quieter, more religious and more serious. He still had to divorce his wife, Mabel, but this didn't finally happen till 1921.

At the end of 1918 I finished third class and the War ended on 11 November. There were big celebrations and bell ringing at the school. We were told all the soldiers were coming home. And they did, bringing with them the Spanish flu epidemic.

Schools were closed for six weeks in 1919 for the epidemic, to our great joy. No one could go abroad without a white wire mask covered with gauze, especially in the old steam trams. None of our relations were affected but we heard that 10,000 people died throughout Australia, more than were killed at Gallipoli. I was too young to fully understand but I knew it was serious because of those masks we had to wear.

Dad's other brothers Bertie and Ollie returned home from France, intact. More "boots, beards and braces" in our kitchen but I was awfully glad to see them. Uncle Ernie was still tender with me and called me "sweetie" and "love", cuddling me closer than ever when he came. I loved it. He was the only person who ever cuddled me. He was my first admirer and he always held a special spot in my heart.

Ernie often came to see us in Bull Street, as did Dad's brother Bertie who told us ghost stories and promised us one shilling if we'd walk down to the cow bail near the back fence in the dark. We never did . . . even for the money. He really scared us. Bertie sadly died at forty, as did his son. We rarely saw Uncle Ollie.

Another "uncle", Charlie McNaughton who was married to Dad's Aunt Harriet, owned the Albion Hotel in Hannell Street, Wickham, and on occasions used to visit us with a very large bag of boiled lollies and a two-shilling piece for each of us when he left. Such largesse! Mum duly collected the money after he'd gone, much to our frustration. He was a big comfortable-looking man with white hair and a moustache who always sat the wrong way around on chairs. .

Despite the mostly sunny weather, life seemed always grey in my mind: grey earth, grey skies . . . even school seemed grey. I attribute this to my mother. Mum never let me play, I had to look after young children or run messages until it was too late in the day to play. As a child I never played, except in my mind. I found it hard to play when I became an adult and I think that's why I became lazy and indifferent.

I didn't feel hostile to my father, I even loved him, but he didn't spend a lot of time with us, even on weekends. We dealt with my mother.

She had another baby that year, my sister Eva, born at home. Mum wanted her to be called Nancy but Dad went down and registered her as Eva Edgecomb. Mum sulked for a week. I thought at the time, "Why is mum having more babies? We have too many kids already." I knew I'd have to help look after the new one.

The local midwife, Nurse Whiteman, who went about her duties on a bicycle, delivered Eva. Winnie, then aged five, paid her threepence for delivering Eva in a special ceremony. That was quite amusing and Winnie was thrilled with it. Mayfield was not very big and I'm sure Nurse Whiteman delivered for all the local poor, like us. She also had a small private hospital in Hanbury Street where the more affluent were confined.

"Ernie, put Bertie's boots on!" That is a phrase I heard many times in 1919 and I still remember it with affection. I heard it first at nine years of age when Grandma Sharp came to look after us when my sister Eva was born. She was telling my brother Tom to put his younger brother Bill's boots on, but, forgetting our names was referring to her own children of twenty years before: Ernie and his younger brother Bertrand. She was just forgetful . . . the years of looking after Ollie and Ernie and Bertie had left their mark. She was only sixty and didn't have long to live.

Cynthia still denigrated me even though she was now in second year at high school and doing well. Her new complaint was that as well as being ugly I was unloving. She didn't mind Mum's attitude or the chores she was given. She did everything Mum expected of her: all the housework and sewing and mending. To me she still had a "slave temperament" and paid heavily for it in later life. She was loyal and caring underneath everything, but took out her anger and resentment on me, not Mum.

She wasn't always unpleasant to me. I remember her teaching me to count to ten before I started school in Gosford. She taught me three numbers every day. I felt immense pleasure in her teaching me. She was often asked to take us younger children to various parts of Newcastle, parks, libraries and she seemed to enjoy it.

She sometimes took Tom and me into Newcastle Beach, which was quite a way from where we lived. We went to the "ladies' reserve" to swim. Bushes divided the ladies' reserve from the main beach where Tom had to swim. We wore black sateen homemade costumes and I always had a glorious time. I jumped for joy when I felt the water rushing over my bare feet. I loved the combined feeling of soft sand between my toes, the cold rushing water on my legs, the heat of the Australian sun on my body, the salty freshness of the air and sheer blueness of the sky circling my head. It was utter sensuous pleasure.

I always returned to Mayfield on the tram tired but happy with my Dorothy bag full of shells and sand and my fair skin red and sore.

I was intrigued by the terraced houses in Newcastle city near the beach. I felt that was where I should be living. (In my mind, I was really a London child with a nanny and a night and day nursery.) The terraces reminded me of pictures of London streets. The houses in Church Street, Mayfield, had elegance, but these slummy ones in Newcastle Beach and Wickham were more appealing to my mind.

I stared at the buildings around the beach as we walked to the tram with Cynthia.

"I'd like to live there."

"Well you never will so forget it."

"I might. One day. When I'm rich."

"You'll never be rich."

"Why not?"

"Because you're selfish."

"I'm not."

"Anyway, no one's ever going to marry you because you're so hideous."

She spoke to me like this all the time, but I never held a grudge. I believed her. I was hideous to look at. I told lies. I was selfish and uncaring. And mean. I thought she probably had good, sisterly reasons for being nasty. But I did feel angry and belittled.

I was very loving and maternal as a young girl so her accusations puzzled me. I wasn't perfect, I stood up for myself but so what? If I was so ugly why didn't she keep it to herself? Why hurt me? I instinctively knew I might need her in later life ... so I took it all.

Advertisements in the *Newcastle Morning Herald* from circa 1920.

Mr Harold C Crebert of Roe St Mayfield killed in action, France Sept 26 1916.

FIRM JELLIES: stand the mould in a basin of water containing a good handful of Salt and Soda.

Wet Umbrellas should never be left open to dry as the silk stretches when damp and is liable to split. The right method is to close the umbrella and stand it, handle down, to drain.

10 · Messages to the terminus

My teacher in fifth class, Mr Stove, was famous for caning the boys in the old house at the back of the school. I thought he was as black as Satan and ten feet tall, and his fingers poking into your back was something to deeply disturb you. When I met him years later I towered over him as he was only five feet four inches tall and seemed vulnerable and unthreatening, even likeable. When he was my teacher I hated him.

School at this stage was important to us. During my time there, Mayfield school was rebuilt. It had been old and rambling, consisting of three or four rooms and two portable classrooms. But the new school — two storeys, if you please — was very modern. I was now one of the "older" girls and well settled in.

The new building was completed in 1920 and had a sewer connected with doors to each toilet. Luxury indeed! It was renamed Mayfield East Superior Public School.

I did most of the messages for the family after school — as well as being the baby-minder. One of my hips is higher than the other from toting babies around on my hip. Great was my joy when Dad built a billycart to take the youngest baby for an outing . . . we never had anything so practical as a pram. I'm not knocking baby minding, I always liked the little things, but I yearned to play with other kids.

I must have walked hundreds of miles for messages. We lived about a mile from school and the "messages down to the terminus" were about another mile. It took me a half hour to walk to school and a half hour to walk to the terminus and another half hour to return

All the roads were gravel. Travel was by walking if you didn't have a bicycle or horse and cart. There were very few cars, and the footpaths were gravel. The rough roads had no curb or guttering and the streets were lit with gas lamps, not electricity.

The "terminus" was the Mayfield steam tram terminus to Newcastle city. It sat at the corner of Maitland Road and Hanbury Street. Maitland Road was the main road into Newcastle city. Hanbury Street went to Waratah

Steam tram in Mayfield, before 1922. (Photo: Bert Lovett collection, Norm Barney Photographic Collection, Cultural Collections, University of Newcastle, NSW)

where there was a rail link to Newcastle city. There were bush and tea-trees on one side of Hanbury Street in those days with frogs croaking in ponds. The terminus was where most of our few shops were, although there was a single small weatherboard grocer's shop in Vine Street.

The steam trams had a small engine tram at the front with usually just one passenger carriage behind. They ran into Newcastle from Mayfield. They were very noisy and gritty with a bell that went "clang clang clang" loudly as they left.

Sometimes I walked to the terminus on sweltering summer days with not a cloud in the sky or a soul in the street. Days when I thought I might die from the heat and relentless sun. That's when Mayfield seemed like a desert, like the most isolated place on the earth and all I could think of was to get away from there and from the blazing BHP furnaces and screaming whistles. There were days when the tram rail lines smouldered and the tram steam engine looked as though it would burst from the heat. That's when the driver and conductor looked pale and angry, with sweat on their uniforms, although they were mostly in good spirits.

Once I walked home from the terminus in teeming rain, my clothes soaked because I forgot an umbrella and there was hell to pay when I got home. I remember walking to the terminus in winter when the light faded fast as the sun sank like a stone at five o'clock. I had to walk back shivering in the night air.

This endless walking as a child seemed to be over enormous distances, but that was because the terminus was up one long, long hill and down another and I was a terrible dawdler. I loved the smell of freshly cut grass, the scent of flowers and the sounds of chittering birds, crickets and bees. I liked the mystery of the gum trees in the dark and the crispness in the winter night air. I especially loved the hiss of the steam trams and the shouts of the tram guards.

Mayfield was still very rural then. I'd cut across the paddocks at the back of our house, no houses there then, up to Crebert Street and then go up and down Hanbury Street and turn into Maitland Road. The names of those streets were embedded in my mind, as if I couldn't fully experience a street unless I could say its name automatically.

On the corner of Hanbury Street and Maitland Road was the Waratah Hotel, an old one-storey dark, red-brick building with white frosted windows with waratahs painted on them. After that was Brown's paper shop and toyshop, then later a shoe repair shop which we never patronised, because Dad mended all our shoes. He had a last and a "little hammer" he was always losing: "Where's my little hammer gone?" Dad also cut our hair, at least the boys'. We girls mostly had plaits, though sometimes he cut my hair short too. I hated that.

Next on Maitland Road was Witherspoon's very tidy and clean grocer's shop, an allotment next door where he kept his horses and carts for deliveries, then the butcher shop.

I spent a lot of time in the butcher's with its sawdust on the floor, and a big sign that said "No smoking" and another which said "Smoking and Spitting in this shop is an offence against the Law". Men were terrible spitters in those days; it always offended me. They would spit anywhere in the street.

Mr Alexander McGregor was the butcher and he was a very civil man. In answer to my timid request of a nice roast for about two shillings he would always reply, "Right you are." I always felt safe in the butcher's shop; they were always bright and clean and no swearing either. One day a woman asked him for a "couple of pounds of snags" and he gave her a sharp look and said calmly "we call them links of love".

The scales in the shops all had "scales made in Dayton-Ohio USA" written on them, which always intrigued me.

Beyond the butcher's there was nothing but the Misses Parkes' drapery shop. Many an hour I spent looking in their shop window coveting the big

A crowd waits for the first electric tram to arrive in Mayfield terminus, 1923. (Photo: Newcastle Region Library)

Mayfield terminus, 1920s. (Photo: Cultural Collections, University of Newcastle, NSW)

celluloid dolls which served as models to show off baby wear. These dolls came from Japan (priced at nineteen shillings and sixpence). They were the same as Nellie Norgard's and I don't think I ever wanted anything as much in my life.

I had an imaginary friend called Rosie who came with me on these expeditions, so I had someone to talk to about my dreams about dolls. I imagined Rosie lived in a big house with rooms full of dolls, prams and toys galore and a mother and father who doted on her. She was always happy to accompany me down to the terminus shops.

Mum often wondered why it took me so long to do the messages, but Rosie and I used to scan all the shop windows and discuss what we might buy that week. We knew every doll in Brown's paper shop window. I usually paid the paper bill at Brown's. It was about two shillings and sixpence a month; a newspaper cost one penny, so I often had a reason to linger. *The Newcastle Morning Herald and Miner's Advocate* was delivered to us every day except Sunday.

Rosie always liked the doll in Misses Parkes' window too, and I didn't like to tell her that that was the one I wanted most. Rosie was short-tempered and jealous. I told her Nellie Norgard had one (with a handkerchief pinned to its bonnet to stop its face from fading) and Rosie said her father would immediately buy her one if she asked him but she wouldn't because it might hurt my feelings. Rosie was perceptive and a loyal friend, though a bit of a snob.

No one in my family ever knew about Rosie, or about my imaginary adventures . . . I kept that world to myself. I pretended to be playing with Rosie at home when no one was watching. Everyone thought I talked to myself.

On the other side of Maitland Road, later, was Mrs Hunter's shop that sold fruit and confectionery and Mr Giles the (new) chemist who was a very sweet-looking man who looked like the actor Leslie Howard. Later on in 1921, Vaisey's shoe store was built near Church Street and then further down, in 1925, a new drapery store called The Coliseum was built. We began to have a few stores and shops to choose from.

My trips to the terminus were usually to the butcher's or to pay the paper bill. Groceries were usually delivered. A typical grocery order was six pounds of potatoes, six pounds of sugar, three pounds of butter, two plugs of Champion tobacco, one tin of jam, one tin of Golden Syrup, one bag of oatmeal and one bag of flour. My father grew most of our own fruit and vegetables in the back garden, and Chinese market gardeners from the Hunter River waterfront brought around baskets of fruit and vegetables to sell.

The Chinese market gardeners wore straw conical hats and carried poles over their shoulders, watering cans on each end, and were forever watering their geometrical, weedless gardens. Dad was friendly with them. I don't know who gave whom tips on growing vegetables but he helped them with letter writing.

One of them took his cart into the markets in town to sell fruit and vegetables and would then make the rounds of the local houses with his left-overs. With clock-like precision we were there to open the gates to the market gardens for him on his return to be rewarded with any "spec" fruit he would endeavour to throw at us. My mother, poor as we were, at last rebelled against our subservience to Chinese "coolies", as she called them, and the practice was stopped. Trust mum to do that.

SOME ITEMS FOR SALE AROUND 1920

The Girls Own Annual Book – 9 shillings
Father Tuck's Annual Book – 4 shillings and sixpence
Chums Book – 9 shillings
Solid gold Nellie Stewart bangles – £2 pounds 2 shillings

11 · Roast lamb, jam, baths and Methodist Sundays

School, baby-minding and running messages dominated my week but weekends were different. On Fridays Mum baked enough biscuits for the rest of the week and Saturday was bath day. In the morning, water was heated in a kerosene tin on a fire between two bricks in the backyard and put into a zinc tub with two handles. We had no bathroom in our house so we had our bath on the back verandah. We had our hair washed and brushed very firmly. Afterwards, we were given a penny to spend and we would walk to the terminus to buy an apple on a stick or a lolly. It was pleasant but not good for our teeth, which were never properly looked after.

If Tom and I didn't go to the pictures in the afternoon he would caddy on the golf links across from our house. My brothers had a better time on a Saturday than we girls; they all caddied for the BHP golfers wearing plus fours. The going rate was nine pence for nine holes. Riches indeed. No caddying on a Sunday, but Tom was never stuck for threepence. He milked the builder Mr Gane's cow when we didn't have our own. As well as being paid he received enough milk for the family. Tom was a very silent person but I don't think he missed much. He thought of lots of ways to make small amounts of money. He was never in debt in his life.

Saturday was also hot baked dinner day. Nothing was cooked again until Monday except vegetables to go with the cold left-over roast on Sunday. We mostly had roast lamb and vegetables on weekends, and chops or sausages or pork (never chicken) on other days. Mum made cheap desserts like sago and rice pudding, junket, fruit jelly, custard and banana custard. I don't remember being hungry.

Often Mum would make grape and blackberry jam, and also melon and lemon jam. When it was melon and lemon jam time the whole family gathered around the kitchen table to dice the jam melon.

There were fruit trees everywhere on our place though admittedly some were very old and the fruit wasn't top grade, but we had good grapes and gooseberries. There were quinces down by the creek and four very old pear

Steelworks golf links with Bull Street behind, early 1930s. (Photo: Cultural Collections, University of Newcastle, NSW)

trees and some fig trees on the golf course opposite our house. Dad planted a lemon tree in our backyard, which lasted, I believe, for 60 years.

The golf course had been part of an old estate that was owned by Newcastle's earliest collector of customs, Mr Simpson, the only port official for the town. Convicts built his house there, Waratah House, in 1848 and cultivated his land. We didn't know that then.

One weekend Cynthia took me into Newcastle to the Bolton Street Park to see the Prince of Wales (who visited Australia in July 1920 to thank Australians for their participation in the War) and I thought how lovely he looked, without a crown, with his happy smile and lovely golden hair shining in the sunlight. I had been well trained to love the royal family.

On Saturday nights our straight hair was put in rags, strips of old black lisle (rayon) stockings around which our hair was twisted to make a mass of curls for the next day. On Sunday afternoons, we were put into white voile dresses with blue sashes for Sunday school at the Methodist church. In winter, we wore red and blue coats with our curls and thought ourselves very fetching.

The only thing I liked about Sunday school was that it had a library and we could take a book home. I was into Elsie Dinsmore books, about an American, her house and her marriage. She had numerous children. I was about ten and I remember saying, "This Elsie Dinsmore has a baby every few pages." Mum pounced on me. No more Elsie books. I knew nothing about conception or birth and was bewildered. I never understood why there were no more books for me.

The Mayfield Methodist church was a strong establishment in our suburb. Some of the best families belonged to it: the Goninans, Winns, Trewarthas, Morrisons, Vaiseys, Cookseys, all top business men and many others including local aldermen.

The church was inaugurated owing to the influence and finance of Mr William Arnott, the biscuit manufacturer, who started his biscuit company in Newcastle in the 1800s. He was famous for his Sunday school classes and for his kindly nature. His grandson William was also a devout supporter of the Methodist church — a tall commanding figure, he was known in his Bible class as Long Bill and I think was partly responsible for founding the Newcastle YMCA.

Grandson Long Bill's Bible classes were very popular, particularly those held in the old Arnott "Holme" in Crebert Street. I remember it was called Holme because a holme meant a small island or islet or piece of flat ground near a river. Maybe William Arnott saw the house as an island retreat from the outside world.[3] The Bible classes always ended with afternoon tea where only the choicest of Arnott's biscuits were served. Long Bill's brother Sam and sister Leslie sang in the church choir. Another brother, Arthur, joined the Salvation Army and rose to the rank of adjutant. I always believed that the S-A-O in Sao biscuit stands for 'Salvation Army officer' but I've never been able to confirm it. But all that was well before my time in Mayfield.

---

3. It was eventually sold to Isaac Winn in 1898 and renamed Winn Court. In 1921 it was acquired by the Church of England and became St Elizabeth's Girl's Home and, later, St Alban's Boys Home. In 1988 it became Annesley House for the needy and now has been rebuilt as Uniting Annesley Court Mayfield for retirees. Annesley was William Arnott's wife's name.

12 · My father the bushie

My father occasionally gathered us around him in bed and read us some Dickens or stories about Br'er Rabbit and Br'er Fox. He always acted out Br'er Rabbit's cheeky words when Br'er Fox flung him into the briar patch in frustration: "Born and bred in the briar patch, Br'er Fox, baa-orn and bred!" Br'er Fox never outfoxed Br'er Rabbit.

Other times Dad would carefully open his violin case, take out his fiddle and play us a song about Simon Bonbello, a musical fellow who played on his cello each day. Or he played "Come, come, come and make eyes at me, down at The Old Bull and Bush" . . . and other songs. He didn't pay all that much attention to me, although, as I've said, he used to call me his "little Miss Sunshine", which I loved.

He was a wonderful carpenter and built a workroom for himself in the back garden to which he often retired. He had a collection of *The Bulletin* magazines there, various books and a hidden bottle of whisky. *The Bulletin* had a pink cover and was famous. Founded by J. F. Archibald and John Haynes in 1880, it was full of original stories and poems and much Australian nationalist sentiment.

Whenever I saw Dad take a swig from that whisky bottle, no niceties like a glass or ice, he warned me, "Don't tell Mum." Of course, I didn't. He wrote a lot of letters to *The Bulletin* out there and would probably have written stories or articles as well if he'd had the time and encouragement. He lived in his own world, somehow separate from us, a loner at his workbench. We all thought that he just wanted time by himself without Mum nagging him, but he never said that to us.

During the week, he would pedal off to distant Dudley to teach in the one-man school. He watered and tended his beloved vegetable garden before he left. He was often late coming home because, as we knew, he stopped off at the pub for a drink. Mum would not have alcohol in the house. We never saw him drunk, he just needed the occasional swig.

Later he taught for many years at Waratah Public School. Being a bushie at heart, he used to love teaching nature study. I believe he used to take his class out to Waratah Hill, now Braye Park, and teach them how to survive if lost in the bush. Years later, Bill Taylor, a returned RAAF serviceman, told our family that he and five other men were lost in the jungle in New Guinea in the Second World War and he was the only one who got through. He said that what saved his life was what he had learned about bushcraft survival on Waratah Hill when he was in "Sharpie's" class at Waratah Public.

Most weekends my father went to Raymond Terrace or Ash Island on the Hunter River, where our grandfather had a boatshed and go fishing or shooting with him. On rainy nights when he was there, I prayed to God to protect him from the perils of ship or boatwreck on the river. I now guess he was snug in the shed drinking rum with his father. He was great mates with his dad: he was the eldest and most dependent son.

We had a milking cow called Nellie, which stupidly somehow produced a bull calf we called Johnny. One day, out of need, Dad decided to slaughter the bull for food. Our neighbour Mr Lempke didn't like us and reported our slaying to the local police sergeant. It was illegal to kill animals privately for consumption, they had to be sent for demotion to an abbattoir. Mr Lempke must have wondered afterwards why my father wasn't called up before the bench. What he didn't know was that the sergeant, being a friend of my father's, was in on the act and also had his larder stacked with portions of Johnny's remains.

Dad caught all the fish we ate. He also shot wild ducks. Once, when he'd shot some wild ducks and no one would eat them, I said, "I'll eat one with you, Dad" and he gratefully cooked one for both of us.

He often came home late on Sunday with a stinking fishing bag and clothes smelling of fish and wood smoke and whisky. Sometimes he had bags of oysters and prawns. I supposed he went off to get away from us but we never questioned his right to do so.

He was a great friend of Theo Towns, a local professional boat builder who used to give him lessons in boat building. He was always building a boat of some kind in our backyard: skiffs and punts. He was a man of his hands and a man of the country. When he was a teacher at Minmi briefly early in his life, he taught all the boys how to shoot, and those later bushcraft classes at Waratah and Dudley schools were legendary.

He grew gooseberries, loganberries, grapes and vegetables but, sadly, never flowers. I used to often think of my grandmother's garden and how I missed it. Dad also kept bees so we often had honey.

The Hunter River foreshore at Mayfield, c. 1932. (Photo and information from "Along the Hunter at old Mayfield, NSW", F. J. Harborne, 2001, Newcastle Region Library)

He made his own fishing and prawn nets out of twine and then tanned them by boiling up a bag of wattle bark in the old copper and dyeing the nets in it. He dried prawns and smoked fish so that the smell of fish permeated the whole place.

He mended our shoes, nagged us to clean our teeth and was forever cutting my hair short, like a boy, much to my embarrassment. I hated going to school with it short. It was white and thin and I suppose he was encouraging it to grow a bit stronger. It certainly did that.

When he had an excess of tomatoes he would send me around to sell them to the neighbours. Even though they were round, firm beautiful red tomatoes and the neighbours readily bought them, this chore was always shameful to me. I'd love to have some of those tomatoes now.

He was always going to give someone the "father of a hiding" but the only time he ever hit me in anger was when I turned a somersault in bed and put my foot through a window. The worst thing he could think of to say was, "God damn, jump on the flaming thing!" He would sometimes go into a

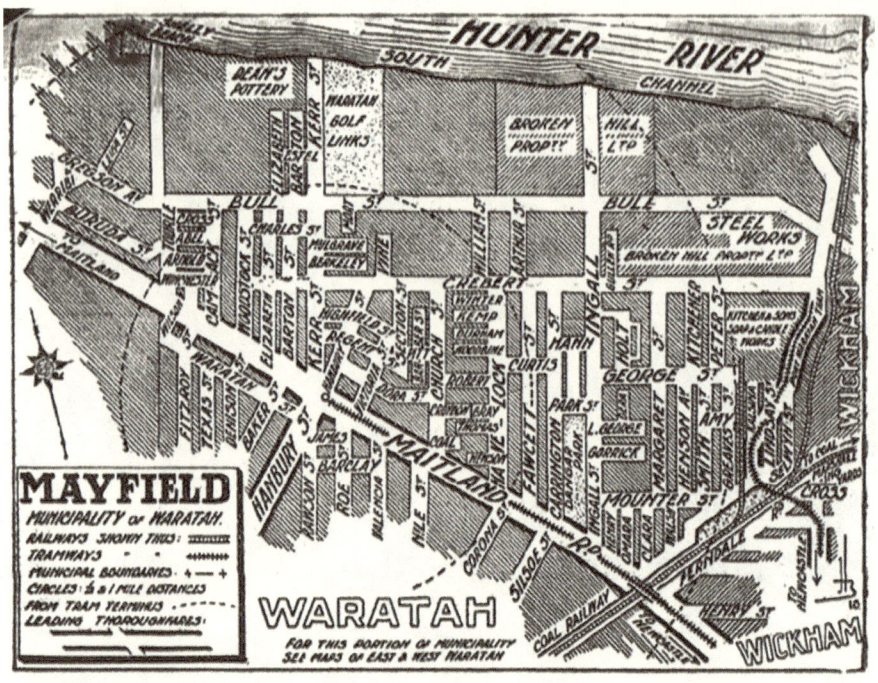

Mayfield street map, 1925, *Wilson's Street Directory*. (Image: Cultural Collections, University of Newcastle, NSW)

towering rage over something and stalk out and take it out on the garden.

We didn't have any holidays or go anywhere, but one day Dad took some of us to Raymond Terrace, where Grandfather had his boatshed, in a rowing boat he'd built. It was an isolated boatshed on the Windeyer's property. He rowed all the way up the Hunter River, we didn't live far from the river in Mayfield, but it was a terrible long trip. When we got there he said he was "going out to shoot a haul for bait", meaning to net some small fish or prawns for bait. But I thought he said, "shoot a horse for bait". This set me worrying and praying he wouldn't be arrested and sent to prison if he was caught.

We weren't allowed to have pets, but somehow a cat wound its way into our place. We named it Percy and Dad was always threatening it with extinction until the day it caught a rat. Thereafter it was the best cat in Mayfield. He loved it so much that one weekend he went to Raymond Terrace and missed it so much he sent a message back for us to put it in a sugar bag with a hole cut for its head and to put it on the bus. He had to walk about a mile to collect it. I can still see Percy with his pink mouth open wide and Dad feeding it oysters he was opening. He didn't take Percy in the boat with him when he went fishing but the cat would sit on the wharf waiting for him to return and take a flying leap into the boat before it had pulled in. Later on, Percy was hit on the head by a cricket ball and became a bit funny but Dad still loved him.

Dad often went to Sydney to see shows (musicals) like *Chu Chin Chow* and *Our Miss Gibbs*. He stayed with one of his well-off sisters there but never asked my mother to go with him. I actually don't remember him ever taking Mum out anywhere. Certainly, I thought he didn't love her, though he was loyal to her. She was jealous of any female schoolteachers he talked about at home, but philandering wasn't his style. I thought secretly that it was a pity it wasn't a more loving marriage, as neither seemed particularly happy. Perhaps their love had faded? I certainly hoped for better for myself when I married. But that was looking a long way into the future.

Waratah House (Simpson's Folly), top c. 1920, bottom c. 1930. (Photos: John Turner collection, Cultural Collections, University of Newcastle, NSW)

13 · Simple pleasures

Our home life in those days consisted of very simple pleasures. We walked down to the river to see the derelict Waratah House or to the top of Bull Street to see the "burned down" house, which had belonged to the Breckenridges, who owned a somewhat exclusive shop in Newcastle.

Charles Simpson, Collector of Customs, who built Waratah House, was given a grant of 36 acres in 1831. The area is now bounded by Crebert, Kerr and Ingall streets and the Hunter River. He named his house for the waratahs that grew there in profusion and it was the furthest north it grew. He had his convicts row him by boat down river to his office in Newcastle. He established extensive vineyards and orchards. I remember the pear trees in the middle of the old golf course that had been his land. They were a mass of white blossom in spring, however, their fruit was very small and inedible . . . bitter and hard as stones. This history was unknown to me when as children we wandered in and out of the old rooms of Waratah House and the surrounding land. I remember the old wallpaper in the house particularly well. All that land along the river was known as "The Folly" because Waratah House was known as Simpson's Folly. It was demolished in 1933 to allow BHP to erect a pipe mill.

On our side of Bull Street, starting from Ingall Street and heading west, was an old Chinese market garden, then old Mrs Norgard, her daughter Mrs Pritchard and then her son Mr Peter Norgard. Then the Gleasons who had a small mixed business; then a small creek with watercress growing in it; Mr and Mrs Lempke; then our place (there were no street numbers in those days); then Mrs Nelmes; then a vacant block of land; an old house in which the Gullivers lived; Mrs Russell (about whom I write later); then Kitty Kuhn who lived with Mrs Casino, her sister who kept fowls and lived on a large block of land in a dilapidated two-storey stone house right on the footpath. I would take them up a billycan of milk and Mrs Casino would give me a few eggs. They were two old crones to me, dressed in old threadbare clothing and corn-bag aprons. Kitty Kuhn was, and looked, slightly mental. Mrs Casino was different. She once showed me very grand wedding photos and told me she had travelled in Europe. Next came the Minters and Durhams, and then on the corner a convent. We often peeped through the palings and watched the nuns praying.

On the opposite side was a boatshed. I forget who owned it. Then, heading east, Mr Latham who owned the next boatshed and where the New Year's Day regatta was held. Then came Cox's dairy farm, followed by a Chinese vegetable garden. Next was the BHP golf course where my brother Tom caddied. Then the massive steelworks.

This area I have described was bounded by Ingall Street on the east, the Hunter River to the north and Kerr Street to the west.

Mayfield had been the most sought-after suburb in Newcastle before the steelworks was built. Wealthy grocers, butchers and storekeepers lived there: Mullaleys, Winns, Rundles, Vaiseys, Breckenridges; and managers, dentists and doctors. The iron founders — Goninans — as well as the Morrisons, Bearbys, Witherspoons, McGregors, Schofields and Trewarthas — had beautiful brick homes with tennis courts and servants and big gardens in Mayfield. The Trewartha family owned a grocery store in Hunter Street (Lane and Trewartha) with the best bacon, jams, sauces, teas and coffees in Newcastle. Old Mr Trewartha greeted everyone with "Good morning, good morning, good morning", his dear old face wreathed in smiles as he ushered us in. I loved going in there, with the sawdust on the floor and the assistants always grinning.[4] When the steelworks started, all these families or their descendants moved to the suburbs of New Lambton or, later, Bar Beach. But when I first came to Mayfield there they were all in full flower, and I was aware, even at the age of ten, of a great contradictory split in Newcastle society.

---

4. The store was bought by Rundles in 1939.

14 · An intrepid ten-year-old

Grandmother and Grandfather Sharp sold their property in Wallsend and moved to a house in Mary Street, Islington, in 1920.

Grandma Sharp only ever let me down once and I don't think she knew she was doing it. I was about ten years old and one morning I was given threepence to go to town on a message. It was one penny on the tram to Newcastle and a penny home to Mayfield. When I left school to do the message I thought I would be very daring and take the bus to Newcastle (the *Endeavour* or the *Irresistible* as they named the buses in those days). The bus fare was one and a half pence but what did I care? The bus stop was outside the school and saved me a long walk.

My message done I started to worry about that extra half penny, so I walked to Grandma's new house at Islington, an inner suburb of Newcastle. I thought she would give me a penny, grown-ups always gave me a penny, but Grandma didn't this time. And I didn't ask. She was standing in the vegetable garden making desultory conversation with someone in the street. I suppose I wasn't that noticeable to her, after all she had many other grandchildren. I soon left and walked the rest of the three miles home. I bought a lolly on the way home with the halfpenny and returned the full penny to Mum.

Was there a to-do when I finally arrived home though! It was dark and they were worried sick. I doubt if I told them the truth. My life was studded with lies and evasions. All my family kept their doings to themselves and I was no different. Still, I felt resentment building up inside me against the family pressures.

One Thursday soon after this I was told at school that Arnott's biscuit factory would be selling broken biscuits at sixpence a scoop at 7.30 am the next day. I rushed home and asked my mother if Tom and I could go and get some. She was usually hesitant about saying yes to my requests but this time she said yes. After all, broken biscuits were food, and all to be had for two shillings.

Highly excited, we set our old Westclox alarm clock for 6 am. That would give us time to get dressed and walk the mile to get the steam tram at the

Mayfield terminus into Newcastle city. "Hell Fire Jack" was the name given to all steam tram drivers and the tram guard would blow his whistle shrilly. For one penny each he would deposit us at Union Street, Cooks Hill.

We had clean well-ironed pillowcases with us (the ones with tape to close them) and we alighted from the tram and rushed up the hill on Union Street, past Cooks Hill Intermediate High School which Cynthia attended, past a few more shops and there was the biscuit factory with a line of underprivileged children, all clutching pillowslips and waiting for the factory to open. If it had been already open the children would have hoped that the broken biscuits weren't all gone, but we actually did this trip many times and there were always some biscuits left.

A 1920s celluloid doll from Japan.

For sixpence you got a big scoop and I'm not talking ice-cream scoop. They were huge scoops and the pillow would be bulging by the time we had three scoops, all for the unbelievable price of one shilling and sixpence.

With four pence for our fares, my brother and I had two pence left over to take home. Oh, what an exciting adventure it was, and we were always home in time to have a hasty plate of porridge and be at school by 9.30 am.

Looking back, we were the poorest of the poor, going to so much trouble for broken biscuits, but we didn't realise it then. It was an adventure to us.

I still dreamt about the celluloid doll — the one in the Misses Parkes' window (cost nineteen shillings and sixpence) — for months before each Christmas but it never materialised. At Christmas 1920, when I was ten, I had especially asked Santa Claus for the doll. I was so disappointed when it wasn't at the foot of my bed on Christmas morning that I disappeared for hours. Nobody could ever pry out of me where I'd been. I'd been down to the terminus, in the Christmas day heat, gazing tearfully into the small draper's shop window where there were two celluloid dolls as models for baby wear. It probably was good for my character because I never again set my heart on anything. I took the cold fact that I would never have one to my young heart. I never again considered Santa Claus anything but a cold-hearted miser even though I still regarded him as a reality long after my

Arnott's factory, Union Street, Cooks Hill (date unknown). (Photographer unknown)

friends found out he didn't exist. Such are the contradictions with which we live.

When I arrived home that Christmas Day, Mum asked where I'd been but I didn't tell her. I didn't even tell her of my disappointment. She wouldn't have been sympathetic I thought, so as usual I kept it to myself. As far as the future went that was the safest thing to do, even if it wasn't to be long before some confronting truths were aired in our family.

Meanwhile we had an invasion from the "Old Dart" to cope with.

15 · The Pommy invasion

In the next two years (1920–21) there was big change in Mayfield as well as in my life. The English firm John Lysaght had decided to build an ironworks plant at the end of Ingall Street, to add to the general background of thumping, banging and whistling of the steelworks. They built it on reclaimed mangrove swampland between the end of Ingall Street and the steelworks, pumping out sand to a depth of five feet (1.5 metres) filled in the swamp. On this land they built a plant that in its heyday rolled out over a million tons of galvanised and corrugated iron each year.

Lysaght was a sheet steel manufacturer that began in Britain in 1857 but soon found Australia was its largest customer. Besides making pre-painted sheet steel other Lysaght products included material for motorcars, refrigerators, washing machines, stoves, air conditioning units, roofing and cladding, truck bodies and rail wagons.

Work in the plant in Mayfield could only be carried out by skilled workmen, none of whom could be found in Australia, so two separate groups of men had to be transferred to Mayfield from British works: ninety-five men from the sheet rolling mills at Newport on the Usk River in Wales and twenty-eight men from the galvanising works at Bristol on the Avon River in England. With their families, the total reached two hundred and twenty.

Lysaght planned to house them all near the works at Mayfield so they set about buying all the land they could around us. My grandfather owned our house, Mrs Nelmes' house, a vacant block of land, the house where the Gullivers lived and the land that went right to our little creek at the back. Lysaght bought all this land from him and on those vacant blocks they built Avon Street (named after Bristol's river). Gullivers' house was also sold to them and Mr Bob Miller of Lysaght lived in it with his wife and two girls, Ruby and Edith.

The area in Avon Street, where fine brick houses were built for the English and Welsh skilled migrants, and the whole area defined by Avon, Vine, Bull and Usk streets (Usk Street was named after Newport's river) were nicknamed "Pommy Town" by the local residents. The area is identifiable today

Hunter River foreshore at Mayfield with Lysaght's in background (including chimney stacks) and Ryland Brothers in the foreground, c. 1932. (Photo and information from "Along the Hunter at old Mayfield, NSW", F. J. Harborne, 2001, Newcastle Region Library)

by a stately avenue of tall palm trees off Industrial Drive in Avon and Mena streets.

The migrants with their wives and families were lured out to Australia with the promise of good jobs making galvanised steel and specially built homes to rent. Around eighty-six homes were erected, most of them still standing today. Of course, some of the workers were housed in dwellings already built and a few chose to rent houses elsewhere.

There was a grand parade of the new migrants through the streets of Mayfield when the workers arrived in March 1921, which we all dutifully watched. Each of the migrants' houses were stocked by Lysaght with free provisions.

I never minded the Pommy invasion like others did. They came with their English and Welsh accents and I was enthralled. One of the most memorable sounds of my childhood was a group of Welsh workers, half-tiddly on their way home from the pub, singing *When I Survey the Wondrous Cross* outside my bedroom window.

> When I survey the wondrous cross
> On which the Prince of glory died,
> My richest gain I count but loss,
> And pour contempt on all my pride.
>
> Forbid it, Lord, that I should boast,
> Save in the death of Christ my God!
> All the vain things that charm me most,
> I sacrifice them to his blood . . .

Such music! Such harmony! It must have been good for me to remember it.

One of the benefits of the settlement was that the immigrant children came to our school and one boy, in particular, took my fancy: Jack Hunt. He was good-looking, gentle and Welsh. I never said a word to him but I thought he was fascinating. He was very quiet and thoughtful, not like the Australian boys. I was fixated for a long while.

It was to these iron mills at Lysaght that my brother Tom later went to work after he worked at Ireland's grocery distribution centre in Mayfield; but a lot was to happen to our family and to me before then.

16 · Cynthia, school and me

I was in sixth class when my sister Cynthia was suddenly whisked away to Queensland. It was 1921. She was fifteen years old. She wanted to complete high school but my father decided that as she was past the school leaving age of fourteen she must go to work for his sister Maude, who was married to a wealthy pastoralist named Gilbert Lauder. They'd married in 1910 when she was twenty-three and he was forty-six. They had a large sheep station in southern Queensland near Charleville. Cynthia was to be housemaid to my father's five nieces. The reasoning was that the money she earned would help support our family. No one thought of her continuing education.

I remember being on Newcastle Station with the whole family and an important-looking train steamed in. It was the overnight from Sydney to Brisbane and it stopped at Newcastle for a half hour. A very pretty woman — my aunt Maude who I'd never met but who for some reason we always called Aunty Lil — emerged from a carriage with a crowd of little girls around her.

The family was en route to Queensland from Sydney where they had been holidaying. Everyone sat in the railway cafeteria with cups of tea and sandwiches, with long gushy farewells between Mum and Dad and Cynthia. The rest of us stood and sat around bewildered, with no idea what all this meant. The scene is stamped on my memory because at the time I was pleased to see the last of Cynthia. Now, I thought, there is no one to tell me how ugly I am and I might, if I was lucky, get that pink silk dress I always wanted.

I was still obsessed with pink silk. I was always stuck in blue and hated it. What Cynthia had to do with this I don't know but in my infantile brain I worked out that with one less to keep there might be more for me. How silly I was. Mum had my two younger sisters, Winnie aged seven and Eva aged three, both of whom she seemed to love more than me, so I was just a nuisance. There was no way I was getting a new dress.

I thought that Cynthia looked rather forlorn as she boarded the train with our unknown aunt and all those little girls. She just wanted to please our parents and had no clear idea of what was going to happen to her. She knew I was smug about her going but she couldn't hide her tears.

"I'll miss you," I lied.

"Take care of Winnie," she said. I nodded but Winnie was the last person who needed my care. She'll look after herself, the bossy little thing, I thought, but I knew I would be looking after her and Eva every day. And there was a new baby due the next year, although I didn't know it then.

Cynthia waved till she was out of sight. I was happy to see her go but even at age eleven I sensed her anxiety. Little did we know she was being sold into another sort of bondage and that our pretty aunt and her five young daughters weren't all they appeared.

Home life resumed as usual except that now, as the oldest sister, I had to help with the house cleaning and washing up as well as baby-minding and message-going. As well as school.

School wasn't a worry that year. I was in 6A now and good at English, arithmetic and problems, but I was beginning to think that on no account would I go on to senior high school . . . another five years of home life would be too much to endure. I was having stronger and stronger feelings of rebellion.

My teacher in 6A was Miss Olive Champness, one of the teachers that I truly loved. She instilled in me a passion for and understanding of English poetry and literature, which I have never lost. She read my compositions to the class and gave me every encouragement to read and write. Not that I was a great writer — I knew I wasn't — I just wrote honestly.

She was a great lover of Christina Rosetti and her poetic style and talked for hours about a particular poem, *At Home*, which she made us learn by heart. It was one of the poems that Cynthia had recited at school so well. It always had a profound effect on me. Miss Champness made me think about it and its relevance to me.

> *At Home*
> When I was dead, my spirit turned
> To seek the much frequented house:
> I passed the door, and saw my friends
> Feasting beneath green orange boughs;
> From hand to hand they pushed the wine,
> They sucked the pulp of plum and peach;
> They sang, they jested, and they laughed,
> For each was loved by each.
> I listened to their honest chat:
> Said one: "Tomorrow we shall be
> Plod, plod along the featureless sands,
> And coasting miles and miles of sea."
> Said one: "Before the turn of tide

We will achieve the eyrie-seat."
Said one: "Tomorrow shall be like
Today, but much more sweet."
"Tomorrow," they said, strong with hope,
And dwelt upon the pleasant way:

"Tomorrow," cried they, one and all,
While no one spoke of yesterday.
Their life stood full as blessed noon;
I, only I, had passed away:
"Tomorrow and today," they cried;
I was of yesterday.
I shivered comfortless, but cast
No chill across the tablecloth;
I, all forgotten, shivered, sad
To stay, and yet to part how loath:
I passed from the familiar room,
I who from love had passed away,
Like the remembrance of a guest
That tarrieth but a day.

Somehow, she saw possibilities in me, despite my ragged clothes and unkempt appearance. She spoke to me more as a friend than a teacher. She wanted me to go on to high school and sit for the Leaving Certificate. She thought I could be a teacher or a journalist. I didn't agree with her. I didn't want to stay at school and go on to teachers' college or university. My ambition was to leave home and get a job as soon as I could. In sixth class, we had to make up our minds where the future lay. My father, being a schoolteacher too, thought the only decent career open to a woman was teaching. He pleaded with me to consider this but I had different ideas. I knew I was too shy to ever stand up in front of a class and could think of no alternative but that of a typist. I never had much imagination about my future.

At that time in sixth class children either took special classes and sat the examination for high school (which went on to the Leaving Certificate) or sat for the QC (Qualifying Certificate) and thus determined our future. The QC mostly led to the lesser schools and not to university. A big decision for an eleven-year-old!

I took the latter course and ended up with a QC. I was a fool not to listen to my father and Miss Champness but at that stage I was more determined than them. However, my determination was about to be sidelined by a fateful encounter on Newcastle Beach.

17 · The big lie

It was a late September morning in 1921, early spring but unseasonably hot. My sisters Winnie, Eva and myself were at Newcastle Beach with Mum who was pregnant again. We had been having fun swimming in the sea and playing in the sand. While we were slowly packing up to go home in the late morning, an older woman friend of Annie's came over and began talking to her.

It turned out the friend hadn't seen Mum for a long time. She gazed at us all playing around in the sand and asked Mum if we were all her children.

"No," said Mum pointing at Winnie and Eva. "Those two are mine but she" — pointing at me — "is Will's."

Mum thought I was too far away to see and hear this, but I did hear. I was shocked.

I said nothing, but on the tram going home I asked, "Mum, why did you lie to that woman? Saying I wasn't your child."

Mum turned pale and said nothing. She didn't correct me or explain herself, she just looked embarrassed and, as was her way, went silent.

I said no more but there was a sick feeling in my stomach. I'd never seen or heard my mother lie before. When she fell silent I felt what she said might be true: that I *wasn't* her child. If so . . . whose child was I? And why had she pretended to be my mother all these years? That's lying, that's against her religion! How dare she disown me! I knew she never loved me. Maybe this is why? Maybe I'm an orphan! And who is Will? Is that a man or a woman? What's going on here? And why, for God's sake, this awful silence! Is it so horrible to talk about?

As soon as we arrived home, instead of unpacking my things I ran to our neighbour Mrs Lempke and asked her if she knew why Mum had said what she did. Mrs Lempke was very close to our family and always knew "everything".

"Didn't anyone ever tell you?" she asked, clearly surprised by my question. "Annie is not your real mum. Your real mother was Annie's older sister, Wilhelmina. She was called "Will", short for Wilhelmina. She was married to your father before Annie. She died soon after childbirth having Bill, when you were two years old. You and Cynthia and Tom and Bill are all Wilhelmina's kids. It's no secret. After she died, Annie went up there to Dolgelly — somewhere in the outback near a town called Boomi — to look after you all. Then she married your father when they came back to Gosford. I'm sorry I thought Annie would have told you about it. Or Tom? You don't remember your mother?"

"No. I don't. Mum's never ever mentioned it or even my real mother's name," I said in tears. "So, she's my stepmother? I always thought there was something not right. She's never loved me. She's my stepmother! My real mother died! Will? Wilhelmina! Oh God!"

"Well, actually she's your aunt as well, isn't she? She did a big thing taking you all on for your father's sake. You should be grateful to Annie. She's been very good for you."

"No," I burst out, "no, she hasn't."

"Don't be unfair, Jean. She probably thought you always knew and didn't want to bring it up. Cynthia would know, she was old enough when it all happened. She would remember. Didn't she tell you?"

"Nobody told me!"

"Nobody?"

I ran home in tears. I felt as if my whole life had been a lie, that I had been criminally deceived. My anger grew as I ran. Tom was in the backyard.

"Did you know our real mother died?" I stormed towards him. "In childbirth, with Bill. Annie is our stepmother. Our real mother's sister. Our mum's name was Wilhelmina. We had another mother. Our real mother is dead!"

Tom looked at me confused. He didn't seem able to speak. For some reason, he wasn't completely surprised.

"You were four," I said. "You must remember something?"

"Just a vague feeling of something sad happening years ago and someone cooking my dinner. I thought that was mum. I always thought Mum was my mum."

"We all did," I said. Tom didn't seem all that fussed. He looked concerned but he wasn't about to blame anyone. He was like that.

"You'd think she would have told us . . . by now."

"She probably was going to. Some day."

"She was never going to tell us. Nor was Dad."

The rest of the family never understood my despairing angry reaction. I didn't understand it myself. The betrayal was deep for me. I was hurt. Deceived and abused. I felt I was on my own now, forever. I could trust no one. I wanted to scream.

Dad wasn't much help. I'd overheard him say once he'd been married before but I didn't realise it was to my mother! He shrugged and said he thought I knew. He told me how much he'd loved Wilhelmina, my mother, but he felt he needed someone to help him raise us children. It was sad but I had to get on with life, he said. He thought Annie was doing a good job.

"She's treated me like a slave," I said. "And Cynthia, too."

"She's pregnant," Dad said. "You have responsibilities as older children of the family. You were treated no different to the rest. Don't start to bloody whinge now . . . "

"She's never mentioned mum's name to me. My own mother! She let me think *she* was my real mother. She's a fraud."

"Jean, she's looked after you as best she could. She's put up with me and my habits and our lack of money. She's always thought of you as her children, like a mother. You know that."

"She doesn't treat us like she does Winnie and Eva. She loves them more than us."

"She does not! As far as I'm concerned you treat her as if she's your mother. Understand?"

"I can't and won't ever treat her as my mother. Ever again! Because she ISN'T!"

"I'll give you the mother and father of a hiding in a minute, Jeannie . . . "

I didn't care if he did!

I stormed out of his shed and ran right down to the end of our backyard. I picked up a big piece of wood and bashed it against the lavatory door until Dad yelled at me to stop, that I was frightening Nellie, our cow. I stomped off to Avon Street and up to the terminus and back, kicking anything I could on the way, so I would calm down.

Annie was preparing dinner by the time I returned. I marched into the kitchen and confronted her.

"Why didn't you tell me?'

Silence. She was cutting up a pumpkin with a large knife. She knew what I was talking about but she was having difficulty cutting through the pumpkin skin. She pretended this pumpkin was all that mattered.

"You didn't tell Tom or Bill either? Did you think we'd never find out?"

Silence. More pumpkin cutting, which wasn't going well. The skin was too hard. Then she stopped:

"I didn't think it was important."

"Not important? That our mother had died? That you weren't our mother?"

"She was my sister."

"I know that. But you've never mentioned her name. In all this time, not once did you say her name. I didn't even know you had any sisters except Aunty Maggie."

"I had a brother called George, too. My twin brother Cecil was killed in a horse and buggy accident when he was fifteen. I was a twin you know."

This sounded pathetic. I had never heard of either of them.

"I'm not talking about them," I said.

Silence again. She stared at the pumpkin in frustration and put down the knife.

"I did what I thought was right. What the Lord wanted."

"The Lord wants you to be truthful. And kind."

"I am kind."

"It's not kind to lie to your children."

"It's unchristian to say that, Jean. I didn't lie."

"You didn't tell us. That's lying."

"When was I supposed to tell you? When? Cynthia could have told you. Why didn't she? She knew it might upset you. So did I. I don't want any more trouble, please."

"You're not my mother. I'm never going to call you Mother or Mum again."

"What am I then?"

"My aunt . . . my stepmother."

"I've been looking after you as a mother for years . . ."

"My mother was gentle and kind. And loving!"

Annie then did something I'd never seen her do. She lost her temper. She picked up the pumpkin and, for a split second I thought she was going to throw it at me, but she turned and threw it onto the floor in front of me where it split open. I was shocked. Shaking, she pointed the knife at me.

"See what you've made me do! You wicked girl! Go to the bedroom and shut the door. Come back when you've washed your mouth out with soap. And ask God to forgive you for saying that."

I ran into my room and slammed the door. I screamed at the top of my voice, long and loud. Finally, I fell onto the bed and began crying, making sure everyone could hear me. I had never felt so desolate in my life. Or so resentful. I wasn't going to ask God for anything. Or wash my mouth out. I tried to think about my real mother and if I remembered anything of her. I only remembered a feeling of someone being nice to me and putting on my shoes. No face. No image, just a feeling. Was that my mother? I clung on to that feeling as only a sullen little girl can. I felt it was the only "mother love" I had or would ever have.

I felt a raging anger all over my body. Raging because I had felt guilty at not loving my "mother" — Annie — but had hated her. I had a huge affection and warmth inside me, a loving nature, which only found an outlet in toys or imaginary friends. I had been denied a mother's love from her. She treated me like a worker, a domestic servant, she gave me no affection or love but gave massive affection to her own children. I felt no love from her and had been lied to about her being my mother. She had replaced my mother and hadn't even had the good grace to tell me.

No photo of my mother was in the house nor anything that belonged to her. She was not honoured in any way yet she was Annie's *sister*. There was no trace of her. She, who might have given me love, was snatched away while I was a child when I didn't realise what had happened. No one thought it wise to tell me or to try and make up for that loss. I felt a massive victim. My whole being was packed with resentment and anger. It didn't matter if it was logical or not, it was there. I was angry at such treatment, angry at Annie's lack of empathy, lack of decency and lack of emotion. What sort of human being was this person acting as my mother? What sort of inhuman witch was she? I felt I had been mistreated all my life and refused what should have been my right.

I resolved, then and there, cruelly perhaps, that I would never fully cooperate with Annie again. As soon as I could I would get away from her and the whole miserable situation. I decided to go to domestic science school and learn shorthand and typing so that I could get away from the atmosphere at home and my cold-hearted stepmother and get a job.

And then, for me, the bright lights and pretty clothes!

Later, my father secretly showed me a picture of my birth mother Wilhelmina which he kept in his shed. When I asked him why he'd never shown it to us he said that he thought it would have been unfair to Annie.

Annie Sharp, née Hibberd (left), and sister Margaretta Hibberd, date unknown.

What about unfair to us, I thought, but didn't say it. It was to be the only picture I, or any of us, ever saw of her. The good thing about all the fuss was that Dad felt free to tell us about her and what had happened before we were born.

It took weeks to tell. He spoke to us alone in his shed, away from my "mother" Annie, because it was clear she didn't like the story being told.

18 · Wilhelmina, the lost love

The day and moment Dad remembered most, he said, was sitting in the Dolgelly hotel's tiny lounge on an early evening in autumn, May 1912, and staring out the window into the darkening, flat landscape. "That was the gloomiest moment of my life," he said.

The body of his beloved wife, Wilhelmina, our mother, was lying in an open coffin on the table in the dining room. She was clothed but most of her body was covered with a white sheet with only her face showing. He had refused to cover her face and had delayed the funeral as long as he could. The air was chilly and there had been a light frost in the early morning. That frost remained embedded in his memory. All frosts reminded him of Dolgelly.

Wilhelmina had been pronounced dead by a doctor from Moree some three days before and the nearby Boomi town authority had issued a death certificate.

Dad said that in that dismal moment he thought that everything was lost, that he'd never recover, that his hopes and dreams had died with Wilhelmina. "She was so smart," he said, "so sensible. Her common sense got us through. I thought she was invincible. What was I going to do without her?"

Dad's father and mother were sitting in the lounge with him that moment. On hearing of Wilhelmina's death, they had come directly, all the way from Wallsend–Plattsburg. Dad's father, our grandfather, also named Thomas Sharp, had been on the phone in the lounge for hours completing arrangements for the funeral and contacting Wilhelmina's family to arrange for her sister Annie to travel to Dolgelly immediately. He also informed most of Dad's brothers and sisters. Our grandma Janet sat beside him knitting incessantly.

His father walked slowly over to where Dad stared out the window.

"You need to pull yourself together, Tom," he said gently. "You must think of your kids now. Janet and I will take the baby and look after him for as long as we can. Your mother says she'll do that only if you agree. It'll take the burden off you. Would you be happy with that?"

"Thanks, Dad, I suppose so," Dad said in a daze. He didn't really want to part with any of Will's kids, he told us, but he knew it wouldn't be forever.

"I've spoken to Will's sister, Annie Hibberd, and she's on her way from Minmi to help mind the kids for the time being. She'll be here after the funeral tomorrow. Is that all right with you?"

"Annie? She's against alcohol, she won't stay here."

"No, I've spoken to her about that. She'll stay as long as she's needed she says. She'll do it without pay. She's been here before with you so she knows your kids well. She sounds ideal. I've discussed this with Janet and we think it might even be a good idea if you were to ask her to marry you. I think she would."

"Marry her?"

"She's over thirty Tom, she knows the children; all those Hibberd girls liked you I remember and, you never know, it might just suit her. The kids are her sister's after all. She's their aunt. You have to be practical. You should pray that she agrees. You can't survive on your own."

Dad was shocked. He said the idea of marrying Annie for convenience was abhorrent to him. Wilhelmina, his great love, wasn't even in her grave — please! Yet he knew his father was a street smart old Scot who knew what it took to survive. No romantic, his father could see the possible cost in the future for his son and what a practical solution this might be. "It isn't a matter of choice," the old Scot told Dad. 'It's your only hope. If I were you I'd get down on my knees and beg her. No other woman will take on four children."

"Dad, all right, ease up," our father apparently said as he pointed towards the dining room. "Will's still warm."

Dad said he couldn't think straight at that moment. He couldn't imagine a life without Wilhelmina. Marry Annie? The religious teetotaller? Even thinking he might felt like betrayal.

"I'd been in love with Will for fifteen years, Dad, built her a house; we've been married seven years, had four children. What? I'm just going to forget all that and move on?"

"No, Tom, you won't forget all that but the welfare of *hers* and *your* kids comes first!"

"Where were we that night anyway, Dad?" I asked as we sat huddled by the hurricane lamp in his back shed.

"In bed, I hope. All three of you."

"We always went to bed early," said Tom.

"How did Mum die then Dad?" I butted in. "Did she die just having Bill? What happened?"

"It's a long story," said Dad. "In a way, her dying is my fault. I overestimated her strength. I called the doctor too late."

"What doctor? Tell us from the beginning," I urged him.

"Really? You want the lot? The story of your mother?"

"We do. How did you meet her, when did you get married, how did we all end up in Dolgelly?" Tom was as inquisitive as I was. Everything Dad said was new to us.

He was surprised that we so urgently wanted to know so much about our mother. I suppose because he'd long tried to stifle his pained memories of her. Didn't he realise that children want to know about their lost or birth parents?

"I'll just tell you about her dying first," he said. "Let me get the sad bit over first."

We didn't care where he started. He settled back in his chair.

"I'd been a teacher in Boomi but we took over this hotel in Dolgelly. It was a big opportunity I thought."

Dad said they were just starting to make the hotel pay when Wilhelmina became pregnant with Bill. He described how, when the baby was due, she decided to go alone in a horse and trap to have the baby in Moree hospital. He had to stay and run the hotel.

"Truth is she felt she needed a doctor for this birth. She had some sort of premonition or the baby felt big or something. I wanted the doctor to come up from Moree but it was too expensive (they charged a pound a mile) and Will would have none of it. She decided it was cheaper to go to Moree in a horse and trap with a hired driver. I didn't really want her to do this. There was a midwife of sorts in Boomi but Will was so stubborn."

"She left in the trap for Moree very early one morning in late March. It's a big thing for a horse to pull a cart for thirty-five miles in a day. Most of the time the horse walked, with plenty of rests. The driver may have changed horses. Anyway, it took all day."

"Some miles out of Moree a storm broke and Wilhelmina and the driver were soaked. The storms in Boomi and Moree don't muck around; they're mostly huge deluges. Apparently, she arrived at the hospital and couldn't stop shivering. A healthy baby Bill (actually, he was named Donald Wilhelm but we always called him Bill) was delivered but Will became ill with pneumonia.

"Against the advice of the doctors she left the hospital as soon as the baby was born, desperate to get back to you kids and me. I got a message saying that the baby was born and healthy but she had pneumonia. I urged her to stay in the hospital. She wouldn't listen. She had been warned she was too ill to travel but, being Will, she was unstoppable. She travelled the thirty-five miles back in the trap she'd arranged, rugging herself up with the baby and umbrellas."

"By the time she arrived back at the hotel she was so sick I put her straight to bed. Her immune system broke down and she contracted meningitis. She had a fever, headaches and was vomiting up all the food I gave her. She had really cold hands, her skin was pale and she complained of aching in her limbs and a stiff neck. She had rashes all over her. She insisted the bedroom be dark with the blinds drawn. I wanted to call the doctor from Moree immediately but she was in a sort of delirium and refused to let me do it. "A pound a mile," she kept saying. 'We can't afford it Tom.'"

"I shouldn't have listened to her," Dad said. "I should have sent for the doctor straightaway. I eventually did. It's a lot of money but this was her *life*! When I rang the doctor, he came as fast as he could. But he could do nothing when he arrived except try and make her comfortable. He came too late. She died in our bed at the hotel six weeks after Bill's birth. I was there with the doctor when she died. She was in such pain . . . "

At this point Dad was on the edge of tears but I knew he would never cry. We felt like crying though.

Neither my brother Tom nor I remembered any of this tragedy even though we were there. I don't remember anyone being sick or any of the drama surrounding our mother's death. Cynthia must have known though. I asked Dad about my toy dog being "slaughtered" and hung out to dry. He said that happened on the day of the funeral when we were left at home alone for a short time. Dad said that I was inconsolable and when he saw the dog he reprimanded Cynthia and Tom for being so cruel. He thought that they were probably distressed by the atmosphere around the funeral.

Dad also told me he had seen me kissing Ah Fong sitting on the verandah steps later in the afternoon and had heard what we said.

"For some reason, I thought all you kids knew. How could you not? But, of course, you were all so young you forgot," Dad admitted. "I wish I could have. I was never the same. Poor Annie, I've been no bargain."

He said he was actually thankful that Annie came up when she did. Grandma and Grandpa then took the baby and went on the long trip back to Wallsend, travelling by buggy to Moree and then by train, like we did two years later.

"Annie came and looked after you kids but she always wanted us to leave the hotel and go back to Newcastle. She was as stubborn as Will. It took a couple of years to arrange. We moved to Gosford and Annie and I were married in the registry. We didn't want to bother you kids with that."

Many years later Dad told me that Annie had become pregnant in Dolgelly and he had no choice but to marry her, like his father had suggested. Annie was, in fact, always anxious to get married, certainly before they returned to Newcastle.

A week later we asked Dad again to tell us how he met Wilhelmina and how they got married and went to live in Boomi.

He said he fell in love with Wilhelmina when he'd first met her at Minmi in 1897 when he was nineteen and she was twenty. He met all three girls in the Hibberd family. He attended Wallsend–Plattsburg public school from 1882 till 1893 where he was encouraged to be a pupil teacher. However, when he left school he started working as a miner, like his father, in the famous Back Creek coalmines at Minmi. Minmi, Plattsburg and Wallsend were all coalmines close together west of Newcastle. When he first met Wilhelmina she was training to be a teacher. Because he'd already been a pupil teacher at Plattsburg school she persuaded him to leave the mines and take a three-month course at Fort Street Model School in Sydney to qualify as a primary teacher.

They became engaged in 1899 but had to wait till 1905 to marry because her mother Thomasina died at fifty-five from coronary thrombosis (heart attack) in 1899 and Wilhelmina had become the sole support of her sick father and younger siblings, including Annie.

Wilhelmina's father died from cancer in 1905. By then, Dad was the single teacher at a new school in Boomi in the far north-west of New South Wales. He personally built a house there for Wilhelmina and himself and handmade most of the furniture. He sometimes sent money down for her to buy soft furnishings and sheets and blankets. When she bought the goods at Winns department store in Newcastle, one of my father's sisters who worked there would say to her, "There goes some more of Tom Sharp's money."

Wilhelmina was the headmistress at Wallsend–Plattsburg infants school at twenty-five after winning a scholarship for teacher training at Blackfriars in Sydney. She was her birth family's sole breadwinner for six years.

When her father died Wilhelmina disposed of the family house at Minmi. The family had rented it from John Brown, the famous mine owner, for two shillings and sixpence a week. A friend called Aunty Smith took in her sister Maggie (Margareta) and her brother George.

Dad told us they were married at Plattsburg in 1905. They honeymooned in Katoomba then settled in Boomi. They took Will's younger sister Annie to live with them. Dad had been the first teacher at Greenbah "provisional school" in the Moree district in 1901. In 1903 he was transferred to Boomi which had only twenty-six pupils. This grew to fifty-five by 1910.

Cynthia was born in Boomi in 1906 and Tom in 1908. Annie took housekeeping, cleaning and child-minding jobs with local graziers. In 1910, when I was born, they moved to take over the hotel at Dolgelly to "try and make a go of it" as Dad said. I realised later that what they took over was probably the lease and a liquor licence. Dad never fully explained why they made this move. Annie was fanatical about abstinence and told them she wouldn't live in a place where alcohol was sold. She returned to Minmi.

Dad knew how hard it was for Annie to come back after Wilhelmina died and be forced to live in the hotel when alcohol was against her religion. He said that she took over the duties of mother to us children with enthusiasm and goodwill but always wanted him to sell the hotel.

I thought to myself when I was older that while Annie may have been too religious to live in a pub, she wasn't too religious to get pregnant to Dad. She was a handsome and capable young woman Dad said and although he didn't say so I guessed Dad sought comfort from her sometime later no matter how much he had cared for Wilhelmina. He told me years later, in confidence, that Annie used to pray to God for forgiveness every time they made love, even after they were married.

By 1914 Dad sold the house in Boomi and all the furniture for not much money. He was grateful that old Mrs White in Gosford would take us in. He couldn't get a job with the Education Department again till 1916 because he'd resigned in 1910 so he had to sell those lamps to make ends meet because their money ran out. They were very hard years for him, he said. We kids never knew about him and Annie getting married in Gosford, we thought they'd always been married. Mrs White got sick he said and so we had to leave

The only photo of Wilhelmina Susan Sharp (nee Hibberd) Jean ever saw.

Gosford and go to our grandparents' house in Boundary Road, Plattsburg, before moving on to Bull Street at Mayfield.

Tom and I gobbled up every bit of information Dad gave us. We were still very young so maybe he didn't tell us everything. We'll never know. He'd so loved Wilhelmina and we could see how painful it was to talk about her.

I wondered again if Cynthia remembered Wilhelmina dying, after all she was six years old when it happened. I looked forward to her return from Queensland so I could ask her why she had never said anything to me about it. However, when she did return, she was in no state to talk about anything.

19 · Whatever happened to Cynthia?

While Cynthia was away in Queensland we moved houses. My grandfather sold our Bull Street house to two elderly unmarried sisters named Cazneaux and we moved to Vine Street, just around the corner. My grandfather had bought a block of land in Vine Street and transferred, piece-by-piece, an old house he bought in Tighes Hill onto the block. When it was finally habitable we moved. We paid a solicitor twelve pounds each quarter as interest on a loan to buy it. I well remember how my stepmother Annie — I never called her Mum again only "Annie" — scraped and saved for that twelve pounds and how I was entrusted to take it in to the solicitors — Braye, Cragge and Cohen — and bring home the receipt. This kept us safe for another three months. When Dad died years later, the house had to be sold because he had never managed to pay off the mortgage, just the interest.

The Vine Street house was another small weatherboard, with a front verandah and a rear that backed onto a football oval. The number of bedrooms was the same but there was a kitchen *plus* a back verandah for dining. The garden was much smaller but Dad still grew vegetables. I still had to share a bedroom with Winnie and Eva, and Tom and Bill shared the other bedroom.

I wasn't as attached to this house as I was to Bull Street but, interestingly, one of my sons played a soccer match on that football oval thirty-three years later and told me he looked in at the backyard of the house where we had once lived and thought of me as a young girl there and smiled. It still exists, that house and the oval.

On 1 January 1922 Annie had another baby, a boy called Gilbert. My favourite childhood ditty became: "The trouble with a baby's that, eventually it becomes a brat." And another brat it was for me to look after in my spare time. Damn.

In the beginning of 1922 I went first to Wickham school and then to the newly opened Newcastle Central School. Miss Bocking was the headmistress. It later became Newcastle Central Domestic Science School and, even later, Hunter Girls' High School. This is where I learned dressmaking, cooking, drawing and artwork, English, maths, shorthand and typing. This was a "lesser" intermediate high school that didn't necessarily encourage students to do the Leaving Certificate or qualify for university or teachers' college. I had set my path.

At Wickham school, Miss Horton was our first-year English mistress. She was a well-groomed lady and her large brown eyes softly glowed behind gold-rimmed glasses. Her voice was cultivated but could be raised in anger. I thought she was very sophisticated and she created quite an impression on me.

One day in the first term she told us to "write a composition about anything you like but try and to put some conversations into it". This was right up my alley. I wrote a little story about the Hunt family, about my fascination with Jack Hunt and about his stepmother and his two sisters (Margaret and Rosalyn), naming them by their real names and telling what I thought was an ordinary little story about them and Jack. Of course, the story betrayed my feelings about Jack but I couldn't see this.

The next day at school Miss Horton told the class at 2.45 pm to finish their work and to sit quietly with their hands folded. She then took a chair and sat in front of the class. Imagine my horror when she took out my composition and read it out loud to the A class. After she had read it she said, "Now that's what I call a good composition."

Was I covered in glory? No! Not the slightest. I was hugely embarrassed because one of my friends in class, Lillian Hawthorn, had been at Mayfield primary with me and knew the Hunt family very well. She would know my guilty secret and spread it: that I loved Jack Hunt. I don't know if she ever did spread it and, sadly, I never had a conversation with Jack Hunt, even though his name remains magical to me, even today.

It was the time when I was first started to notice boys and hoped they would notice me. I was pretty sure I was plain and unappealing but that didn't stop me having crushes. I wore the best clothes I could and always kept my hair well brushed.

"Maybe they won't notice I'm not pretty," I thought. "It's personality that counts . . . and clothes."

Later that year at school, Miss Horton showed how sarcastic she could be. I'd never seen anyone being deliberately sarcastic before. It shocked me. One afternoon she was reading a story about Turkey to us. The hero stabbed someone with a scimitar. She stopped reading, took off her glasses and asked: "Does any girl know what a scimitar is?" A dead silence greeted her. I had a hazy idea that it was some kind of oriental sword but as I rarely spoke I remained quiet. Her exasperated look of scorn remains with me.

She said quietly, without a trace of humour: "It is a small pair of scissors. Right?" Everyone nodded. She glared at us and shook her head.

"Now girls tell me what he was stabbed with?"

With one voice we all replied, "A small pair of scissors, Miss."[5]

That must have really finished us in her eyes because she gave us a scornful look that I have never forgotten. We all saw it. She didn't correct us. She just glared at us and shook her head again only this time in pity. I didn't ever see her again. Perhaps she asked to be transferred to another school where there were more intelligent girls of twelve years of age. In the end, I think all that Miss Horton taught me was the power of sarcasm. It was one of the faults I was accused of later in life and I believe I picked it up partially from her. I'm sure she never meant to teach me that. I always really liked her.

At this time, Cynthia returned from Queensland.

We met her at Newcastle Station in almost the same place on the platform where we'd said farewell the year before. Of course, I was anxious about seeing her again. Life had been peaceful without her but now I wanted to know what she knew about our birth mother. It wasn't going to be easy to talk to her, it never had been, but this was different. We both had the same dead mother.

I expected a fiery, grown woman to emerge from the train, look down her nose at me and immediately order me about. Nothing could have been further from the truth. A thin, humble, pale and unsteady figure crept from the carriage. She looked around apprehensively. She hardly spoke. She didn't look at me at all. She seemed drained of energy and enthusiasm. How she had changed! Gone was her spirit and fire — it appalled me to see such a wraith. She had not one word to say, she just mumbled a few hellos. Barely sixteen, I thought it may have been shyness on returning but it was to be permanent. It took a while for me to realise how spiritually broken she was.

Nothing was ever said or explained, but she told me later she'd been treated as a servant, not a relation, at the sheep station in Queensland. Our aunt made her work long hours, early morning till night. She and her husband crushed her spirit. Cynthia never talked at length or in detail about

---

5. A scimitar is a short, curved, Middle Eastern sword.

this but it must have been extreme. The sad thing is they were our relations but I've realised since that no one can destroy you as efficiently as your own family or extended family when they have a mind to.

In bed that night I talked to the back of Cynthia's head.

"What happened up there?"

"None of your business."

"It must have been bad."

"Why?"

"Because you look . . . haggard."

"I do not!"

Pause.

"It was awful."

"Did they beat you?" (As if this was the norm.)

"Of course not."

"What did they do then?"

"Made me work."

"Just work?"

"Yes! Just work. Isn't that enough?" (This said with great sarcasm.)

"What work?"

"Cleaning rooms, toilets, the dairy house, the kitchen, washing up, doing the washing and ironing, sweeping the path and the house, mopping the floors, making the beds, churning the butter, scooping the cream, feeding the chooks and animals, helping the cook, peeling potatoes, stringing beans, cleaning the silver . . . I did everything, as well as looking after the children. No privileges. No rights. I was . . . "

"A servant?"

"No, just a poor girl from the city. And they told me I was staff, not a relation."

"You got paid though?"

"Dad got paid, not me. They sent him money. At least I helped out with our family."

When we were older, she told me that the father yelled at her and the children treated her the same, ordering her about unkindly. She had to obey them. That would have been hard for Cynthia. There was probably more to it than she told me.

"I couldn't complain because they were Dad's family."

She had written to our father pleading with him to bring her home.

My father didn't seem to notice or care about any of this. Not outwardly, anyway. I often wondered if he even really knew. Cynthia would never be game to tell him the truth. It was hard enough Cynthia coming home to a new house and a new baby. Telling Dad his sister was brutal was no priority.

I often think about this episode and its effect on Cynthia. It was a shock to me that she could be destroyed by a single year with another family, albeit our relations. I was surprised her confidence was so easily undermined. Maybe she wasn't as self-confident when she was younger as I had imagined. Maybe they had been overbearingly cruel to her and she didn't tell us the worst of it.

I did wonder whether something else had happened that she couldn't speak about, something awful with the men up there. She was a very pretty fifteen-year-old girl without the protection of her family. She never hinted at anything like this to me but if something like that had happened I know she would never, ever talk about it. I began to realise that life wasn't always fair and that you couldn't always rely on the wisdom of your parents.

Cynthia shared a bedroom with me, eight-year-old Winnie and three-year-old Eva. Gilbert slept with Annie and Dad. Dad decided Cynthia should work for his mother and father who had moved to a townhouse in Islington, a suburb of Newcastle. She came home from there at weekends looking even more forlorn. She told me later grandfather treated her as a servant, too, and would say to her roughly: "Clean Bertie's boots!" Bertie was my father's younger and very handsome brother. Or "Get Bertie's dinner!" No kindness in it. This coming from an old coal miner! When the working class gain a bit of power they can be very uncaring, especially to their own. I was never a big fan of Grandfather Sharp, even if he did give us the house in Bull Street rent-free.

Cynthia survived this stint of drudgery at Islington and left to work at the Paragon, a Greek café in Beaumont Street, Hamilton. She was a nice-looking grown-up young woman now with lovely thick wavy hair, very clean and sweet smelling. She wanted to study nursing at Wallsend hospital, but she couldn't because of the depressing poverty at home and the pressures on her. She felt she had to get a job with more money so she could contribute to the housekeeping. She never felt the bitterness that ate into me, she never rebelled, she saw the facts of life as they were: she must help all she could — her family were suffering and she must help. She was good-hearted. Perhaps too good-hearted. That is how I see it now . . . I didn't then.

I did eventually find a moment to ask her about our birth mother's death. She just said, yes, she always knew her mother had died but she had no explanation about why she'd never told me about it. She said; "I couldn't." That's the most she ever said to me, but at least the knowledge of our common history was bringing us closer.

She was a naturally conscientious worker and the Kristofferson's Paragon Café of Hamilton got a treasure for their money, as she worked long and late hours. She never complained. She was also their "slave" but this time a better paid and appreciated one. Towards myself, all the talk of my ugliness had gone, but she was still silently hostile. That didn't disappear completely until later although I could feel it abate as she grew older. All the time I was at high school Cynthia was either at Islington or at the Greek café in Beaumont Street.

As her harsh treatment of me abated I realised that she had changed permanently. Cynthia's time in Queensland was the start of our mature relationship.

She became embarrassed when I mentioned our early childhood. She still had a caustic tongue when it suited her but she seemed to want to be liked and accepted by me now, something she never cared about when she was younger. This made her timid and nervous. A far cry from the bullying disparager she had been. Thankfully she increasingly became my best friend. The fact that we were full sisters played a big part.

Late that year, 1922, our dear grandmother Janet died suddenly. She was only sixty-three. She had just returned from a day's shopping when she had a heart attack and died in her kitchen at Islington. Worn out, I thought at the time, from caring for too many people. I took it very badly because she was the one gentle, loving force in my life and I loved her dearly.

There was a big Methodist funeral in Islington and the entire family of nine children and twenty-eight grandchildren plus wives and husbands and many friends attended. It was as big a funeral as she deserved and as it ought to have been, with lots of tears and saddened faces but it still seemed inadequate to me.

It took me a long time to recover from my grandmother's death.

20 · Tom, my starstruck brother

My elder brother Tom didn't have as much influence over me as Cynthia, but because he took me to the pictures and because I spent so much of my early life around him, I had an unexpressed deep affection for him. He meant a lot to me even though we never talked intimately. I felt he got a rough deal in life.

He was born in Boomi in 1908 and had a great sense of humour that had nowhere to go and he always called himself an " '08 baby".

He was named Thomas Patterson (Patterson was his father's grandmother's middle name) and there must have been much pride in his birth: sons were of prime importance in those days.

Never a big "noise" in my childhood memories I don't know how he rated at school but he always boasted he was never caned or "got the cuts", the slang name for getting caned.

Tom was an avid reader of the Nelson Lee library of school stories (Nelson Lee was a famous detective with a sidekick called Nipper) and the Sexton Blake detective novels, and he bought them whenever he could afford them.

He ran messages for neighbours and caddied at the steelworks golf course. When he was eleven he milked our neighbour Mr Gane's cow night and morning and received about five shillings a week, which he hoarded under his mattress with his Nelson Lees.

He left school at fourteen, when I was in first-year high school, and went to work for Ireland, a groceries distribution company in Newcastle. David Cohen's and Ireland were very big in Newcastle then. Most children left school at fourteen to work and help the family budget. Big families and little money was the rule in our world.

He was at Ireland for a few years (working 8 am till 4.30 pm) and then went to work at John Lysaght iron works. He worked there for years and years and liked it. He worked shiftwork from 6 am to 2 pm, which was called the "morning shift", or 2 pm to 10 pm for the "afternoon shift" and 10 pm to 6 am for the "dog watch". He was an ironworker, it was tough work but he was good at it.

He was of a cheerful nature, an ardent fan of Greta Garbo and would sometimes see her movies several times over.

Movies and dancing were his main interests, apart from soccer. He played with "The Orbs", made up mostly of Lysaght employees.

We were very much into hats in those days and he would often come with us to visit the hat shops. He'd parade around in front of us in different hats to our great amusement. If we brought them home he would try them all on and parade them in the kitchen for us. He made us see exactly how we would look in them.

Movies were his greatest joy though. He would come home and re-enact them. Drawing himself to his full height, all 5'8" of him, he would say: "Come up and see me sometime . . . " or he would pretend to be a southern belle in New York.

Movie houses were his way of life. The Strand, the Lyric, Herbert's at Islington, the Show at Mayfield, the Waratah Town Hall and the Royal were the movie palaces where his imagination caught fire and took him away from the humdrum of his work and young life. Tom never had a real chance in life, but his love of movies made an indelible imprint on my life. I never told him how much I did love him.

He ended up later in life working on the wharves in Newcastle, never rich or successful materially, a heavy drinker but a decent man. I was always proud of him.

For the record, I post here Tom's top movie loves and theatres he attended, and which he always lovingly recorded:

THE STRAND THEATRE, NEWCASTLE (sixpence entry, opera glasses one shilling)
Arthur Shirley in *The Mystery of the Handsome Cab* by Fergus Hume.
Constance Talmadge in *Her Night of Romance*.
William Diamond in *The Sunset Trail*.
Norma Talmadge in *The Only Woman*.
Theda Bara in *Carmen*.
Clara Bow in *It*.
Charlie Chaplin in *His New Job*.
Clever Mary.
Richard Dix in *Manhattan*.
Edmund Lowe in *The Brass Bowl*.
Buck Jones in *The Man Who Played Square*.

Agnes Ayres in *Worldly Goods*.
Buster Keaton in *Sherlock Junior*.
Tom Mix and his horse Tony, and Duke his dog in *Teeth*, a full-blooded drama of the west.

THE MAYFIELD THEATRE
Tom Mix and Tony in *The Last of the Duanes*.
John Gilbert in *Man's Mate*.

THE WARATAH THEATRE
George O'Brien in *The Roughneck*.
Bessie Love, Ray Stewart and Hobart Bosworth in *Sundown* (seven wonderful reels).

THE WALLSEND THEATRE (matinee /night prices: one shilling; reserved: one shilling and fourpence)
Mary Pickford in *Dorothy Veinon of Haddon Hall*, supported by Estelle Taylor (wife of Jack Dempsey).
All Mack Sennett two-reel comedies.

UNION PICTURE THEATRE, Hamilton and Newcastle
A five-act feature *The Disciple*, featuring William S. Hart.
Any Mack Sennett comedy.
A Village Scandal, with Raymond Hitchcock and Fatty Arbuckle.

21 · The prettiest girl in Mayfield

While she worked at the Beaumont Street café, Cynthia had many admirers. Among them was a man named Walter Bryant, whom I thought was hilarious as he insisted that the world was flat and that deluxe was pronounced "de-loox". He taught Cynthia how to play the zither. She went out with him for about two years.

Cynthia continued to work at the Paragon for the rest of that year (1923) and into the next. I used to cheekily borrow her clothes to wear when I was going out with my girlfriends while she worked Saturday night "stuck at the Paragon". I was thirteen or fourteen then. She always found out and there was hell to pay on Sunday morning.

Cynthia: "I didn't say you could wear my clothes!"

Me: "I didn't wear them."

Cynthia: "Don't lie. You've always been a liar. You think I don't know?"

Me: "You're at work anyway. You don't need them."

Cynthia: "They're my property. You don't even iron them afterwards. Look at this blouse."

Me: "I put them back on the hangers."

Cynthia: "They always look soiled. You make such a mess with them. Creases everywhere. Stains. You have no right."

Me: "There's no stains!" (There were never stains!)

Cynthia: "You're just as selfish as ever. And a liar! DON'T TOUCH MY CLOTHES!"

Me: "I haven't got anything decent of my own."

Cynthia: "Bad luck. If I catch you again I will scratch your eyes out."

Me: "Charming..."

Cynthia: "You don't even love Mum. You don't respect anyone."

Me: "Stop saying that!"

Cynthia: "It's hurtful."

Me: "You're her vassal so you can't see anything. All that holiness doesn't fool me."

Cynthia: "You don't know what you're talking about."

Me: "Don't I? I know a thing or two about hypocrisy. I have to live with it every day."

Cynthia: "Shut up! Shut up! Just don't steal my things."

Me: "I didn't steal them!"

Cynthia: "You did."

Me: "I borrowed them! You're my sister."

Cynthia: "Without permission."

I was thick-skinned then and used to smile smugly to myself, as if I had a perfect right to borrow from my own sister, whatever she thought.

I was still the "selfish, unloving Jean" but at least she talked to me.

I knew it was difficult for her coming back to a new and chaotic house, with everything changed and a new baby plus a three-year-old after her traumatic time in Queensland. The eldest in the family and a former star at school, now a nobody. Arriving back without any idea what to do next in her life and a family that could barely support itself. No school or university to go to, only drudgery to look forward to. A small overcrowded house. No confidence in herself.

I sensed all this but I didn't care because I had too many problems of my own. However, it depressed me seeing her work at the Paragon café for so long. I could see that without education or training Cynthia was at the world's mercy, always doing menial jobs or desperate for a reliable husband. That wasn't for me, I thought — I didn't want to end up in a milk bar or looking after other people's families. That was all my stepmother ever did to earn money. I wanted to achieve something, be independent and have my own life.

Dad and Annie didn't seem too concerned about me, didn't seem to actually care. Perhaps they had too many other worries. They didn't drive or advise us coherently — they left it to us to work out. Dad did try to push me to do the Leaving Certificate and do teaching but after he failed he just let me go where I wanted, as if it was all too much for him. I suppose he was unhappy and preoccupied, with more kids to bring up.

Although we were the children of a primary schoolteacher (admittedly a former miner) and we were bright at school and my father had started married life with great expectations for us, everything seemed to unravel. None of us went to university or even teachers' college. To see Cynthia, with her high intelligence, working permanently in a café was disheartening.

What a sad life ours seemed to me. Could none of us ever break out of this kind of world? It made me more determined than ever to try to make something of myself.

Cynthia eventually left the Paragon and went to work in Winn's department store's tea-rooms in Hunter Street, Newcastle. Their very nice dining room was presided over by a Miss Adams and was well patronised at lunchtime by leading business men. It was a must for anyone having a day out in Newcastle.

Winn's was a much-respected department store rivalled only by Scott's, which stood where the store occupied by David Jones is now.[6] Scott's didn't stand a chance against Winn's when it came to café catering which was the only place to have lunch or afternoon tea ... their cream cakes were legend.

It's hard to write about my sister Cynthia at this time without seeing the span of her life, as I knew it later. Her broken spirit was difficult to accept after her childhood. Thank goodness, we became the closest of friends. I couldn't have borne it if we'd stayed enemies.

Around this time (1923–25) I found that boys were starting to notice me more and I was thinking more and more about clothes. I was going to the pictures and picnics with my school friends and meeting a few young men.

My body was maturing in all the ways the female body does. My periods began sometime in these three years but no one spoke to me about that or other developments in my body: my legs changing shape, my breasts growing, abdominal pains and so on. I only talked about it with the other girls at school who were as ignorant as I was. We had to find out everything ourselves, although the occasional female teacher was helpful.

I passed all my examinations at Newcastle Domestic Science School and gained my certificate of proficiency in shorthand and typing. The three years of high school seemed to pass in a flash.

I started fourth year in 1925 but left after one term, as soon as I turned fifteen, to get a job somewhere as a secretary. I didn't want to finish school or do the Leaving Certificate because it would be a waste of time.

How stupid I was to be so engrossed in the present. I couldn't see the broad horizon. Time is so devious. You would imagine someone would have touched me along the way, tried to convince me or point me in another direction, but no one did. I was too headstrong, too conditioned to "no play" and wearing virtual rags. All I wanted was to be out of the painful

---

6. Jean is writing in 1988. David Jones department store closed in 2011. At time of publication the site is being developed as a boutique hotel.

humdrum of family life and into my own thing. Oh dear, how important I thought clothes were. I thought my whole life depended on them.

I didn't want to end up like Cynthia or Tom. Better to work in an office, I thought, than as a waitress, no matter how hard working and conscientious that waitress may be. So, I walked out of school and announced to Annie and Dad that I was looking for a job. They weren't happy but there was nothing they could do or attempted to do.

Cynthia had to repay my stepmother's "mothering" in hard cash when she was earning money, however lowly the job. Unlike me, she always did, generously and consistently. She never held any resentment and when our stepmother died she felt the loss deeply.

I began to think that the personal will of my siblings and myself was undermined by the attitude of Annie and Dad. They didn't do it consciously, I know, it was how they'd been brought up, the way things had always been. I was the exception in our family because I was the one standing up to them. No one else rebelled. I sensed what Annie and Dad were unconsciously doing to us, the influence they had, making us accept our lot, and I resisted. Their attitude subtly destroyed our chances of improving ourselves. It wasn't their fault; negativity and acceptance were ingrained in them. I knew there was something better, a better life for us, but it involved struggle. They wanted us to accept the status quo and cause no trouble. I knew that what was happening was sucking the fight out of us, the way we lived stopped us from growing intellectually. I wanted my own children, if I had them, to grow . . . expand. Not to be like us, forever cowed by the world.

It was the start of my feelings of deep depression, of fighting a sense of hopelessness, which I tried to rid myself of. They were the same feelings that I had in later life. A feeling of despair, of not being good enough, of being somehow worthless and the strong idea that there was no choice but to accept the worst life dished out to you. That, coupled with my suppressed anger over my dead mother, was difficult to deal with.

During the next two years, I had various secretarial jobs and also menial work cleaning houses. The jobs were always short-lived and temporary. Occasionally I served behind a counter in shops.

Home conditions spurred me on to become more proficient in shorthand, typing and bookkeeping and at seventeen (in 1927) after answering job ads in the paper for many months, I finally had some positive interest

Hunter Street, Newcastle, in the 1920s, not far from Pateys Lane where Jean worked. (Photo: Cultural Collections, University of Newcastle, NSW)

from Brambles carrying company in Newcastle who recommended me to another firm.

I became girl Friday and general factotum in the office of one of Newcastle's leading signwriters, Miller's Signs. They specialised in hoarding advertising and old-fashioned petrol-pump painting. For the next four years, I found myself amongst the most amusing people. I found that signwriters were energetic and frustrated artists. They started to educate me and I lapped it up.

The office was in Pateys Lane, a mean little lane off Newcomen Street. There, at one pound a week plus cunning pilfering from the petty cash, I developed a style of my own.

The men there liked me, fussed over me, teased me, flattered me; we had a lot of fun together. I was a young woman whom they seemed to value beyond just as a girl Friday. They thought I was smart and amusing. It gave me a lot of confidence. They were interested in life at large and everything that was happening in the world, much more than I had experienced at home. They made me feel that I had a right to a better life, not just an ambition for it.

They consciously tried to give me general instruction about international events. About people like Don Bradman and his batting feats in Australia and England, about Jack Lang and the New South Wales government, about Harry Hopman and Wimbledon, about the details of the Depression worldwide and the rise of the Nazis and Hitler in Germany. Also about people and events like Nellie Melba, Phar Lap and the Melbourne Cup. They were the first people to open me up to wider interests outside my family. I went on picnics with them, had lunches, even went to movies with one of them. There was no actual romance there for me but they did wonders for my self-esteem.

I only received one pound a week to start off with, but after paying five shillings a week in fares, I had fifteen shillings to spend on all the pretty clothes I wanted. I was supposed to pay five shillings a week board but Annie found it hard to extract that from me. It was the beginning of the Depression years in Australia and a lot of people couldn't even find work.

In those days, I made my own clothes on an old White sewing machine and shoes were only about five shillings a pair. A good rush hat was one shilling and could be decorated with ribbon. Of course, a good hat could be had at the Bon Ton or at Miss Duncan's, both in Hunter Street. I survived.

Dentists were too expensive to patronise and, as my teeth had never been attended to, at seventeen I had to have an upper denture fitted for about two guineas. This was an embarrassment to me but I soon found out that plenty of people my age had dentures.

To give an idea of what influenced me at this time, this newspaper description of the bride and bridesmaids and relations at a Newcastle wedding in 1928 took my fancy at the time:

> She wore a Julie Frock of ivory crepe-de-chine with ostrich feather and pearl trimmings. The train which fell from her shoulders was lined with lemon Georgette and trimmed with ostrich feathers and seed pearls. Her veil of hand-

made Brussels lace was held in place by a coronet of orange blossoms. She carried a shower bouquet of tuber roses and cactus dahlias, a gift from the groom.

Attended by her sister wearing a frock of powder blue crepe-de-chine trimmed with silver lace and handmade flowers with a loose panel from the shoulders and her cousin in apricot crepe-de-chine made on similar lines.

Both bridesmaids wore silver lace hats with silver ribbon streamers, the former carrying a bouquet of apricot rosebuds and the latter blue delphiniums and asters, gift from the bridegroom.

The flower girl (a niece) wore a petal frock of pink crepe-de-chine and a silver lace hat and carried a silver basket of pink roses with a gift of a gold armlet from the bridegroom.

Bride's mother wore a black gown of charmante with jet trimmings worn with a black hat of plush with a jet ornament. She carried a posy of red roses. The BG's mother wore a frock of grey embossed crepe-de-chine with a black Georgette Hat and carried a posy of red carnations.

The bride left in a cinnamon brown beaded Marocaine frock with hat to tone.

I bought a red beret and had a navy-blue dress and cape to go with it. I thought, with my bobbed hair, I was very fetching as I was one of the first girls in Newcastle to wear a red beret.

I started going out with boys in a much more rebellious way. Often, I deliberately chose boys whom I knew my parents would dislike. I was always in big trouble if I came home late but I began to ignore Annie and Dad and do as I pleased. I was a regular brat and I wouldn't, of course, take orders from my stepmother.

"Why are you home so late?"

"None of your business."

"Who were you out with?"

"No one."

"I'd like to meet some of these boys who take you out."

"Why?"

"I want to make sure they're good boys. I don't like you going out with people I don't know."

"Why should you know them?"

"You're too young, Jean, you can't see what people are really like."

"I like all boys and I like kissing them, if you'd like to know. And they can kiss me if I say so. Whenever they like."

"You're going to get into trouble one day, Jean. They don't stop at kissing."

"I won't stop them. They can do whatever they want."

"You'll get pregnant, you silly girl, and then where will you be?"

"Like you did you mean?"

"Go to bed! And pray to God for forgiveness."

I enjoyed baiting my stepmother. She was so easy to get the better of. Verbally she was limited to Methodist dogma and conventional morality. Little did she see that I was quite capable of looking after myself. I was aware of the sexual dangers and I was very careful with boys who were mostly very careful and gentlemanly with me. She needn't have worried; I was a fast learner, I wasn't going to get caught. I respected God but I didn't need him to look after me regarding men. That was my business.

Dad was terrified that Cynthia and I would marry one of the steelworkers from the area, men whom he used to give the glassy stare to if any of them dared to ask us out. He was always bringing home uninteresting schoolteachers and introducing them to us. He needn't have bothered. We weren't attracted to the workers or the teachers from his school. We longed for other things, other places, and romance.

I got the surprise of my life when I was sixteen. Bill Claridge, a very decent, straightforward working-class Welsh boy who lived in Mayfield and took me out a lot, walked me home after the pictures one evening and stood at the gate in front of our house in Vine Street. It was only about 10.30 pm and I think he was trying to pluck up the courage to give me a goodnight kiss when he looked at me longingly and said unexpectedly:

"Gee you're pretty, Jean."

I nearly dropped dead. No one had *ever* told me I was pretty, ever, in my life. I was sure I was plain, though I hoped at least tolerable, especially after Cynthia's brainwashing. I knew my clothes helped me a lot. And Bill Claridge was not just anyone, he had a bit of style and I was a little bit taken by him.

"Me pretty?" He must be lying I thought. He was embarrassed for something to say. He just wanted a kiss.

"You're the prettiest girl in Mayfield. Didn't you know that?"

He seemed so sincere. I wanted to burst into tears. Certainly, I kissed him. Anyone who is kind to me and calls me the "prettiest girl" gets a kiss. Even now.

It was a shock, although I know now that most sixteen-year-old girls are naturally attractive in some way. I like to think I wasn't only attractive to men but maternal, loving, intelligent and a good companion. That I was unselfish and caring despite what my family might think. I thought I dressed well, given I had so little money. I knew that boys looked at me a lot so I thought I must have something. I didn't know if it was clothes or what, but I loved the attention.

I started to feel confident. I began to go out with different men, older men and accepted their compliments though I never really believed them. I was always wary. The Newcastle men and boys were very polite to me, not sexually insistent but very patient. They were all gentlemen. Sometimes maybe a bit too gentlemanly, a bit too polite, sometimes, I suppose, rather dull and reserved.

After Bill Claridge's compliment I told Cynthia that a boyfriend said I was pretty. "Of course, you are," she said coldly. Why did she say I was ugly all those years? I never dared ask her but I later supposed it was because she had been unhappy and jealous.

"Am I pretty?" I asked Tom.

"Jeannie, you're my sister. It's like asking me if Mum is pretty."

It was always hard to get a compliment out of Tom, but years later he said to me, to my great delight, "I'm proud of you Jeannie. And all you achieved. You got out."

I had one boyfriend with a motorbike, much to everyone's horror. Vic Poole. His father owned a bicycle shop and Vic was going to inherit it. It wasn't even a motorbike shop so no one need have worried. I wasn't going to marry a bicycle shop owner I can assure you. And I wasn't running off with a wild bikie either. He wasn't one, even though he looked like one. He had a leather jacket and a big, noisy Harley-Davidson. I was pleased to let them think what they like, the worse the better. It was quite thrilling to be on the back of that bike anyway, the thunderous roar that frightened everybody and the speed Vic would ride at which, of course, terrified and thrilled me.

Vic used to come to our house a lot and look at me sitting in the kitchen at the table and say, "I'm looking forward to the day I eat a chop off that tablecloth, Sharpie." I would reply, "You might be waiting a long time, Pooley." I kept him in his place.

I couldn't get the adventurous and accomplished men and boys I wanted in Newcastle... just Mayfield boys and I wasn't going to marry one of them. I wanted to get out of that place. I knew those boys were loving, kind and loyal but I knew they were stuck there and their horizons were limited. That wasn't for me.

Cynthia became engaged to a young man called Tom Wyndham. She fell very much in love with him. I don't know what he did for a living but he eventually went to live in Adelaide and they kept their affair alive by correspondence. At this time my stepmother's sister, Aunty Maggie (or Margreta as she later wanted to be called) came to live with us. She had lived in Fiji with her husband. Cynthia as usual was left to cope with the family as well as working. Something went wrong, there was some misunderstanding with Tom or he'd met another girl. Cynthia returned the ring by registered mail and that was that. I remember our little brother Gilbert looked at a photograph of Tom and said, "Rotten old Tom Wyndham made Cynthia cry."

Cynthia and I still fought occasionally but gradually we realised our common interests and the bond of being full sisters. As we grew older we had more in common and conversed as equals. She never talked to me about Tom Wyndham though, that was too painful. It was a deep, deep loss for her and it took her a long time to recover. It should have been a warning to me about my own future with boys but in those days I thought I was invincible.

Dental advertisement in the *Newcastle Morning Herald* from 1920s.

AE Vesper
PERFECT ARTIFICIAL TEETH

Dentist FG Holloway. Old, Young or nervous patients may have any number of teeth extracted in a few minutes without feeling the slightest pain of inconvenience — no swollen gums or after effects. *Gold fillings* — ten shillings and sixpence.

For speech, mastication and restoration of the youthful appearance on the face by removing lines and wrinkles my artificial teeth are unrivalled.

22 · "I suppose you must all love babies?"

After four years at the signwriters in Newcastle I'd managed to save ten pounds and I was ready to move on. I'd enjoyed being there but I wasn't satisfied. I wasn't that good a typist or secretary . . . it didn't suit my nature . . . and I hadn't found anybody I wanted to marry. I was still stuck in the world I grew up in: dull old Newcastle. I felt it was time to make an effort to get out. They knew at the office about my restlessness and were keen to keep me so they offered me a transfer to work in their office in Martin Place in Sydney. I accepted.

In 1931 I moved to a boarding house in Strathfield, much to my parents' surprise. I commuted by train to the city office in Martin Place. My parents were used to my independence now. Dad did not really want me to go but he said he would help all he could.

It was quite an adventure to go to Sydney on the train with a suitcase of clothes, to travel to my new accommodation found for me by my employers, and to start a new job.

The office in Martin Place wasn't as friendly as old Patey's Lane, but soon some of the boys from Newcastle moved to Sydney too and I felt more at home.

Even so, after six months, I still wasn't happy. I was a restless twenty-one-year-old and I knew by then that I had to make some tough decisions: get more training or be stuck as a second-rate secretary for life. The only option for me was nursing. I thought I'd make a good nurse — I'd been nursing children and babies all my life.

I applied to all the hospitals in Sydney and Newcastle for general nurse training. All of them refused me. I was disappointed. I assumed it was because either I hadn't studied the right subjects at school, didn't have enough education or I was considered too old. Too old at twenty-one?

However, one of the hospitals that refused my application, Crown Street Women's Hospital in Surry Hills, informed me about an obstetrics (midwife) nursing course at the hospital. It was only one-year long and was purely maternity training. I didn't require general nursing training to qualify and there were no fees. It was essentially live-in, meals and board paid for. I immediately applied.

I was accepted almost at once. I jumped for joy when I received the letter at work. The people at the office were thrilled for me. I resigned from my job at the end of 1931 and after an enjoyable, tearful send-off from an office party I went home for Christmas with news of my new plans. Cynthia was pleased and promised to help me financially as much as she could. Dad said he would too although I knew he and Cynthia had no extra money. Dad was still on three pounds ten shillings a week as a primary schoolteacher and it was the middle of the Depression.

It was one of the best Christmases I ever had at home in Mayfield, living with the expectation of a new venture in Sydney and the support of the family. I look back on it now as the beginning of my struggle for what I called in my old-fashioned way "my place in the sun". I hoped this next move would change my whole life. It did, but not in the way I was expecting.

On 12 January 1932, I entered the Crown Street Women's Hospital to become an obstetrics nurse.

Possessing nothing but enthusiasm and hope, and six black-printed cotton frocks, two pairs of black shoes, six pairs of black stockings, four sets of stiff collars and cuffs, a black coat and a plain black hat with a brim. I was ready to really live. No money and no wages to be paid for twelve months. All I had to look forward to was hard labour of fifty-six hours a week on my feet, but it didn't matter, I was happy and excited.

The first person to greet us was Sister Edna Shaw. Kind and smiling she said to us: "I suppose you must love babies." When I say "us" I mean the group of new trainee nurses who were to do the midwifery course of twelve months as opposed to another group of general-trained nurses who were to do the course in six months. They were already well trained in hospital routine and nursing in general and had certificates to prove it. We had never read a thermometer, given a bedpan, been in a theatre or worn a uniform. We were the original raw recruits.

It was a large hospital, old and sprawling. We were taken over to the nurses' home and allotted rooms. I shared mine with a large awkward-looking girl from Balgowlah.

It was a bare room with two single beds, a dressing table, a wardrobe, a brown linoleum-covered floor and two nondescript mats beside each bed. It opened out onto a wide stone balcony, which in turn faced onto Foveaux

Crown Street Women's Hospital in Surry Hills, Sydney, in the 1930s. (Photographer unknown)

Matron Edna Shaw with nurses and babies at Crown Street hospital. (Photo: Sam Hood collection, Mitchell Library, State Library of New South Wales)

Street. In the group was Mavis Munro, a fellow trainee who eventually became my best friend at the hospital and friend for life.

It's a wonder the "no wage" condition didn't deter me from nursing. All we received was board and lodging, laundry and our uniforms. I don't know how I managed but I remember having a small bank account of ten pounds at the start of the year. I occasionally received gifts of ten shillings from my father or sister which helped. I had forgotten about shoes and stockings wearing out and the unforeseen expenditure of a small suitcase for taking on district work delivering babies in poor homes. The dearest outlay for the year was a pair of surgical scissors and a pair of Howard Kelly forceps. It left a hole in my bank account to buy them.

On that first day, we were informed that our hours of duty were 6 am to 2 pm one week and 2 pm to 10 pm the following week. No day off and our only break was what was called a "long weekend" from 2 pm Sunday to 2 pm Monday every second weekend when we changed shifts.

The night nurse called us at 5.30 am the next day and after a wash and a tooth-clean we struggled into our new uniforms, complete with caps and stiff collars fastened with a stud and our stiff cuffs. I forget how we fastened those. We trooped over to Sister Giles' office on the first floor where we studied a roster and found out where we were to go.

The first morning I was posted to the first-floor maternity ward, which consisted of two big wards with about twenty beds in each and a bungalow attached with another ten beds. Each bed had a white swing cot beside it, nearly all with a baby curled up inside. Some babies were sick and our job was to wash the patients and make the beds or change the sheets.

Some nurses were allotted the task of changing and bathing the babies and some to make up the cots. The babies to be bathed were swathed in khaki-coloured cuddlies or shawls. We nurses took them out to the nursery where we were shown, with plenty of harsh words from the sisters, how to do the job expertly. Sisters always spoke sharply to trainee nurses, especially new ones.

Today nurse training is very different; no novice is allowed to handle mothers and babies until they have learned their craft on models and have a thorough grounding in hospital routine with all the whys and wherefores, but we were thrown in headfirst.[7] Apart from hurt feelings and tears we managed to become quite adept, despite our lack of experience. The making

---

7. The author is writing in the 1980s.

of a hospital bed was a technique all its own and we were drilled in neat, mitred corners and smooth surfaces. All my life, my own beds were made in the way I was taught at Crown Street.

Breakfast for the patients was then served: a plate of porridge, two pieces of toast and a cup of tea. If a lucky patient had an egg she would write her name on it and we would boil if for her. Then the nursing staff took it in turns to go down to the dining room on the ground floor for their own breakfast. Food there was a little better as we usually had porridge and some sort of protein. We were slaves and had to be fed to keep our energy up.

Then back to the wards to pan the patients, tidy the beds, do the flowers and have everything in near perfect order for Matron Clarke and Sister Shaw to do rounds and thoroughly inspect everything.

The nurses then disappeared to change into clean aprons and look hopefully at the letter rack to see if any news from the outside world had filtered through to them. Then back to the day room for morning tea and afterwards any treatment for patients. The resident doctor would then do the rounds. Each patient had an honorary doctor and gynecological specialist and often one or other would call and see any patient that needed special care.

Babies would again be changed and taken out of the terrible khaki shawls, changed and generally inspected. I once asked where the shawls came from and received the news that prisoners at Long Bay jail knitted them. That's what they looked and felt like, too. I could feel the pain in those shawls.

Dinner was next and the patients had a substantial cooked meal of red meat and vegetables, which was sent up from the kitchen in tin dixies to be served by us. Stewed rabbit or tripe was given to those on a white diet.

Occasionally a loud alarm bell was rung and all untrained staff rushed up to the labour ward to witness an actual birth. This so horrified me on the first occasion I saw one that I would have run away if I could have found the front door.

All trained nurses or students would flock around some unfortunate woman and see a small human being emerge and give a roar of indignation at such treatment or perhaps just remain motionless and then be held by the heels and given a smart slap on the bottom. If there was still no response he/she was given resuscitation. This viewing was called a "witness" and we had to witness about 200 during our training.

At 1 pm we were set free and those who had the energy went out. Most of us stretched out on our hard, narrow beds and had a snooze. After that

Nurses and babies, Crown Street hospital, 1930s. (Photo: Sam Hood collection, Mitchell Library, State Library of New South Wales)

we had a hot bath (in the common bathroom) and dressed in our street clothes and either went out or studied a textbook on obstetrics, *A Practice of Gynaecology* or *A Short Practice of Midwifery* by Dr Henry Jellett, a man whom we learned to hate. We all also had rather a happy time together gossiping and laughing.

The following week we had the luxury of sleeping in and started our duties at 1 pm and carried through till 9 pm. Matron Agnes Clarke lectured us once a week in a small room beside pathology and the morgue and a Dr Selwyn Harrison gave us a lecture on infant care about once a month.

Crown Street was quite close to the city and for leisure we often walked into town to see a movie or went down to the botanical gardens to study, admire the flowers and trees or just rest.

On Saturday 19 March 1932, when we'd been training for just over two months, Mavis Munro and I walked over the Sydney Harbour Bridge on the day it opened. We were among 300,000 people at the ceremony.

For months, we'd watched the two spans of the bridge approaching each other. We thought they would never meet. It looked for a long time as

Jean was in the crowd at the opening of the Sydney Harbour Bridge, 19 March 1932. (Photo: Sydney Harbour Bridge albums, NSW State Archives)

though they would miss each other by ten or so feet, but in the end there was only an inch or two in it.

We wore our hats and gloves and joined the huge crowd that walked across the grey painted structure and then we caught the Luna Park ferry back and the tram home to Crown Street. The atmosphere was electric and exciting. We hadn't wanted to miss this moment. Our "bridge across the harbour" was going to "change Sydney" the newspapers said.

We didn't see the right-wing New Guard leader Captain de Groot in military uniform on horseback as he infamously cut the ribbon in front of Jack Lang, the Labor New South Wales premier. As he did he called out, "In the name of the decent and respectable people of New South Wales." He was opposed to the socialist policies of Lang.

We were too far back in the crowd to see anything but we soon heard about it from others and read about it later. Captain de Groot had been a soldier in the First World War and opposed Labor and all it stood for.

Apparently, De Groot had been able to blend in with the New South Wales Lancers, also on horseback, because he was in a First World War military uniform. He said later his action was in protest that the Governor of NSW, Sir Philip Game, had not been invited to perform the ceremony.

None of us approved of what he did. It seemed over-dramatic and pointless. Later on, I remember a white painted graffiti sign on a wall, "Lang Is Right!" When Jack Lang lost government over the nationalisation of the banks the sign was altered to "Lang Is Right . . . OUT!"

One Friday in April 1932, I dropped in on my old office in Martin Place to say hello to everyone at the signwriters and let them know how I was handling nursing. I was surprised to see all the men wearing black armbands.

"Why?" I asked.

"Don't you know? Phar Lap is dead," they said. "Died yesterday in the US. Those bastards kill everything."

I was amused that men would wear black armbands for a racehorse but I guess Phar Lap was no ordinary horse. He was legendary and had won the Melbourne Cup and other big races. Even I had heard of him. He had captured the Australian public's imagination in those Depression times, just like Don Bradman, although in those days I wasn't much interested in sport.

The men gave me a black armband and I wore it back to the hospital, which mystified the other nurses. In some ways that armband began an interest in racehorses that stayed with me all my life. I even started going to Randwick races with one of the registrars. I was starting to feel I was "somebody".

23 · Bedbugs and breech births

Slums surrounded Crown Street Hospital and most of our patients were poor in the extreme but all loved their babies, poor little things. In those days, if a girl was three or four months pregnant and single she could live in a block at the hospital called "the cottage". She was only required to help fold the hospital laundry — a handyman would take the linen to the wards.

Every girl was called "Mrs" and after she had had her baby, the hospital would have it adopted. If she wanted to keep the baby she was sent to an annex at the bottom end of Darling Point Road, a beautiful home on the harbour. The building was demolished and today there is a lovely park on the land the house used to occupy.

The hospital did their best to find the mother a job where she could have the baby with her or board the baby while she worked. A baby bonus of five pounds was given to the mother and the hospital didn't charge a penny. It was a kind hospital and Sister Shaw (later the famous Matron Shaw of Crown Street) was the kindest and most considerate woman I ever knew; she should have received an OBE[8] at least.

After we had a few months' training we were sent out on district rounds. Many women in those days gave birth at home and we would be sent out with a senior nurse with our little suitcases and dressed in a uniform covered by a black coat and wearing our plain black hats with a brim.

We didn't always have our fare and many a police car or milkman would give us a lift, including if the trams had stopped running for the night. On one memorable occasion, we were sent a special car to collect us, which was sheer bliss. Most of the cases were around Surry Hills in Crown Street, Riley Street and Florence Street. Sometimes we went to The Rocks or over to Rosebery or Paddington.

We were not fully trained at this stage and I participated in some terrifying cases. We always took about twenty pennies with us as we had to ring

---

8. Order of the British Empire, a similar award to the Order of Australia. It was given by the British monarch to British or Commonwealth citizens for outstanding services to the arts, sciences, welfare or to the military.

Corner of Hargrave Street and Charlotte Lane, East Sydney, 1927. (Photo courtesy City of Sydney Archives)

the hospital for help or advice every two hours from a public telephone. Impacted shoulders, breech births, umbilical cords tangled around babies' necks, premature babies, prolonged labour, transverse lies, brow presentations, footling, perineum tears during birth, all fell to my lot, but during this time we never lost a mother or a child.

Some homes were so poor that we had nowhere to sit and we would watch bedbugs crawling over the bed. Once we were sent to a house in Paddington and when we examined the patient there were two legs hanging out of the vagina. We had been warned not to pull on legs as we would have a terrible problem on our hands so we inserted our fingers under the legs (in sterile gloves), found the baby's mouth and pulled the head down forwards. Otherwise it would have caught on the pelvic brim and we would never have been able to get the infant out.

Fate must have been kind to us that day because we left a healthy mother and baby. We were very pleased with our achievement but came to earth next day when the sister visited the patient for after-care and discovered that in our zeal we hadn't shaved the patient. Not that we hadn't thought of it but we reasoned that she might have become infected while we were removing the pubic hair.

Most babies are easily delivered but we had quite a few impacted shoulders. One woman was having her eleventh child and was fully dilated but nothing happened when she pushed. The other nurse said she could feel something hard and something soft. I went to a public phone and rang the hospital.

The night sister told me we must be mistaken but we insisted on help. Straight away Sister Shaw came and gave her one cubic centimetre of pituitrin[9] and out came a large baby with a big hard lump on its forehead. The head could not get through, a face presentation can never be delivered, so we were lucky it was only a brow but it took a long time to get over the shock of that.

Later we were sent out on "district". That was easy. We washed the mother, took her temperature, and bathed the baby and saw that it was all right.

The mothers and babies at Crown Street were always treated generously. Every baby born there was taken down to Matron Clarke's office when the mother was discharged and given a pair of booties and a bonnet.

On Christmas Day Sister Shaw visited all the patients and took toys and clothes for the other children. Lady Whaley, a hospital benefactor, took her in her chauffeur-driven car. Lady Whaley was as kind to the poor as Sister Shaw was; she even sent her ampoules of perfume to give out.

Christmas Day was a great event. For months we hoarded empty soft drink bottles and sold them. Newspapers were sold to butcher shops or greengrocers and with our meagre savings we bought paper streamers and balloons. On Christmas Eve we would make a great show of them. Sometimes we had Christmas bush and Christmas bells.

The hospital had a small mobile organ and all staff that could be spared followed it around each ward and sang Christmas carols to the patients. One of my poignant memories is singing to the pregnant girls at the cottage and giving each one a small bag of sweets and a pair of booties. What the patients thought of us would be hard to imagine. The doctors in training donated churns of ice cream for the patients' dinner and for us poor nurses too.

---

9. Pituitrin is a proprietary name for an extract of bovine posterior pituitary hormones formerly used in obstetrics and since displaced by purer preparations. It was used then as a narcotic.

Christmas dinner was always lavish. The plum pudding gave us indigestion but we always ate some because it was chock-a-block with threepenny pieces. As we weren't paid wages, these threepenny pieces were much sought after. However, it wasn't too long before I was a proud, paid, professional nurse with my own money to spend.

24 · First love

After I graduated in 1933 I stayed on at Crown Street as a staff obstetrics nurse for a year. I worked in the surrounding poor suburbs, delivering and looking after mothers just as I had in training. I also assisted the new trainee nurses on district visits and births. I lived in the hospital in slightly better accommodation than when training. I dated a number of doctors in those days, which was a thrill, though it was usually short-lived. Nursing took up most of my time and the doctors were usually overworked interns with even less time than me.

At the end of the year I was offered a temporary hospital obstetrics position in Merriwa, a small country town in the upper Hunter region of New South Wales. It had about one thousand inhabitants and the hospital was pretty primitive. I was looking for something different so I took the position. It was a new experience to be a trained nurse whose knowledge and skills were valued. I delivered many babies in Merriwa and ran the obstetrics unit there for three months.

I then applied for the position of obstetrics sister at Cootamundra hospital in the Riverina district of New South Wales. This was a much larger and richer town than Merriwa and the hospital was also bigger though still lacking the modern equipment of Crown Street.

I worked in Cootamundra for nearly two years.

During my time there I met David C, a grazier's son, who came into the hospital to have his broken arm put in plaster. He had broken it falling from a horse while mustering sheep on the family property. He kept hanging around after he accidentally met me at the hospital.

He was a nice-looking, sweet-tempered and gentle boy who invited me to the pictures and to a bachelors' and spinsters' ball, a huge country affair in those days. I had to scramble to make myself a decent dress. He then took me to a tennis day on his father's property. I, of course, had never played tennis in my life and made a complete fool of myself. I met his parents, who seemed to like me and we even had lunch there. We saw a lot of each other from then on. He was twenty-seven, I was twenty-four and in my prime, I thought.

We fell very much in love. I was smitten. He was all I ever wanted in a man. Gentle, educated, caring, full of wit and loving. He said he wanted to marry me and take me to live on his property. He was going to have his own property that his father would set up for him. I was only too happy to accept. It was a dream.

He wanted to meet my parents. I was reluctant because I knew he would see our poor, inadequate house in Mayfield with kids everywhere and probably think less of me. He said he didn't care about all that, he just wanted to meet them before we married. I thought that was fair enough. He was impressed my father was a schoolteacher. He reassured me not to worry about my family, that he loved me too much for that.

So, reluctantly, I arranged for him to come to Mayfield. I went home for a week's break and he came up on the train for the Sunday.

I met him at Newcastle Station and we caught the tram out to Mayfield. I explained my father had never owned a car and he laughed. We walked from the terminus together. He looked so handsome and I felt proud. However, I could see his expression getting more thoughtful and serious as we walked down Vine Street and looked at the houses with the steelworks behind.

Annie and Dad welcomed him with open arms and he stayed for Sunday dinner and talked non-stop with Dad. He appeared to be quite at home with everyone, even with Cynthia, Tom and Annie. They all liked him. Later we had a walk on the steelworks golf course and he said he liked my family very much.

I went on the tram with him back to Newcastle Station. He was enthusiastic about the family and our marriage. We kissed hungrily at the station and he said he'd see me back in Cootamundra. I waved him goodbye.

That was the last I ever saw of him. I never heard his voice or saw him again.

He didn't contact me in Cootamundra when I returned and when I enquired about him I was told by the housekeeper at his property that he had gone to England with his father. I never believed that. Wherever he went, whatever he was thinking, he never reappeared. And never explained. There was no letter or phone call. Just silence. Forever.

I was deeply hurt. I had been very much in love with him and thought we were well suited. I would have been a good wife to him, I knew. He had proposed and I had accepted. That seemed to count for nothing once he had seen my family house and met my parents.

Cootamundra District Hospital, date unknown. (Photographer unknown)

I felt ashamed. I'd underestimated what a poor background would mean to him. Or maybe I had never realised how poor we were. I kept thinking . . . was it the lack of paint on the walls or the smallness of the house? Or the furniture? Or the steelworks dominating the area? Or my brothers and sisters and their unsuitable clothes and rough speech habits? I supposed it was everything together, too much for him and his family.

As a person, I obviously meant little to him. Not without a background. Were my parents *that* unimpressive, *that* disappointing? My siblings? Did our love count for nothing? What about our wonderful times together? I knew he loved me, he couldn't deny that. Clearly not enough.

I never blamed him or felt bitterness towards him. All I felt was sadness, anger and regret. He was a nice boy, who always treated me well, apart from this. He had a lovely nature. If anything, I blamed his parents, the way he was brought up and the unfairness of life.

It took me a long while to recover from the pain of this rejection. For a while I didn't think I was going to. It was the start of more severe bouts of depression that would haunt me all my life. The depression wasn't so much about him as about my family and my inner anger at my childhood. It was a rage of despair and it was many years before I understood it.

When it was certain he was never going to contact me again I left Cootamundra and went back to Sydney where I asked for, and received, my old job back as a Crown Street staff obstetrics nurse. I stayed there from

1935 till 1938. I must have delivered or helped deliver over 400 babies in that time.

My tough old grandfather Sharp died in 1936 and I attended the funeral in Newcastle. He was eighty when he died. He had willed what he had equally among his nine children and my full brother Bill (Wilhelm) whom he and Grandma had brought up until he was five and considered him one of theirs. The Sharps came from near and far to hear his will read and attend the funeral. Uncle Ernie didn't endear himself to the family when he said in the car on the way to the funeral: "I wonder how much the old boy left . . ."

Uncle Ernie had done quite well in life as had his brothers Oliver — who at that stage somehow had a big property near Charleville in Queensland — and Bert —who owned a bus that ferried workers to the steelworks. Uncle Ernie had owned a truck that carried for a big firm but then started a Sunday paper agency in Mayfield and ended up with plenty of money and a Packard car. For that comment he made about grandfather in the car, he was called the "family Scrooge".

I had never been a fan of Grandfather Sharp but I recognised what he had achieved in his life. He didn't leave that much money after all, despite his property acquisitions. Certainly, he didn't help my father because, as already mentioned, when Dad died a year later he still owed all the money on our Vine Street house.

During all this time, my sister Winnie was doing general nursing at Newcastle hospital, following in my footsteps. She was working hard, she told me, and enjoying it. She was bright enough to go university, but that opportunity was never presented to her.

In Sydney, I was invited out by various doctors, interns and other men and I desperately played the field. I needed all the attention I could get. I had numerous "affairs". I had three abortions, I'm ashamed to admit, in that time — a period when it was completely illegal. All my abortions were by hospital doctors who had ways of getting those things properly and secretly done. I never went to a "quack" to have an abortion, to amateurs where the risks were great. I knew many doctors very well and they, in their secret and responsible way, looked after me. They didn't look after me emotionally though. Only my best friend Mavis and my sister Cynthia cared for me in that way. They knew what I was going through.

I'm not proud of those abortions and the clandestine and illegal way they were done but it was a necessity. It's taken me a long time to admit that they occurred. I've always been very closed about this part of my life. I always seemed to be in love with someone or other, though I know now it was all in reaction to my grief over David C abandoning me. I was careless and lucky not to do myself permanent damage. I was still a rebel and thought I could take care of myself.

25 · No one left to be proud of me

Although my dear father had had a bad cough for many years I was upset in late 1936 to learn that he was diagnosed with tuberculosis. He had to go to a sanitarium, or private hospital, in Wentworth Falls in the Blue Mountains west of Sydney. I took the train up there several times to visit him but he never improved. The doctors eventually admitted the disease was too far advanced. Towards the end of that year he deteriorated rapidly and my visits became more frequent, more so than even Annie's and Cynthia's, who had to come from Newcastle.

He and I talked a lot about Mayfield and his life there, and at Wallsend and Minmi. He reiterated how much he had loved my birth mother Wilhelmina when they married, how close they were and what a struggle it had been to get on with his life without her.

He had been faithful to Annie but, as he said, first loves are always the strongest. I was proud of my father then and how hard he had worked for his family, including me too, despite the setbacks. The lack of money wasn't his fault. I felt I was the closest to him of all the children, though I never said that out loud. He still called me his Miss Sunshine. I felt this was ironic as I had grown up to be a rather sad person.

I was alone with him in his room at Wentworth Falls on 6 January 1937, the night he died. I had come from Sydney after a couple of difficult deliveries and I was dog-tired. It was hot. I sat by his bed that night, knowing he was very ill. Late at night he asked me for a glass of water but I was too tired to get it. I fell asleep in the chair beside his bed.

When I woke up he wasn't breathing. I checked his pulse and heart. He was dead. He had died while I was asleep. I called out and the medical staff came running in. I've always regretted not getting him that glass of water.

I asked to be allowed to sit in the room alone with him for a while. While sitting there I began to understand what a major event it is in your life when one of your parents dies. I tried to imagine that his soul had left his body and was now going to protect me but all I could feel was that he was gone ... into the unknown. I prayed to God to let me feel him but I only felt that he no longer existed for me. All I had was my memory of him. I was now on my own. Except for Cynthia.

I thought the angels might sing and spirit his soul into the air when he died but, of course, that didn't happen. He had just stopped breathing. His body went cold. I touched him, felt the coldness and then a wave of sadness. Tears welled up in my eyes but I couldn't cry. This was my father, who I'd known all my life . . . who I'd lived with since my mother's death and who tried to look after me as best he could. He'd watched me being born in Boomi. It was his ducks I'd said I'd eat in Mayfield when nobody else would. He was the father who always left a storm lantern for us on the back verandah for the backyard toilet in Mayfield.

The doctor came back and I finally started to cry. He stood patiently till I finished. My father meant nothing to him, but still, he waited. The attitude of doctors to death intrigues me. Generally complete indifference, though respectful. Isn't it a fellow human being? There's always universal joy at childbirth but not universal sadness at death.

I was the only one of the family there. Annie wasn't there, she came next day. I couldn't say how much she grieved. She never showed a lot of emotion. I didn't blame her whatever. My brother Tom had to hurry up from his honeymoon! He had married Rita on 19 December 1936. He came up with Annie and Cynthia, and Gilbert and Winnie came later. Tom had been working at Lysaght and contributing a lot of his money to Dad and Annie in Mayfield while Dad couldn't work. Tom was such a decent man and always loyal to them both and stood by them. In 1938, he and Rita had a lovely girl, Dale.

I had cared about my father too, even if sometimes I had wanted more from him. I hoped he knew that. Now the supporting bond, the father–daughter anchor of him, was gone. Annie was never my supporter, it was only him, I thought.

No one anymore to tell me I've done badly or well. No one left to be proud of me. Cynthia now seemed like a mother to me, a mother/sister. We went back so far, I was no longer very close to Tom. It's odd how we don't like feeling alone in the world, though we mostly are.

Dad was only fifty-nine when he died.

When Annie came up, and then Cynthia, Winnie and Tom, we jointly paid for a van to take Dad's body back to Newcastle for a funeral at Beresfield crematorium. Cynthia by then had a job in a small firm as a bookkeeper, a job at which she excelled; Tom was working at Lysaght; and Winnie, then twenty-three, was nursing at Wallsend hospital.

After the funeral in Newcastle, Cynthia introduced me to her new boyfriend, Jim. His real name was Harold Stanley but she always called him Jim for some reason. He was a chubby man in his early thirties and was trying to buy and pay off a barbershop at the edge of Newcastle city near Hamilton. He had a moustache, a mildly sullen, defensive manner and kept his distance from everyone. When I spoke to him he seemed to have very little to say. Maybe he was shy? Cynthia said he was from a respected Newcastle family and trained as a men's barber; they were going to get married one day.

After the wake, I cornered Cynthia at breakfast when no one was around.

"Cynthia, are you really thinking of marrying him?"

"Of course."

"Are you sure?"

What I wanted to say was, "Cynthia, he seems only capable of speaking in monosyllables."

"Of course I'm sure."

What I wanted to say then was, "That man will *not* make you happy." But I didn't. I said, "All right."

"There's a flat behind the shop he wants to buy so we'll have somewhere to live. We get on very well, Jean."

I wanted to scream from the rooftops, "You're too smart for him, Cyn!"

But I said, "Well he seems like a decent man."

"Thank you," she said. Then she said: "Have some faith in me please. He's more intelligent than you think and even if he's a barber he loves me. I don't criticise your boyfriends. Even when they desert you."

"Oh, thank you," I said, with as little sarcasm as I could.

She always knew what I was thinking.

I thought Cynthia was compromising. Yet who was I to criticise them if they loved one another? My misgivings were that he had all Newcastle's limitations in his manner and she would be trapped in the same world where she grew up. As it turned out, he would take advantage of her slave temperament and dominate her in a way that I dreaded. None of this appeared to concern her though, nor did it later on. She was always happy with him. He was what she wanted. He was dependable. He was loyal. That's what she needed. Her sights were set low, I thought, for a girl who had promised so much at school.

They did not marry for five years. It took place in 1942 when she was thirty-six. I was present.

I didn't know it then but my own life was about to change dramatically as well.

26 · A second-class railway ticket to a new life

I went back to Crown Street hospital and my unexciting, though stressful, single life delivering babies. At least I had a good job.

In early 1938 my best friend Mavis Munro married. I was her bridesmaid and the wedding was in Sydney. I thought I looked very fetching. I know this because everyone told me so, especially the photographer whose photograph of me I kept for a long time.

Years later, laughing at herself, a slightly disappointed-in-marriage Mavis said to me, "You know, Jeannie, I married an amateur. Me, who's had experts!" Then she laughed. So did I. She had had lots of boyfriends. She didn't really care and they were happy enough, although she did marry a very ordinary man.

We were still friends, even forty years later. I maintained a lot of friendships through my life but I'm particularly proud of my long friendship with Mavis.

My young sister Winnie was also married in June 1938, to John Ayton whom I never knew much about. I went to Newcastle for the wedding and was the bridesmaid. It was a lovely event. I was disappointed that Mr Ayton wasn't the stylish husband I would have hoped for our dear, bright scholarship-winning Winnie but she was married before I was and they seemed very happy. Another good, decent but struggling man in our family, I thought, even though I liked him. Winnie would be struggling all her life, I imagined, quite rightly as it turned out. The marriage lasted though and she was happy. John owned a coal-carting truck and they also built a small grocer shop with a house attached in Swansea south of Newcastle. They lived behind the shop for years, happily raising a family.

It wasn't what I wanted. I longed all my life for some style, to have style ... in any of our lives. Style, comfort and love. I wanted them more than anything.

Towards the end of 1938 I decided my work prospects and relationships with men were going nowhere in Sydney. I was getting bored with, and tired of, city life. I had quite liked life in the country at Merriwa and Cootamundra

Jean as bridesmaid to her sister Winnie in Newcastle, 1938. (Photo courtesy Cheryl Small)

so I scanned the newspapers for another job away from Sydney. Of course, part of me was also looking to find a life partner. I was always maternal, and I thought there were better chances for me in the country. I wasn't conscious of this then, I was conscious only that I was restless.

I applied for a position as sister at the maternity unit at the Warialda District Hospital advertised in the *Sydney Morning Herald*. Warialda is a small town in the northern tablelands of New South Wales near the Queensland border. Perfect, I thought. I did not admit it to myself but I secretly hoped there would be less female competition.

Within the week, back came a letter from a Mr J. Weinthal of the hospital board accepting my offer and enclosing a second-class single railway ticket to Warialda.

I immediately gave a month's notice to the hospital and prepared to travel. I was now twenty-eight. I had a little money saved although it was still technically the Depression. I didn't need to inform my mother or family — I could write and tell them from Warialda. In any case, I had no idea how long I'd be there. There was no tenure guaranteed in the offer.

One afternoon in the late spring of 1938 I collapsed with a sigh of relief into my corner seat of a second-class carriage at Sydney's Central Station on the North-West Mail bound for Moree. My heavy suitcase with all my worldly possessions safely stowed in the luggage rack overhead and my handbag and the latest copy of *Women's Weekly* and *The Bulletin* on my lap.

It was a quiet day, no shouting schoolboys or giggling black-stockinged girls in school uniforms and white and navy panama hats — nobody returning flushed with glory from the show or sunburnt families returning from beach holidays at Manly and Collaroy going home to the even more sunburnt country in the dry inlands of Murrurundi, Moree and Warialda. Just the regular North-West Mail travellers and me.

I had been intent on finding a window seat facing the engine and that was easy as it wasn't crowded. It felt like an adventure. I was off to experience something new. Nothing warned me that by accepting the little green piece of cardboard in my hand that I was off to something that would change my life forever and that my carefree if sometimes impecunious existence was left behind with the shriek of the steam whistle of the train as it left the number one platform at Central Station at 4 pm.

It was a long, slow journey to Moree, through the night with constant stopping at almost every town on the way. Impossible to sleep, it was also rather cold, especially as we headed further inland. The carriages creaked continually and swayed and shuddered whenever we came to a halt. Which was often. Sometimes we were stationary for what seemed like hours, as if we were changing engines or repairing carriages or taking on water for the steam engine.

At Singleton, a young bloke about twenty-three or twenty-four years old boarded and came into my compartment and started spouting poetry to me. He seemed obsessed with Omar Khayyám: "Never blows so red the rose as where some buried Caesar bled." I think he was living in some kind of fantasy world. He was on his way to becoming a jackaroo at Midkin Station near Moree.

"There are 78,000 sheep on Midkin Station," he kept saying. I thought to myself: "Well, those poor sheep will hear a lot more of this poetry I suppose."

Later, I developed a toothache and fell into a troubled sleep and woke up at Narrabri. We had a cup of tea there, in the middle of the night on the cold platform. A few desolate passengers who couldn't sleep huddled around the tiny station cafeteria counter. A lot of people got off the train here. Men in broad-brimmed hats and tight pants were waiting on the platform for women in white shoes and cotton frocks who were tumbling out of the sleeping car with cranky children and lots of luggage. They should have tried sitting up all night with a toothache.

We arrived at Moree in the early morning, about 7 am. I had breakfast at the station: toast and more steaming tea in thick white cups. I knew I had been to Moree when I was four when my father brought us down from Dolgelly, but I hardly remembered.

Within two hours I changed into the "slow" train to Warialda, which was still fifty-two miles (eighty-four kilometres) away. I only spent an hour or so in Moree waiting for it to leave. It was a "mixed train" and went from Moree to Inverell each morning and returned to Moree in the evening. A mixed train was one passenger carriage attached to the back of a goods train, carrying grain and farm equipment. It stopped at every possible opportunity to pick up and unload.

It was a slow train all right. The slowness gave me time to study the countryside.

It was flat and desolate-looking at first, with here and there a solitary homestead surrounded by darker foliage trees, tanks and windmills, and occasionally a paddock of ripening wheat. The sidings had funny names: Pallamalawa, Binegar, Yagobi, Gravesend, Hadleigh . . . and, at last, a "Warialda Railway" sign at a siding called Kellys Gully.

It wasn't total desolation that greeted me but Kellys Gully is small and not the best way to be introduced to the fine and fascinating town and district of Warialda. When the steam train shuddered to a halt I was expecting a small country town but not one as tiny as this one looked through the carriage window. I didn't realise that Warialda railway station was built at Kellys Gully, a small siding five miles from the town.

27 · Who's in charge here, you, me or Doctor Wheatley?

Scarcely had my foot landed on the platform when a kindly voice said, "Welcome to Warialda, Sister." The Reverend William Powell took my suitcase and led me to his car — I think it was a Willys Knight or an old black Chevrolet Tourer — standing just outside the station. Reverend Powell met all incoming hospital staff with a sweet smile and an outstretched welcoming hand. He was quick to assure me that this was only a railway town (a siding). When the railway first came the civic fathers thought that trains would make Warialda too noisy and dirty and so they had the station built five miles away.

Bill Powell (as Reverend Powell was called by everyone) proved to be always kind and a friend. He was probably in his late fifties then, very upright standing, grey-haired and gentle. Although only a reverend I soon found out he lived at the vicarage of the Church of England in Warialda.

He told me as we drove into the town proper that while the town had a population of less than a thousand it served a large area of sheep and wheat stations and properties in all directions. The big ones were well known in the district and had exotic names like Coolatai, Gournama and Croppa.

The largest property in the area was called Gunyerwarildi, north of Warialda near the town of Croppa Creek, and owned by the stately Mackay family. It was a massive sheep, wheat and cattle farm of over 100,000 acres. Reverend Powell joked that Dr Wheatley, the local doctor, once quipped that the social pecking order in Warialda was "the majority of us, then one step up to the McMasters (another rural family), then the Mackays, then God". The Mackay family never shopped in Warialda. They preferred Inverell (a nearby large town) or Sydney, a fact that didn't go down well with the townspeople.

The names of these properties plus the names of the surrounding towns eventually held a magic spell for me that I was never to forget. It was as though they had existed since time began not just the hundred or so years they had. Perhaps it was Aboriginal names that gave the feeling of ancientness but it immediately fascinated me in a way that Cootamundra and

Merriwa hadn't. I felt a familial and timeless connection to the town and district.

Bill Powell's old car carried me from straggling Kellys Gully on a gravel road through mostly rough scrub-covered country for five miles, then around a highway corner, through a bit more scrub, past the showground, through the historic old township — primitive to my city eyes — past two banks opposite each other on a corner — over an old and rickety wooden bridge, around a street corner past the sandstone Presbyterian Church, past a few more paddocks and a small muddy lane with an old slab cottage on one corner — to the hospital grounds on another corner.

The hospital was approached by a gravel drive enclosing a rose garden, which was maintained by Mr Colin Pyrke (the owner of one of the local general stores — a sort of country Woolworths) and his staff, which added a pretty touch to the hospital approach. Reverend Bill drew his car to a halt in front of the hospital and ushered me into the day room — in fact the dining room — around midday. The staff were at morning tea.

As we walked in the usual hospital aroma of disinfectant assailed my nostrils but, strangely, another two smells challenged it. One was the smell of floor polish but there was also a smell of wood smoke, which seemed to

The rickety bridge at Warialda (photographed in 1968). It has since been rebuilt.

be mixed in with it. This made the aroma very unique. It was something I noticed immediately and never forgot.

The matron, Erma Gallus, was there, a thin, strained, suspicious-looking woman in her forties, with sharp features and intense blue eyes. She was flanked by the day sister and three experienced nurses. They bade me welcome, made a place for us at the table and plied us with hot scones and tea. Matron got down to business straightaway.

"Long journey?"

"I haven't had much sleep."

"When did you finish up at Crown Street?"

"Two days ago. Delivered a baby the day I left."

"Goodness, you should have had a holiday. Mightn't be so hectic here although we've got two mothers due this week. It's good you've come. The doctor is away at the moment. On his honeymoon."

"Oh."

"I'll show you your quarters and your unit when you finish your morning tea."

Afterwards, without fuss, she led me over my future domain, the Jessie Carlyon Maternity Unit[10] completed in 1935 and reached by a walkway from the main hospital. It was just called the maternity unit. Apparently, the previous sister departed for Moree only two hours after I arrived.

The maternity unit consisted of one public ward of four beds, a room for private patients and a labour room. It was connected to the main hospital with a covered wooden walkway, a white-timbered structure completely gauzed in and abutting some wild, forbidding-looking scrub. I wasn't greatly impressed with the place.

I thought the whole set-up was primitive — I soon learned that all sterilising was done with primuses, a pump-up heating apparatus that immediately and always terrified me. There was an annex for the sterilisation of both linen and instruments. All other heating and lighting was done using kerosene or wood fire. It seemed as bumpkin to me as the lizards and goannas that roamed in the garden by the walkway. I kept my opinions to myself.

The main hospital consisted of a male six-bed ward, a female six-bed ward, two private rooms, a theatre and a sluice room. The smell of floor polish and wood smoke permeated every room.

---

10. Funded by the Warialda Country Women's Association and a generous legacy from local Jessie Carlyon.

There was no town water in Warialda, all water was tank water. No refrigeration either: we used cool safes made of hessian filled with charcoal and water. We also had a small ice chest, which held a block of ice from the town iceworks.

There was no sewerage and no garbage collection, though there was electricity and septic tanks. The hospital also had its own windmill with a pump. All ironing was done with a petrol iron.

The main building was an old, tired-looking single-storey brick structure with a sweep of gravel in front that led to the front doorway where one could look down at the rose garden.

I was the only maternity sister. Sometimes during emergencies a general nurse and the doctor assisted me. When I had patients, I worked and when there were no mothers and babies in the unit my time was my own. My days turned out to be times of feverish energy or complete idleness.

The matron ran the main hospital with two sisters and three experienced nurses. One sister and one nurse were on night duty. There were also two housemaids, one cook, one handyman and one laundress. One sister at the hospital was madly in love with a bloke called Angus MacIntosh whom she eventually married and who was later killed in Tobruk.

I had sleeping quarters at the hospital and it didn't take me long to settle in. I was soon delivering the two due babies.

Warialda turned out to be a stylish, quiet country town, not at its best in the summer. There was no swimming pool in those days and it was very hot in January and February. I easily made friends with the hospital staff and we often went for walks along the creek or to the pictures held in the Soldiers' Memorial Hall (organised by the local School of Arts). Or we went to church. There were no clubs for women and women didn't frequent pubs. Dancing and balls were strictly limited to autumn and winter.

The most talked about recent event was former nurse Iris Goldman's marriage to Dr Wheatley, Warialda's resident doctor. Dark and vivacious, Iris had been very popular at the hospital and the doctor was a recent newcomer to the district. They were on their honeymoon when I first came to Warialda and I didn't meet Iris until a few months later.

Everyone thought the marriage would never work as Dr Wheatley had been much sought after by the females of the town. The talk was that Iris wasn't up to his intellect. Dr Wheatley himself was a legend in the hospital and after constantly hearing about him I couldn't wait to meet him. In his place, there was a locum from Inverell in my first two weeks.

Dr Arthur Wheatley and Iris soon returned. My first impression of the doctor walking up the ramp to the maternity unit, was of a very attractive, fair, wavy-haired man in his early thirties, dressed in a simple white cotton-duck suit. He had been a ship's doctor and wore his white suit very smartly. I fell in love with him immediately, as we all did, but as he had just returned from his honeymoon he would have scarcely noticed me. Such was his personality and wisdom that, for me, he became the dominating figure of Warialda society, indeed, of my entire world. I had the impression that he was the central character in the play about Warialda and the rest of us, no matter how self-important, were playing minor roles.

There was a common saying in Warialda then that still stands today in my family, a tribute to his influence: "Who's in charge here, you, me or Dr Wheatley?"

Educated at Sydney Grammar and Sydney University, he was intelligent, gentle and suave — all qualities alien to Warialda. He was a man who knew his worth, even though he was sometimes frustrated at the attitudes in the town. He had been brought up in Randwick and had been a doctor on cruise ships for years. I never knew him to say anything to me that didn't affect me in some way. He never spoke without thinking deeply, he never made careless comments. He was considered in everything he did without the slightest hint of self-importance or sense of superiority.

He was the most impressive man I have ever met. His character made a profound impression on my life.

He was an exceptional doctor, a physician as well as a surgeon, and operated when necessary with a doctor from Bingara to assist him, while the matron gave the anaesthetic. They had very few fatalities. The theatre was an old room in the hospital with just the bare necessities. There was no ambulance: Louis Kratz, a local businessman, had an old Buick that was called in when necessary. Dr Wheatley had an old cream sedan Chevrolet for years, well known in the district, which also acted as ambulance in an emergency. When it later fell to pieces he bought a yellow Ford which similarly lasted for years.

Arthur was kind. He never refused medical services for lack of money. He once had a poor patient whom he advised to have his tonsils out and when the patient said he couldn't afford it Dr Wheatley asked how much he could afford. "All I've got is seven shillings and sixpence," said the patient.

"All right," said Dr Wheatley, "I'll take your tonsils out for seven shillings and sixpence". And he did.

Once it was a pound for an appendectomy. His kindness got in the way of trying to make a living though. Some people deliberately didn't pay him at all and many a woman faced up to her second or third pregnancy with only the help of the unit sister (me mostly) because she hadn't paid him for the previous child. Some did have the grace to blush when I had to get him to put in a stitch or two when they were badly torn, something he never refused.

He had a commonsense approach to his job. When a baby was really sick he listened to what the mother had to say first. He told me: "A mother's natural instincts are often the best guide to a baby's illness and her instincts about what to do are often correct."

One night, one of the hospital maids came into labour, much to everyone's surprise because no one even suspected she was pregnant, not even the father of her child. Women in labour do tend to tell the truth and somehow or other Arthur persuaded her to tell him the name of the father. Arthur then rang up Bill Powell to get hold of the father who didn't know she was pregnant. Bill managed to locate him and we had a nice little marriage service in the labour ward before the baby arrived, so it was legitimate after all.

The hospital was full of pregnancy stories. The doctor before Arthur had a young maid in his home who had a baby all by herself, took it up the back and strangled it. Of course, it was found but neither the doctor nor his wife knew she was in the family way. The doctor said afterwards that he vaguely wondered why the bow at the back of her apron seemed to be getting smaller each day.

Warialda turned out to be much more socially rich and had more character than I could have imagined. Being the sister in the maternity ward was the beginning of a long life adventure.

28 · Getting to be part of the "in" crowd

I found out quickly that church life was integral to everyday life in Warialda. Arthur Wheatley was famously agnostic but most people in Warialda belonged to one denomination or another. The chaplains/padres/priests of all these dominations had important positions in the social life of the town.

The sandstone-built Presbyterian church which I first saw when I drove over the old wooden bridge with Bill Powell was presided over by the Right Reverend P. A. Smith. I never knew what his Christian names were as he was never referred to as anything but P. A. Smith. He was on the hospital board and was welcoming and considerate to the "alien" nursing staff imported to Warialda.

The North-West Mission to Warialda first appointed him in March 1908 but from 1918 to 1920 he was a chaplain in the army in the First World War and served in England and France. The story went that the first words P. A. Smith spoke to his wife when he returned from the war were, "Have you fed the fowls, dear?" He was a caring man — his kids were supposed to be the wildest in town when they were small but they were grown up by the time I arrived, and tame as rabbits.

The Reverend Father Healey led the Catholics in the town. He was kind and caring too but you had to be a Catholic. He was never called anything but Father Healey. He ended his days as a monsignor. P. A. Smith eventually became Moderator of the Presbyterian Church. Bill Powell died in Warialda caring for us and his widow became the beloved Warialda librarian.

When I first took up the position of unit sister at Warialda in 1938 many people were kind to me and tried to make me feel at home. P. A. Smith and his wife were two of them. He was a frequent visitor to the hospital, like Bill Powell. He was a wonderful scholar with a degree from Sydney University and was a schoolmaster before he took up his ministry. I saw through him what the clergy meant to people in a small isolated community.

The Smiths asked me to Christmas dinner in my first year at Warialda (1938) at the old Manse and early in 1939 Mrs Smith asked me down one Thursday for afternoon tea where I was to present myself in my best "bib and tucker". There I first met Arthur's Wheatley's wife Iris, Ethel Weinthal (the solicitor's wife), Jean McGregor (wife of the stock and station agent W. D. McGregor) and Mr and Mrs J. A. McGregor Senior (retired but who still owned the stock and station agency) and some others I can't remember.

This was a big moment for me. It was when I realised I had some status in this town, not just as a nursing sister, but as a person in my own right. Mrs Smith had obviously thought I had enough quality, even as a twenty-eight-year-old, to be introduced to the wives of the professional men of the town. The "in" crowd as I later called them.

Iris Wheatley and I were to become great friends and remained so for many years. She was outgoing and witty, the very opposite to me. Nobody made me laugh as much as she did. She was very striking-looking with her black hair and flashing eyes and had a lively, infectious sense of fun. Her mind was uncomplicated and non-intellectual — she had never heard of most of the classic novels or knew anything about poetry or literature. Her great love was flowers and flower arrangements. She told me with a wicked laugh that she had won Arthur after "everyone had set their traps for him and he fell into mine." Although he had married her against local opinion he was eventually to find that she was the best of all of them for him. She was to care for him, physically and economically, all his life. It was her common sense against his education and upbringing and the combination worked.

Iris asked me out for a game of golf soon after that afternoon tea. I remember how surprised I was at the sand "greens" we had to rake after we had used them and the emus and kangaroos that kept running along the fairways. Not that I had any idea how to play golf. We played very bad golf, nine holes with sand greens often sent our scores up over seventy-two but we didn't care, it was fun. Small boys lay in wait at one hole, which was up a bank, and they pinched our balls before we climbed up it. "You can bet it was one of the Cleals," Iris said. The Cleals from Warialda became famous years later when Noel and Les Cleal played first-grade rugby league in Sydney after being stars in country rugby league. The Cleal family was legend in Warialda for their toughness and anti-establishment natures.

P. A. Smith made a special effort to introduce me to the locals after the Christmas dinner and asked me to attend a social welfare meeting in Gravesend, a nearby small town. I cannot recall what the meeting was particularly about but on the way he explained that the north-west area where Warialda was had been an inland sea millions of years ago — he pointed

Hope Street, Warialda, April 1968.

Iris Wheatley (left), Thell Stevenson (from Inverell) and Dr Arthur Wheatley in Warialda, late 1940s. (Photo courtesy Arthur and Iris's daughter Robyn)

out the rocky cliffs around Gravesend that once had been the seashore and the eroding markings on the cliffs where breakers had spent themselves. He also told me that the little creeks and sandy places around Warialda were full of seashells. This proved to be correct when my children later found shells in the creek beds.

Soon after I arrived the matron held a fete to raise money to buy a refrigerator for the hospital. The fridge was called a Snow Queen and I have never seen a Snow Queen before or since.

I had been brought up a Methodist but because of the Bill Powell and P. A. Smith in Warialda, I was eventually christened into the Anglican Church and confirmed by Bishop Mayes from Armidale. Religion is still very important to me.

In many ways Warialda was a lonely place. It was isolated then, which is why social life was so important: the church and its services and various social functions, tennis parties, bridge, golf, dances and balls, lunches and afternoon teas. Dr Wheatley told me later that when he was first in Warialda and knew no one, he was so lonely he would sometimes take his old Chevrolet car and drive out one hundred miles into the countryside and back, just to pass the time and give himself something to do.

I was welcomed into Warialda society in a way I'd never been welcomed anywhere else. I'm still not sure why. Maybe because I had, unknown to myself, finally matured. Or maybe people there were lonelier than I realised. Perhaps they were desperate for new blood and I was exotic to them. I know I was described to the chemist, Harry Wallace, as "that very pretty new sister in the maternity ward." I hoped it was more than just my looks that people saw, though I knew being a sister helped.

I became fascinated with the Wheatleys who were the centre of Warialda life. I had never met anyone like Arthur, not in all my years at Crown Street or in any of the other country towns where I'd worked. He was unique, as was Iris. I was interested and affected by everything that family did and grateful to be a friend. I was even fascinated by their house in Hope Street.

Arthur had brought his widowed mother to Warialda (always Grandma Wheatley to us) to keep house for him. She brought her furniture and settled in the old weatherboard house next door to the Royal Hotel in Hope Street. The right front part of the house had been the former Bank of New South Wales. It served as a small waiting room and surgery for Arthur. It was very old-fashioned with steps leading up to it from the street and a back

Dr Wheatley's house and surgery (on the right) in Hope Street, Warialda, photographed in 1968. It has since been demolished.

door that opened into the house itself. It served very well as a surgery and the doctor could leave through the rear door at any time to have a meal or a quiet rest in the bedroom.

The kitchen of the house was detached from the main building. It was separated from the bedrooms, lounge rooms and bathroom by a roofed walkway and a cemented-in garden called the courtyard. The kitchen itself was old and had a worn-out-looking wood-burning stove, two laundry tubs and a copper on the back verandah. Also on that verandah was a meat-safe with wet hessian over it and a water bag. There were several water tanks at the side of the house and an old car shed where Arthur parked his old Ford car.

This was the house that Iris moved into after she married Arthur and I mention it in detail because the house became the iconic house in Warialda. Iris was very social and loved being the centre of attention and it was the only house in the street of shops in the heart of the town. It was unique. Being the doctor's wife she attracted a lot of people there.

I remember Saturday mornings in particular when graziers and farmers and their children would come to town to meet each other and shop.

Most of them would at some time drop in to Iris and Arthur's house in the middle of Hope Street which was always full of flowers and other townspeople. They would always be welcome, would get a cup of tea and a piece of cake and be encouraged to indulge in the latest gossip. I had never seen this sort of regular Saturday socialising anywhere else and I never did again. It was unique to Warialda.

Iris became pregnant but unfortunately had a miscarriage that first year of their marriage. She was disappointed when they discovered it had been a boy because they had both badly wanted a boy. Little did I know that pregnancy wasn't very far away for me either.

29 · The doctor, his wife, the chemist, the dentist, the hospital sister and me

Iris described the local chemist Harry Wallace to me — somewhat amusingly similar to the way I'd been described to him — as "that handsome, dark, young chemist". Like me, he was relatively new in town, and he was a bachelor. He had arrived in 1937 without much money and was renting the pharmacy from its previous owner who had moved to Inverell. He was twenty-nine, good-looking, hair receding but charming, intelligent and witty.

He was very friendly with the dentist John Arnold and, of course, Dr Wheatley and Iris. One weekend in early 1939, I was invited, along with one of the other sisters from the hospital, to a picnic on the river at Gravesend. This is where I first met Harry.

He showed a lot of interest in me at the picnic and we went on several picnics after that as a group. I was flattered by his attention and quickly fell in love . . . again. He told me that his family belonged to the Exclusive Plymouth Brethren, a protestant religious sect in Sydney and he was an outcast because he had been seen "going to the pictures".

"They [the sect] sent me a note saying 'they had withdrawn from me'," he told me, then said laughingly, "I always thought that made me the original Exclusive Plymouth Brethren and them the outcasts."

I had no idea about the strictness of the Exclusive Brethren and no idea why "going to the pictures" was such a crime. It sounded odd to my Methodist ears but Harry's stories about them fascinated me.

Harry's parents, like mine, had also been poor. His father had been a travelling salesman, selling farm implements and farm chemicals, such as sheep dip. There were five children in the family to feed and educate, something beyond his income. He drove an old Packard on his travels around New South Wales and was much respected. Harry had left school in Sydney after the Intermediate Certificate when he was fourteen. He sold books door-to-door for a living before going to university at the age of fifteen. In those days, pharmacy students only needed the Intermediate Certificate to study at university. It was a Diploma of Pharmacy and they were apprenticed to a chemist at the same time for two years. Harry had to pass a university entrance examination to do the course.

He took three years to get through pharmacy and then worked at various country pharmacies relieving chemists who wanted to take holidays. He spent a long time relieving, particularly in the town of Harden. He'd finally come to Warialda at the age of twenty-seven with a chance to own his own pharmacy. Although he rented the pharmacy he had first choice on buying it if he did well enough. Harry was ambitious and wanted to better himself, as I did, so we were drawn to each other.

Harry and I began to make a foursome with the dentist John Arnold and another hospital sister, going to dances and to the races at Inverell. Harry and I quickly became a couple. We also went on many outings and parties with John Arnold, the hospital sister, and Dr Wheatley and Iris, including trips to Bingara, Barraba and Moree for dances and sometimes picnic races. Going to the races in those days was a popular activity.

Harry was witty and made everyone in the group laugh. He was also very enterprising in business. Arthur Wheatley really loved him and would laugh until he cried at his jokes. Harry told an amusing story of meeting Arthur for the first time in Warialda. Being the new and only chemist in town he walked up to Arthur's house in Hope Street one morning to introduce himself. The doctor was sitting on the front porch in the morning sun reading the newspaper. Harry stopped at the gate and said: "Hello, Doctor. My name's Harry Wallace. I'm the new chemist." No reaction from Arthur. He just slowly folded his paper and stood up. "Is that so?' he said and walked inside. Harry was left speechless at the gate. Dr Wheatley could sometimes be like that.

It was a poor start to their relationship but Arthur soon came to respect Harry (as he was always an excellent chemist) and they became great friends, often going fishing together for weekends. I was very proud of Harry's friendship with Arthur.

Harry's and mine was a whirlwind romance. I had been jaded with my life for some time and I was more than ready for marriage. So was Harry. It was the right time for us both. I felt I deserved it. We had both fallen in love. Sometime in May or June Harry proposed and I accepted.

We became engaged and he had some diamonds secretly sent up from Sydney. He carried them around in his pocket in a tobacco tin lined with cotton wool until I chose one. Of course, I picked the biggest. We had the ring made up and announced our engagement.

We had no money at all. All Harry had was a Pontiac car and a business that was not paid for and the chemist shop that took about thirty-five pounds a week. He rented it from the former chemist, Mr Ditchfield. I didn't have any money but Harry gave me ten pounds to buy myself a wedding dress. Harry's mother gave the wedding reception at her home in Burwood. She also gave us a dinner set. Thus, were laid the foundations of our later life.

Before we left Warialda to be married, Harry borrowed two hundred pounds to spend on furnishing the tiny flat behind the shop. We covered the bedroom and sitting cum dining room floors in green Feltex, an imitation carpet. We bought a cheap bedroom suite, a cane-wood lounge suite (the cushions were covered in tapestry cloth), a dining table and four chairs, a buffet (one end of which opened up as a small bar), a kitchen table and four chairs. There was a built-in cupboard in the kitchen and two shelves to hold saucepans. We thought we were made . . . we had our own little home.

Cynthia gave a kitchen tea for me in Newcastle. She made as big a fuss as possible. It was in Tom and Rita's house in Hamilton where she lived with stepmother Annie after they had had to leave Vine Street in Mayfield after dad's death. Tom and his wife Rita were kind to Annie and our family all their lives and willingly shared their house in Hamilton with them for many years, certainly till Cynthia married. Eventually Annie moved to Burwood in Sydney to live with Eva. I took some leave from the hospital and caught the train to Newcastle. Cynthia invited Winnie, Uncle Ernie and a few of the girls I knew. I think Gilbert dropped in but Wilhelm (Bill) was still working in Queensland on [Uncle?] Oliver's property. Cynthia was determined to give me a good time although I hadn't been in Newcastle for a long while. How things had changed! I never thought it would be Cynthia giving me a kitchen tea and me getting married before her. I realised that Cynthia's real nature was always a need to help others, something she'd done in our family all her life.

I asked her about Jim. Yes, she was still going to marry him, they'd almost saved enough to finish buying the shop and the flat behind it. I couldn't object as Harry and I were going to live in a similar flat at the back of his chemist shop.

"Are you happy, Cyn?"

"Yes. Jim is very loyal and attentive. I've still got a job as a bookkeeper. What's your husband-to-be like?"

"Oh, very intelligent, very hard-working. Decent. Comes from Sydney, really, he was brought up in Burwood with the Plymouth Brethren. They're a dowdy lot of religious fanatics. The women can't wear make-up or cut their hair. Their clothes are all dark or grey. They are not allowed to read newspapers or listen to the radio or go to the cinema or dances. Or read books. They are supposed to inter-marry, not marry outside the clan. They don't have a minister or preacher, just elders, old men who make up all the rules and say all the prayers. They sometimes don't have windows on their churches. It's all very strict. The church service is just religious statements that the elders are moved to say."

"Good heavens."

"Yes. Harry broke away from it years ago, though he still reads the Bible every night. But he's never been allowed to read novels or poetry so the only other books he reads are westerns, like Zane Grey . . . you know . . . *Riders of the Purple Sage* and so on. Zane Grey and *The Epistles of St Paul to the Corinthians* sit side by side at his bedside."

"There'll be none of our old poetry books in your house then."

"Not at all, he's open-minded. He just doesn't read them. We can read what we like. He left the Brethren because he couldn't stand the hypocritical rules. He'll do well though. He's clever."

"Congratulations. You've escaped."

"Didn't you want to?"

"Leave Newcastle? Never. I'm thirty-three. This town will have to do me."

"You're not too old."

"I like it here."

"It always drags me down."

"You have a phobia. If it wasn't about me or Mum it was Newcastle."

"It wasn't a phobia."

"No? I'm sorry. Of course not."

"Anyway, I'll come and visit when I can, when I have kids, if I have kids."

"Name the first one after me, will you? Jim doesn't want any and neither do I."

I had no intentions of naming any of my children after Cynthia but it was comforting to have her as a relative. We had a lot in common. I wasn't surprised she didn't want children, though I think that was more her "Jim" than her.

A month later, full of hope, Harry and I motored in his car from Warialda to Sydney to get married. We had intended to get married in a registry office

Harry, Jean and puppy George, Warialda, 1939.

on a Wednesday morning and go off to the races at Randwick in the afternoon but Harry's mother Josephine had insisted on a church wedding and a reception, even though it couldn't be with the Plymouth Brethren. We had acquiesced and were to be married in the Eastwood Methodist church. I never got along with his mother, mostly because I was a religious "outsider", and never quite good enough for her favourite son. She always referred to me as "that big Jean that Harry married" which I found insulting, even though I was five-feet-six and Harry was only five-feet-seven. He was taller than me, though he was short for a man. I was a normal height for a woman. Was I supposed to be five-feet-two, with eyes of blue? I do have blue eyes. Harry told me that at his twenty-first birthday she presented him with his first dentures but announced it to everyone present, holding the dentures high so everyone could see them. That story finished me with Josephine.

As I wasn't a Plymouth Brethren, I wasn't technically allowed into their Burwood home. Except for the reception. How she managed to have that without angering the Brethren elders and being "withdrawn from" I'll never know. She could obviously make it happen when she chose. We infidels and non-believers weren't supposed to even speak to the family let alone enter the house. I think Harry's mother and father just ignored the Brethren when it came to their family, hoping that no one would find out. The Brethren elders did hound them later in their lives about their family, when they were near death. That was tragic.

Most of my family and friends managed to attend the wedding from Newcastle. There were very few of Harry's relations because of Brethren rules, but I also realised that Harry had very few friends. Arthur and Iris were too busy to come but Cynthia, loyal as ever, was there along with all my other brothers and sisters, and stepmother. I was only sad my father couldn't be there. That would have been sweet.

We honeymooned at Katoomba (just like my Dad and birth mother thirty-three years before). We returned to Warialda in the spring to find a black sheepdog pup tied up on the back verandah as a wedding present from our friends in Warialda. We were thrilled and called him George — he became our greatest and most loved dog.

30 · Married life in the "place of wild honey"

During the first year after we were married I became aware I had to quickly learn about Warialda and its complex social structure. Once you are married in a rural town like Warialda, especially to a "professional man", it becomes vital.

The town was small but the personalities of its inhabitants, and the inhabitants of nearby properties, were strong. Like Dr Wheatley, Harry and I were not locals and so it took time for us to get used to country ways and to be accepted. It was the wealthy graziers who controlled the wider social structure. They decided who were their equals socially and who were not. The town had its separate social structure.

The name Warialda was Aboriginal, meaning "place of wild honey", although I never actually saw or tasted any wild honey while I lived there. The original inhabitants (or owners of the land) were the Kamilaroi[11] although I knew of no Aboriginals around Warialda when I lived there. At that time, the Kamilaroi lived mainly in Moree, some sixty miles away. In those days, the Aboriginal connection was something little spoken about. I learned more about the Kamilaroi and the treatment of Aboriginals later.

The whole town was unsewered and everyone depended on their tanks for water. In a drought, we bought water from the council pump in Geddes Street near the convent. People had very small bathtubs to wash in and certainly no showers. Water was precious. We only used an inch or two of water in our bathtub and then saved the used water to keep a few shrubs alive in the garden.

Most domestic goods and food came by train from Sydney. Ned Faulkner, a local man, had a huge four-horse dray that he took to the station at Kellys Gully each day. He loaded up all the goods from the train to bring into town for the shops. Food that had to be kept cold was surrounded by bags of dry ice.

---

11. Now spelt Gamilaraay. Warialda is the country of Wirraayaraay (Weraerai) people whose language is closely associated with Gamilaraay. In 1838, many Wirraayaraay were murdered at the tragic Myall Creek Massacre, fifty kilometres south-east of Warialda.

Jean, Harry and George the dog in their early happy years in the backyard at Warialda.

There was a bakery in Hope Street, which made fresh bread every day. Only white bread was baked in those days. Milk was delivered to some of the shops in big drum-like silver cans and customers bought it by the billycan (which they supplied) and stored it in iceboxes at home. There was no pasteurisation in those days and the milk was always creamy. With no proper refrigeration we needed fresh milk every day, if we could get it. There was an iceworks in Hope Street and ice was delivered in big blocks by horse and cart to be used in iceboxes to keep food fresh. Most people had their own hens for eggs. Butter came from Sydney or Newcastle but if you had friends on the properties they could often provide you with fresh butter. Most farms milked their own cows, slaughtered their own sheep, kept hens and grew a lot of their own vegetables.

There was no garbage collection, no ambulance, no fire brigade and no tarred roads except in the town. The soil was red in the town but out in the country it was black and an absolute bog if it rained. When it poured we were stuck in town, sometimes for weeks, because many of the roads became impassable.

There was one doctor in town, one dentist, one chemist, two stock and station agents, one or two solicitors, one post office, one newsagent, one hospital, two banks (Bank of New South Wales and the Commercial Bank) and two pubs, the Royal and the Commercial. There was also a hairdresser called Chaddie Snape who came from Inverell one or two days a week.

Colin Pyrke was owner of the local general store. His only opposition came from a store named Hong Yuens, run by a Chinese family. Both stores sold a large variety of goods including clothes, jewellery, shoes, hardware goods, and tinned and bottled foods and sweets. The other major businesses in town were the White Way café, two stock and station agents, Roger Moore's repair garage, a newsagent, Jo Baz's haberdashery and Quinlan's butchery. There was also a saddler (Jim Durkin) next to the chemist shop and a blacksmith down the other end of Hope Street. These were the days when horses and carts were still important.

It was a primitive kind of life but personal and rather cosy, I thought. I grew to love it. I was settled and secure for the first time in my life. There is something about Warialda that is enduringly human and rurally charming. Everyone knew everyone else's business and nobody seemed to mind much what you did. Summers were very trying heat-wise and most had to get away to the seaside in January and February. Yamba was the closest seaside town and beach, but Manly and Newcastle were both popular holiday spots, too. In autumn and winter, it was very cold and there were heavy frosts.

We boiled our clothes in a copper and wrung them out through laundry wringers. We used petrol irons or "Miss Potts" irons, had charcoal foodsafes for meat, butter coolers, water bags hanging in the verandah shade to keep the water cool, wood fires for cooking, and logs for heating in winter.

The wood-fire stove made the wooden houses warm and cosy, and in winter every house had an open log fire in their sitting room. Open fires were a chore to clean out as the ashes were often still hot in the morning. The fireplaces were kept whitewashed or red-ochred. It was well worth the effort though. We all agreed that Pauline Lanagan, wife of the stock and station agent, kept her open fireplace in the best condition.

Taps froze overnight in winter and a bucket of water had to be brought into the kitchen the night before so you had some water to drink in the morning. Kitchen wood stoves had to be cleaned out at night and laid with paper and kindling chips so that one only had to put a match to the paper to get a blaze in the morning. Wood boxes were kept full of wood beside the stove. To get up on a white-frost morning was icy on the fingers until the fire started. Warialda was famous for its blanket of white frosts in winter.

There was no more enjoyable ritual in autumn and winter than gathering around a huge log fire at someone's house (usually Iris's) after dinner with a glass of sherry, brandy or whisky and gossiping into the night. In those days of no television and very little radio, such occasions were cherished.

Bread was fourpence a loaf. There was no cake shop so all cakes were made at home. Milk was fourpence a pint. Eggs were one shilling a dozen, bacon was one shilling and sixpence per pound. Meat was cheap, tenpence a pound for fillet steak and sixpence a pound for lamb chops or cutlets. Sausages were even cheaper.

The main produce in the area was wheat and wool. There was very little else produced except sheep and cattle for meat. The wheat in the district was beautifully clean and was carted at one penny per mile per bag. It was cheap if you thought you could make your own flour and bread from the wheat.

Farm and sheep station owners came to town usually on Saturdays (with their capable, pretty children) either to shop and/or stay for the "pictures" at the Memorial Hall each Saturday night. They came in their hundreds to the

The flat at the back of Harry's pharmacy photographed in 1985. The back stairs had been removed. Jean and family lived here for six years during the 1939-45 war. The burnt building on the left is the old laundry. The flat was demolished in the 1990s.

Warialda Show each year, usually held in May. Apart from the "sideshow alley" it was a great way for country horse-men and horse-women to compete with each other, show their skills and show off their range of produce from their properties. We loved attending "the show". There was a great sense of fulfillment and excitement about it each year, even though I think it was probably one of the smaller shows in the north-west.

During autumn and winter many balls were held, both in Warialda and in the surrounding area, very often to raise money for causes. There was the Matrons' Ball, The Hospital Ball, the Church of England Ball with debutantes, the Bachelors' and Spinsters' Ball (at both Warialda and Moree). There was also the Catholic Ball with debutantes where Normie Baz, whose family owned the drapery shop in Warialda, was the page. There was also the Picnic Races Ball at Baroma and Inverell. The town's one dressmaker, Miss Page (later Mrs Wells), was always kept busy. There was also the dress shop of Olga Mellick.

To go to one of these balls was a major experience. The women went to enormous trouble to be dressed in (often homemade) beautiful evening dresses and gowns. Usually, all the graziers' wives and children turned up, too, looking more polished and glamorous than everyone else (most of their children went to private schools in Sydney or Brisbane), as well as all the town professionals and their wives.

The music would be considered old fashioned today: there were plenty of waltzes, barn dances, Canadian two steps and Pride of Erins. All the men, with the notable exception of Dr Wheatley, were very good dancers. It was *de rigueur* at the time. The good doctor was charming to everyone but had no sense of rhythm or timing and backed off dancing anything but a slow waltz. I enjoyed these dances. It was a great way to relax and let off steam — there was something exotic, romantic and prestigious about them. There was absolutely nothing like a country ball.

David Jones' and Farmers' catalogues came out in winter and summer (sent by mail to Warialda) and the clothes could be ordered from Sydney. The arrival of these catalogues was an exciting event for us women and we discussed their contents in great detail. Shoes were the hardest thing to get because there were no shoe shops in Warialda. The saddler and Pyrkes store had limited shoes and boots, and it was difficult to order them from Sydney without trying them on. As none of us had driver's licences in those days, we had to be driven to nearby Inverell by our husbands for that sort of shopping.

Each year George Sorley would bring his circus to town for a few days, with his elephants, lions, acrobats and vulgar clowns and it was always packed.

There were also various flower shows and other produce shows. We all played auction bridge and there were constant gatherings at each other's houses.

If you liked gambling there were two illegal SP bookmakers in town, working mainly through the hotels. The police turned a blind eye. There were race meetings at Inverell and Moree, and picnic race meetings at Baroma and Moree. These were amateur affairs with amateur and part-time jockeys, where the social occasion was always more important than the racing.

There was a radio station at Inverell (2NZ) which transmitted to the north-western slopes and tablelands. It broadcast the Sydney races, serials, music, factual programs, the news and personal greetings. It was easily picked up in Warialda.

Once married, Harry and I moved into the small flat at the back of his chemist shop in Hope Street in the spring of 1939 with our loveable sheepdog George. As mentioned, I had carpeted the floors in Feltex, a green marbled colour for the living room and rust for the only bedroom. What appalling taste I had. I also had a dining-room suite interspersed with a tapestry lounge with a cane back and wooden arms, a kitchen table and the four chairs.

Twin beds, a dressing table and wardrobe completed our little love nest and it didn't even cost the two hundred pounds Harry had borrowed.

Hardly had the sweet and tender flowers of spring begun to blossom when war was declared on Germany on 3 September 1939. Life changed dramatically.

31 · "Tall, healthy and with their own teeth . . . "

Warialda didn't alter immediately after the declaration of war, but many young men joined up. At first only the best boys were taken — the tall, healthy ones with their own teeth and arched feet. They were picked out quickly and came home on leave in uniform. They joined the 9th Division of the Australian Army and sailed for Egypt to fight Rommel in the desert or joined the Air Force to fight in the Battle of Britain. Iris Wheatley's brother Bill Goldman became a fighter pilot in the Royal Air Force. The Bank of New South Wales manager Lockie Cameron's son Lachlan joined the Australian Army. Lockie's wife Hazel kept telling me about Tiger Tanks in Europe.

Despite the impending conflict overseas we still led a strong community life in Warialda. I quickly learnt to fit into the social structure of the town as decided by the top business and professional people. The big graziers would occasionally, but not always, acknowledge some of the local business people, as well as the professionals, as equals. None of this social structure was openly acknowledged.

The way of things in town was for the professional men's wives and the wives of the stock and station agents, bank managers and headmasters to ring me up and say they would like to "call" on me. They would ask me what day of the week would suit me. This was very trying for me as I was new to the system. It was alien to the way I'd been brought up, even though I was flattered by the attention. There was no refusing them. I had to comply.

The day before they were coming I would put an extra shine on the house and bake a couple of cakes. On the appointed day, I would rise at dawn and give the house a final dust, fill the house with flowers, add the finishing touches to the cakes I had made the day before, filling them with cream or adding icing, then make the sandwiches and scones. After lunch, I would have a bath and doll myself up, put out the best china and silver, all we had, and sit down and wait till they all arrived promptly at 4 pm.

After chatting for about half an hour I would wheel in the tea trolley complete with cakes and sandwiches. My guests would gush over the cakes, even if they could hardly get their teeth into them. Hazel Cameron, the bank manager's wife, came over just before one such tea party and brought me a plate of chocolate éclairs. She also brought the recipe in case anyone asked how I made them. Everyone had to make their own cakes, of course, cake mixtures in packets were unknown and there was no cake shop. I could never make scones or pastry though — my scones were always as hard as rocks.

This whole social exercise was a compulsory ritual. No exceptions. They called on you to look you over. You then returned the call and they made a second evaluation of you. If you complied with their code you were accepted and asked to tennis or bridge or just afternoon tea somewhere — if not you were ignored. Once "in" you were expected to ignore the "outs" — if you didn't you were quietly dropped.

Domestic life was placid and comfortable, although Harry and I never had a compatible relationship. He developed a gastric ulcer and his diet became a constant nightmare. I might add it was not due to my cooking — it was the result of his bad eating habits from living in boarding houses in the years before we met. During ulcer attacks he complained of the boarding house custard and jam he suffered in his earlier life. The ulcers were also due to worry and stress over business. He had a bad experience in Portland, near Bathurst, where he had tried to buy his first pharmacy. He also had bad experiences working at a pharmacy in Kandos, the details of which I never found out.

He lived on milk and milk puddings and the blandest of food. Meat was a no-no and my butcher's bill for one week was one shilling and eleven pence including dog's meat. I was used to hearty meals at home — lamb chops and roasts with lots of greens and vegetables — so it was disappointing to cook meals for my husband only to see him pick at them like a bird. The sheepdog George at least ate his share of meat.

During that summer of 1939 we mostly lived on the back verandah of the flat. The weather "hotted" up in November and we moved our beds, complete with mosquito nets, onto that verandah. We bought a table to eat on out-of-doors and moved our kitchen chairs there too.

I became pregnant and so did Iris (again) and still the War didn't affect us very much. We compared notes walking on the track alongside the Warialda Creek which was lined with weeping willows and was the only cool spot in town that hot summer. Arthur was longing again for a son and Harry was praying for a daughter. They were both doomed to disappointment.

Unfortunately, Iris had another miscarriage and nearly died after another aborted son. There were two very good matrons at the hospital during the War: Matron Dalgarno and later Matron Reading who, with Arthur's help, saved many a life. Matron Dalgarno saved Iris's life. Iris was so ill after this second miscarriage that Arthur had to decide whether to operate on her (with the knowledge that she could die in the operation) or not operate on her and let her die anyway. She had a bad kidney complaint, eclampsia, and was convulsing. He decided to operate. She took fits after the operation so Matron Dalgarno took a hand — she sent a devastated Arthur home to sleep and gave Iris a quarter of morphine (morphia) and poured a lemon drink laced with Epsom salts down her throat. Iris voided urine and went to sleep. Arthur rushed back about two hours later and woke up Matron Dalgarno who was sleeping on the couch on the back verandah of the hospital and asked her when Iris had died. She told him to go back home because Iris was asleep.

I later had an operation at the hospital and I realised what a wonderful nurse Matron Dalgarno was and why she insisted nurses must have rubber heels on their shoes, warm the bedpans, have warm hands and kind hearts. I had always hated her habit of hanging a cigarette out of the side of her mouth when I worked with her as a sister but I realised later this was irrelevant when it came to nursing. She saved Iris's life by knowledgeable, disciplined nursing.

32 · Messerschmitts, Spitfires, Dunkirk and childbirth

As we moved into 1940 the effects of the War took hold. More boys joined up — men not so tall, young, handsome, or with their own teeth — and were taken away. The news from Europe became grimmer.

Butter and tea were rationed but we could still get plenty of green vegetables and meat of a kind. Dr Wheatley told Quinlan, the butcher, he didn't have "time to eat his meat". We traded half our tea coupons for butter with the country people. Clothing coupons were a worry and china and kitchenware became scarce. But having a baby brought an extra 100 clothing coupons. You had to produce a birth certificate to buy a sieve to push vegetables through after the child was weaned and on to solids.

The War started to change people. Small graziers who had lived on overdrafts became rich overnight as wool prices soared. As well, beef and mutton prices soared. The War brought isolated Australia into twentieth-century Europe, with all its machinery, medicines and new weapons of destruction.

We heard about Dunkirk, the fighting in France, the Battle of Britain. Churchill's voice was listened to almost every night from the BBC. All the news was bad and very frightening. We heard about Messerschmitts (German fighter planes), Spitfires (British fighters), Stukas (German dive bombers), fighter pilots, Bristol Bombers, Beau Fighters (two-engined British fighters), night raids over Germany, the Blitz of London, Mustangs (British fighters), Mosquitos (fast two-engined British bombers), Hawker Hurricanes (British fighters), Hawker Demons (two-seater British fighters), Lancaster and Wellington Bombers, German Dorniers (bombers), Focke-Wulfs and Heinkels (German fighters), Southhampton Flying Boats that bombed submarines, Coventry being razed to the ground, but also Vera Lynn songs that gave us hope. We were glued to the radio and newspapers at every possible moment.

My pregnancy immediately affected Harry's view of me and he began mild flirting with his shop girls. He was always extremely thin and being pregnant I quickly put on a lot of weight. Unfortunately, he made me feel unattractive. I thought it was grossly unfair and disloyal. I didn't realise

Jean, George and baby William, June 1940.

that he never really wanted children; all he really wanted was a pretty wife, not a pregnant one. My periods of depression reignited. I started to feel worthless and unloved again, all the feelings I had as a child. Although in those days I was so busy I could easily push my feelings aside and cope. But I knew the depression was hiding inside me, waiting patiently to express itself.

I realised quickly that our marriage was not like Annie and Dad's marriage, that Harry wasn't anything like my father with his loyalty and forbearance. Our marriage was more a tug-of-war, a split bondage, a constant battleground. I felt our "love" itself wasn't necessarily lasting, as I had been led to believe it would.

I gave birth on 29 May 1940 on the night of the evacuation of Dunkirk. It was a healthy boy we called William. Harry was disappointed it wasn't a girl but still proud that we had a child. I was so consumed by news of Dunkirk on the radio that I dreamt, in the haze of anaesthesia during childbirth, that I was on a boat at Dunkirk rescuing soldiers. I had many soldiers on board my boat and I was saying out loud, "I want another one! I'll take another one." Dr Wheatley, who was delivering the baby, said to me, "Well, I'm sorry, Jean, you've only got the one."

When I took my baby in my arms I thought he was the most beautiful creature I had ever seen. I couldn't take my eyes off him. To think, I thought to myself, that little Jean Sharp, that nobody Mayfield girl could produce such a beautiful human being. I'd always been maternal but the joy I felt with this baby was something unexpected. When I first came home I lay on the bed and stared at him for hours.

As the war wore on, the Red Cross became active locally and stalls started appearing on the streets every week. I made many camouflage nets. Many Warialda boys fought in Tobruk where the desert fighting was real enough, but we got very little news and it was too far away to affect us directly. The boys in the RAF in England also seemed remote, though we worried about them all the time.

We lived through two years of warfare. The allies, England and France, fought the Axis powers Germany and Italy, and the United States sent lots of old ships and planes on lend-lease to them. Our son William was robust and growing.

The post office pinned a list of the casualties on the verandah wall of its building in Hope Street. My favourite uncle, Ernie, had remarried in the early 1920s to Ruby. They had a son, Jack, who enlisted in the army just as his father had done in 1916. We were all devastated when he was killed in action. Ruby especially never got over their only son's death. Twenty years later she was still talking about what a "perfect boy he had been" and how he "bathed twice a day he was so clean". It's perhaps one of the more common but not well publicised effects of war: the long years of silent bereavement of mothers.

A well known woman in Warialda saw her son's name in the list of dead on the post office verandah. She was already a widow. She said nothing and seemed to everyone to take it well. Two days later she was found dead in her home. She had taken an overdose of sleeping pills. She left a note saying there was nothing left for her to live for.

In 1941 Arthur Wheatley and Harry both tried to "join up" as they called enlisting but were both turned down because they were the only doctor and chemist within thirty miles and were labeled "essential services".

By now there was a lack of petrol as well as tea, butter, clothes, children's toys and alcohol. Rationing did nothing to help social life during the War but we still managed to have some fun.

Teddy Musk, a publican at Gravesend about fifteen to twenty miles from Warialda, was a great fan of Arthur's, especially in the lean and hungry years of the War. Publicans could sell beer in Sydney without paying rail freight as opposed to country publicans, who were at a disadvantage. Beer and spirits were strictly rationed. Teddy for some reason could always get plenty of beer and scotch for Arthur. Arthur was a god to him, so somehow Arthur always had a half bottle of whisky in the cupboard, which during the war was really something.

Teddy was one of the great characters of the Warialda district. He ran his pub, or tin shed, in Gravesend (on the road to Moree) with his aged mother. He always had a raffle going on for "The Good Sisters". He was Catholic but a terrible playboy. His mother would say to us, "Oh my Eda-mund, my Eda-mund — better he never were born." They were originally from Lebanon. I don't know why his mother had such an opinion of him but I suppose she was the one who knew him best.

He was an amateur jockey, too, and would win at the picnic races (these were private races sponsored by the graziers). He'd shoulder his way through the other horses as he was a better amateur rider than most.

He had more than his fair share of affairs with women in the district. He told me later in his life that the only thing he wanted was children. He had a good fling when he was young, women fell easily under his spell. He took other men's wives, especially well known graziers' wives, which gave him a glow of satisfaction but it was all in vain. He wasn't happy. What he really wanted was his own family, but that never eventuated.

The Red Cross became even busier. I joined and we held a lot of parties and street stalls to make money to send comforting fruitcakes to soldiers and parcels to prisoners of war. Norma Dunstan and I once made seventeen cakes on a Friday for a stall to be held on Saturday. I was the only one with a Mix Master and Norma organised me. She was a good organiser and also a good cook. It was called a "comforts fund stall".

I loved being part of the Red Cross. It gave me stature as well as purpose, and I blossomed.

Most of the POWs were in Germany at that time and we heard stories of how they managed to get hidden messages out in their censored letters. Fred Weinthal, a solicitor in Warialda, had a brother Ray who was one such prisoner. He wrote to Fred saying, "The Germans are wonderful to us, so kind and generous and to tell everybody how grateful we are. Tell it to the Army, tell it to the Navy and tell it to the Marines."

There wasn't much in the way of entertainment during the War. Men and women still played golf and tennis when they could get balls. Arthur Wheatley was a great golfer and won the open championship at Warialda several times. Liquor became even harder to come by and some made beer at home that was called jungle juice. If anyone had a couple of bottles of sherry or a bottle of scotch then they held a cocktail party for both sexes. Sometimes, the men played billiards at the World War I Memorial Hall at these drinking parties or we played two-bob solo at home.

There were two good pianists in our group of women, Meta Loy, the headmaster's wife and Hazel Cameron, the bank manager's wife. We had all-girl parties and sang songs, which we all enjoyed. Meta Loy held a back-to-childhood party and I can still see Iris dressed as a boy with a shanghai (slingshot) in her pocket and Mona Stephenson (another famous Warialda character) in a pram dressed as a baby.

The women I remember from this group were Fay Wilson, Pauline Lanagan (the wife of Lance Lanagan, the senior stock and station agent), Iris Wheatley, Mona and Nell Stephenson (two spinster sisters who owned properties but lived in town in a beautiful house), Hazel Cameron, Meta Loy, Dorothy Lanagan (wife of Athol, stock and station agent), Norma Dunstan, Amy Brown, Tesse Peate, Molly Peate (married to the electrical shop owner), Ethel Weinthal (the crown solicitor's wife), Tessie Burgess, and Margaret Hooke (the new dentist's wife). Basically, this was the "in" crowd.

They were lively, energetic, intelligent women who loved life and got the most out of every day. They were the best group of women I had ever associated with and I felt very much at home. Even though there was a war on I knew I had found my place in the world as we shared so many difficulties and deprivations. I was one of them, no longer just a girl from Mayfield, but a mother, wife and joint worker for the War.

Not all of us were equal though. Pauline Lanagan's sister was married to P. G. Taylor, Smithy's — that is, Sir Charles Kingsford Smith's — flying companion and he used to give her ten pounds a week housekeeping. We all had to get by on three pounds!

We played auction bridge in a kind of a way. I can still see the indignant face of Arthur Wheatley when Iris didn't return his lead. Dr Wheatley was a good contract bridge player and we tried his patience sorely, particularly as we only played auction. People also had homemade-alcohol parties at night. Dr Wheatley was carried out of one such party at the Mactiers' house as stiff as a board, completely wiped out by the jungle juice.

To be honest, Arthur was a heavy drinker and a terrible flirt. He had amorous flings with, as far as I knew, the wife of a district shire engineer and the wife of a nearby town solicitor. Also, various nurses, I heard. I used to think I was the only woman in Warialda who hadn't slept with him. All of them wooed him, not he them. He mesmerised them with his personality and intelligence. There was a heavily repressed sexual atmosphere in Warialda in those days that wouldn't be denied. Never mentioned or discussed openly, of course.

Arthur was never really interested in any of these women. They were distractions, flings, nothing more. Iris never fully understood this, of course, and naturally took it personally. I would have too. She wasn't fooled yet she stood loyally by him. There was never any danger to their marriage.

For all his philandering he was a great humanitarian, still constantly doing major operations for virtually nothing for those who couldn't pay. Getting up in the middle of the night without complaint and driving miles to attend to accidents or the sick. Doing this night after night. Always wanting to do the best he could for people. Crying when someone died on the operating table. Never refusing medical help to anyone regardless of money. In many ways, he was a contradictory character.

The fact that he stayed relatively poor all his life annoyed Iris. The bigger business people in Warialda ended up despising him. These were the capitalist types in disguise who never understood why he did the things he did, why he did things for nothing. He was lost on them. They didn't understand his lack of material ambition, his philosophical nature or his acute mind, his treatment of all people as equals, his great interest in fishing and patience in undoing tangled lines, his drinking and conviviality, his attractiveness to almost all women and his disarmingly intelligent dissection of them all. He was too original and clear thinking for them.

33 · The terror of the Japanese

When the Japanese attacked Pearl Harbour in December 1941 and left it in ruins, perceptions changed drastically for us. The real threat was now Japan. Although the USA declared war on Japan, as Britain and Australia did, we felt that Britain was committed to fighting Germany. The elite of our army (the Eighth Division) was overseas in Egypt which left us more or less on our own. By the look of things, the Japanese were more powerful than anyone had expected. The general opinion was that they intended to overrun the Pacific and cut off Australia so that the USA would be unable to use Australia as a base.

Imagine our desperate feelings at the Japanese attack after we'd already sent the Ninth Division to Malaya. The Philippines was invaded by the Japanese, two important British warships the *Repulse* and *The Prince of Wales* were sunk off Malaya, and Singapore and Hong Kong surrendered to the Japanese. We heard that the whole Ninth Division were taken prisoners of war when Singapore fell.

Britain had been defeated and abandoned us. We were in shock.

An unamusing side effect of these events was that Japanese houseboys disappeared from American films never to return and *The Japanese Sandman*[12] never played on the air or anywhere else. After the raid on Pearl Harbour a saying developed in Warialda: "Don't panic, remember Pearl Harbour." We heard of new types of Japanese warplanes that received nicknames in the press — Zeros and Claudes (single-engined fighters), Jacks (single-engined navy fighters), Zekes (Zero fighters on Japanese carriers), Sally (the Mitsubishi Ki-21 Heavy Bomber) and Betty (the Mitsubishi G4M Attack Fighter). These details overwhelmed me, just the names of planes and places and generals set my mind racing. Always a nervous person, the War set me on edge, knotted my stomach and dominated my mental life.

The Japanese forces landed in New Guinea and the Solomon Islands, our neighbours. The fighting was coming nearer and nearer. We were more and

---

12. A popular song of that time.

Jean and Bill, Warialda, 1940.

more frightened. We read about General McArthur's and the Americans' defeat in the Philippines and how Sydney was full of Yanks (American soldiers). They had plenty of money, nylon stockings and attracted plenty of Australian girls. The Japanese eventually took Rabaul (on the island of New Britain which is part of New Guinea) and we were fighting seriously to defend Port Moresby. We were told very little. The papers rarely were allowed to report the truth. We had to guess it.

The elite Eighth Division was rushed back after the victory at El Alamein in Egypt to help defend Australia in New Guinea. Other Australian divisions in Britain came back, too. Despite this we felt doomed, overwhelmed by Japan.

The Japanese bombed Darwin on 19 February 1942. They could just as easily have bombed Sydney or Brisbane with greater effect. Two hundred and forty two aircraft, in two separate raids, attacked the town and ships in the harbour. One hundred and eighty-eight aircraft came from four aircraft carriers and fifty-four were land-based bombers. There were two heavy cruisers off shore bombarding as well. Two hundred and fifty people were killed and four hundred wounded. Ships were sunk and buildings destroyed, but in the bush we heard only of a "small raid". It wasn't till the end of the War that we heard how serious the Darwin bombing was. In Darwin, residents believed the Japanese were invading Australia and half the population left and came south. Some even came to Warialda, so we heard about it all.

After three Japanese midget submarines attacked Sydney Harbour and killed twenty-one sailors in May 1942 more people left the city and went to the bush and, again, Warialda was a destination. Sydney was close to home for me and when two of the five large Japanese fleet submarines, which had launched the midget attack in Sydney, actually fired some rounds into Newcastle on the way back to Japan, I started to feel a nightly terror about the Japanese invading Australia and bayoneting us all.

34 · A barbershop, two rooms and a bathtub

Amid all this turmoil I went to Newcastle for Cynthia's wedding in 1942. There was an unusual number of weddings during the War, something we accepted as understandable. Cynthia's betrothed, Jim, was not signed into the army for health reasons so he was in the reserves.

It was a small, dignified affair. She and Jim were married in the Church of England at Wickham and the wedding breakfast was held at 68 Lawson Street, Hamilton, Tom's house, with most of the family present except Dad of course. Tom's wife Rita, as maid of honour, was dressed in red velvet. Annie was very active helping Cynthia and I was impressed, despite my still hostile feelings about her. I never understood her but then I was very stubborn. My half-brother Gilbert, the youngest of us all, had enlisted in the Air Force.

My best news was that Cynthia regarded me as her best friend. She fussed over my little boy William, who was now two years old. Winnie was working as a nurse and Tom was working at Lysaght. My younger brother Bill was either working in a factory somewhere as a boilermaker or was still in Queensland working at Uncle Oliver's property, I'm not sure. Eva was training as a nurse.

Cynthia and Jim didn't have a honeymoon but moved into the flat behind the barbershop in West Newcastle. It was a typical barbershop with a striped pole outside, racehorse and rugby league pictures and girlie calendars on the walls, two tip-up barber's chairs, a large mirror, leather straps for sharpening razors, combs and scissors in glasses of water, spray contraptions and some cheap magazines and newspapers in a pile on the wall seats.

You had to pass through a door at the back of the shop to get to the flat. Immediately you passed through the bedroom adjacent to the back of the shop. It was so small and austere that a double bed along with the wardrobe and tiny bedside table could barely fit. It was necessary to negotiate a small passage around the bed and through a doorway to get to the kitchen.

The kitchen and living area was the only other room in the flat beside the bathroom. It too was austere and small. There was a sink, a gas stove, a small crockery cupboard and a tiny fridge in the alcove leading to the bathroom. There was a saloon or café-type table with seats built in against the back window which you slid into to sit. There were no chairs.

It was poorer and smaller than where we'd lived in Mayfield. I was also living in an equally small flat behind a chemist shop in Warialda (though not as small as Cynthia's place) but I knew that Harry wanted to buy a house eventually as we were having a family.

Cynthia had a tiny back garden with one leafless tree, a stack of boxes and no flowers or grass. They had a large young blue cattle dog called Mo, named after the Australian vaudeville character Mo McCackie played by Roy Rene (born Harry Van Der Sluys). Rene and his vaudeville partner Nat Phillips had an act called "Stiffy and Mo" which was very popular at the time. Their style was Australian "larrikin-lair" comedy that Jim liked so much. Jim and Cynthia had been to Sydney and seen the act. Roy Rene later became a radio star with *McCackie Mansions*. He was also in the 1934 film *Strike Me Lucky*, which we'd all seen. Naming a dog after him seemed novel at the time, very Jim.

I visited the flat behind the shop many times after her marriage because Cynthia was not allowed out to visit anyone alone. I remember her as forever there making me cups of tea in that tiny kitchen while we sat at the table and gossiped. She worried about people not liking her. During my first visit there after the wedding, with my son William, I was worried by the lack of space in the flat.

"Aren't you planning on buying something larger?"

"This is all we can afford at the moment. It's all we need. We have each other."

"What if you have children?"

"No children. Jim doesn't want any. He just wants me."

"To wait on him hand and foot?"

Although she wasn't allowed to leave the flat by herself except to shop, she seemed content. She didn't react to my criticism. She just looked at me as if I could never understand her.

"I just hope you'll be all right," I said.

"Jim says I can go back to work for a while later on so we can save up to buy a caravan. Then we can travel around Australia in his holidays."

I was consoled to hear she was allowed to go to work. Glad she could get out of that tiny flat. They did, in fact, buy a caravan eventually and did travel all round Australia in Jim's holidays. It was his one concession to her pleasure and a very cheap way to have a holiday. But they never got rid of that flat although they did eventually, twenty-nine years later, start to build a small holiday "dream house" at Shoal Bay. For a few years he allowed her to work as a bookkeeper in a nearby firm but jealousy eventually put a stop to that.

"I'm happy. You don't have to worry, Jean. Jim loves me. He'll look after me."

It was hard to believe. More relieved than "happy" I would have thought. To me she didn't look at all happy; it was rare for her to smile or laugh. "All that sacrifice for this?" I kept thinking. "Two rooms and a bathtub behind a barbershop in West Newcastle?" I knew, more than anyone, the arc of her life.

I felt sad for her to have to depend so much on her husband for company. He was to continue to keep her on a very tight rein, almost a prisoner, for the rest of her life. I think he did love her, in his way, but he was over-possessive. It was Cynthia's choice though and she never complained, so why should I? At least we had become close friends.

While I was there that first time he came in from his work, haircutting, having closed the shop for lunch.

"How long are you staying?" he said gruffly, asserting ownership of the kitchen. I'd only been there thirty minutes. He completely ignored William. "Need some tucker."

Cynthia scrambled around like a scullery maid to get his sandwich. He sat and ate it in complete silence. Neither of us spoke.

"I'll be going then," I said and he made no objection, just kept staring out the window.

Cynthia saw me through the bedroom to the barbershop door. I gave her a hug.

"Thanks for coming," she said.

I could see that she knew Jim was anti-social, anti-our-family, no great bargain and was unlikely to get any easier. It was a look she gave me then that I remember now. A look that said, "Something is broken in me and this is truly the best I can do, he is my rock, I know you are critical but *please* don't say anything . . . we are sisters . . . I am doing my best . . . please . . . I am happy."

There was nothing I could say. I never did say anything, not in all the years that followed. Yet, I felt pain at the wasted potential in Cynthia. She was so intelligent, so gifted, she should have had more out of her life, she should have been able to give more to the world. If only our family had recognised that and encouraged her more when she was young. If only . . .

William and I caught the tram to where we were staying . . . and the North-West Mail back to Moree that night.

Cynthia was never allowed to visit me in Warialda or anyone else in the family no matter where they lived — even with Jim accompanying her. When my new family and I moved to Newcastle years later, one suburb away, we always had to go to the flat behind the barbershop if we wanted to see her. There was no question of her going out with me on her own. Going out anywhere alone was forbidden. She never ceased giving in to Jim's every whim.

35 · Babies and the Battle of the Coral Sea

In May 1942, the USA sank eleven Japanese warships off the Solomon Islands. This was probably the beginning of the end for Japan, though we didn't know it at the time. It was the Battle of the Coral Sea and we knew the Americans had prevented the Japanese from making a full invasion of New Guinea and isolating Australia. In June, with the famous USA victory at the Midway Islands, we had more flickers of hope.

In Warialda we began to feel very grateful to the Americans. Although, after the surrender of The Philippines to the Japanese under General MacArthur and his withdrawal to Australia, we realised that the War and the threat of invasion was far from over.

Australian soldiers were now fighting stubbornly against the Japanese in New Guinea on the Kokoda Trail and in the Owen Stanley Ranges. We heard names like Guadalcanal and the battle of Milne Bay but we never really knew the details. We knew the Americans had bombed Tokyo. The big sea battles then seemed to stop for a while and we hoped the Australians and Americans had halted the Japanese in New Guinea.

The beginning of 1943 seemed a little brighter after US bombers made their first bombing raids on Germany and many more in the Pacific. The US was now clearing the Pacific of Japanese troops. We didn't hear every detail but we knew the names of significant battles later in 1944: the Philippine Sea, Leyte Gulf and the Marianas.

We still didn't hear much of the Australian prisoners of war in Malaya and Java. The Japanese didn't give lists of prisoners and we didn't hear anything about the fate of the Red Cross parcels we sent. Nobody knew whether their loved ones up there were alive or dead.

Occasionally an isolated letter or two was received by relatives, always in twenty-five words or less, only saying they were alive. Cards were sent back to the soldiers through the Red Cross. One returned soldier told me after the War that he got a Red Cross card in a POW camp with the following message:

Dear Frank, Mum still makes lumpy custard. Oodles of love Pat.

Others I heard about were:

Dear Bill, Mum still tries to make all our clothes! Love Kathy.

Dear Tom, Dad has finally mended the chook-house door. Lots of love, Joyce.

These were clever ways of communicating support and the mood at home. It sometimes took two years before the Japanese delivered them to POWs.

During 1943 when the Japanese seemed to get the upper hand again, the general consensus was that we would be invaded. Someone said we'd all be put out to work in rice paddies for the Japanese. I remember thinking "but there are no rice paddies in Warialda, it's too dry to grow rice". It shows how ignorant we were of Japanese culture and the realities of war.

Harry hired an allotment next door to the shop (owned by Jim Durkin, the saddler) and he grew corn, potatoes and other vegetables in case things grew worse. To get enough water he put a pump down in the creek at the back of the flat and piped water up for the garden. He was always enterprising. He also managed to get a new Buick car for himself by convincing authorities in Sydney that it was needed as an ambulance for the town. Even the police in Warialda were impressed that he did this — they couldn't get new cars for the police. Harry did use it as an ambulance as it was much needed.

The school built an air-raid shelter in the school grounds, but why anyone would spend money to bombard a tiny rural town was beyond my imagination.

Dr Wheatley gave first-aid classes weekly to anyone who would come. Meta Loy, the headmaster's wife, put on a concert that would not have disgraced the Sydney Town Hall. It raised quite a lot of money to help the Red Cross. She trained the kids well and when I asked her where she got all the good clothes from she said, "Grey calico and dye". She had all the mothers sew at her house so she could supervise their making.

Penicillin was developed into an important drug because of the pressure of the War. It had been discovered and developed in 1928 by Alexander Fleming but it took the devastation of war and substantial American money for it to be developed in mass quantity for the troops. Penicillin in tablet form made by May and Baker, commonly called M and Bs, came in towards the end of the War. We were aware of these developments because both Harry and Arthur kept abreast of medical advances.

After the War, one little girl in Warialda, Wendy Wilson, looked over her father's shoulder as he was reading the paper and saw an Air Force parade. She said, "What are they, Daddy?" and he said in his Australian voice, "Airmen darling." Wendy sniffed and said, "They don't look like tablets to me." M and B?

We didn't know it at the time, but the Japanese in Malaya did not give any quinine or penicillin to the POWs nor did they distribute the millions of parcels sent by the Red Cross.

I became pregnant again. This was deliberate because even though there was a war and a threatened invasion, I was determined to have more family.

There's a story behind this pregnancy. I was determined to have another child and I carefully worked out the days of the month when I was most likely to get pregnant. Harry and I somehow kept missing the day every month and I worried that I'd never get pregnant again. Then Harry's mother and father came up to stay briefly and Harry put them in our bedroom and us on the verandah. Unfortunately, this happened on the very day I knew I was at my most fertile. I couldn't let the day pass without a try. There's no way we could make love on the verandah so I made Harry drive us out into the bush to a private spot at lunch time, where I laid out a blanket and we made love. Not that there was much loving about it as Harry had to get back to the shop quickly and was rather put out by the whole venture. Still, I became pregnant. Maybe others were doing the same sort of thing? It wasn't talked about.

People in Warialda were very generous in the war effort. They gave their support with money to the Comfort Fund and Red Cross all through 1944 and well into 1945. I made the trip through town and called on everyone who had a sticker on their window stating they supported a POW. Then I delivered the money to Dorothy Lanagan who was the President of the Red Cross in Warialda. We were doing something for our friends' husbands and sons fighting in the jungles of New Guinea and Malaya. I felt a useful part of the community.

Dorothy Lanagan told me that a sister of hers who had lived in Singapore with her doctor husband had not been heard of since the invasion. She didn't know until after the War was over that her sister escaped from Singapore on a ship that disappeared without trace and her husband became a POW in Malaya. Apart from his grief about his wife when he came back to Australia, he said what absolutely floored him was the way the women POWs looked

Jean with friends at the back of the chemist shop at Warialda, late 1945. (Left to right back row) unknown, Jean (seated), unknown and Margaret Hooke (local dentist's wife); (left to right front row) Bill Wallace, Geoffrey Wallace (obscured), Stephen Wallace, Rodger Hooke and unknown girl.

so pretty in their clothes only days after the War was declared over. They all had kept some of their finery to wear. They believed we would win and had hidden clothes to look their best on the day they were freed. We heard about how hard it was for the male POWs but nobody talked much about the women, nurses and civilians, who were also prisoners. Well, not till much later.

Dorothy Lanagan brought her aged mother from Sydney to live with her during the War. Her mother said to me privately one day: "My lovely daughter Dorothy married behind the altar at St Mary's in Sydney because she wasn't a Catholic. Isn't that awful?" Strange, how this shamed her.

I had my second baby on 23 December 1943, in the heat of summer. It was a boy and Harry was so disappointed he couldn't look at me or come to the hospital. That was difficult to swallow, but as usual I kept my feelings to myself. It was a big baby, howling and cranky, with a big knot of skin and flesh over his forehead. Dr Wheatley remarked, as he dragged him out screaming, "Uh-oh, this one's a fighter." On Dr Wheatley's advice I named him Henry to placate his father but I must admit I always intended to call him Stephen, although that was nominally his second name. Iris finally had a child the following year, a girl called Robyn. There was much relief all round, but we both wanted more kids.

By now older men were joining up, either in the Home Guard, in the Home Guard Air Force in Wangi Wangi on Lake Macquarie, or in the regular Army or Air Force. The men who joined from Warialda that I knew were: Colin Pyrke, the owner of the general store who joined the Home Guard Air Force; Athol Lanagan joined the Home Guard Army; Jack Brown joined the regular Army; Brian Hickson joined the Army and died on the Burma Railway; Frank Moriarty joined the Army; Fred Weinthal, the solicitor general, joined the Army saying later that the others in his unit called him Grandad; Tom Peate, Molly's husband, joined the Army; and Morry Nelson who worked for the McGregor's Stock and Station Agency joined and was killed in New Guinea.

Except for the war effort, life went on much the same. The summers were still very hot and the winters frosty, the spring almost non-existent or rather a rush of delicate colour and perfume in the flowers and was all over in about six weeks. Then the summer heat would start again. Autumn was the best time: a gradual lowering of temperatures and the rains in March gave the countryside a soft glow that was absent in summer. I loved the pastel colours of the countryside and the trees around Warialda in autumn, loved visiting the properties in that time for social occasions. Even during the War the rolling, pastel countryside was magical.

Harry worried about the business all the time. One day I found him sitting in the dispensary after closing time in despair and close to tears.

"What's wrong, love?" I said.

"We're going broke," he replied. "I can't do this, I can't make the shop pay. There's too many unpaid invoices, we owe too much money. I don't have the income."

"I was the de facto bookkeeper and girl Friday in Newcastle," I said. "Let me have a look at the bills and the bank balance. Maybe we can work it out, ask for time to pay? It's always possible and most firms are patient if they know the money's coming eventually."

To my surprise, he was so desperate he let me do it. I sat down with him that night and we checked all the bills and the bank accounts and the record of shop earnings and so on. I had done this for Miller's Signs for years in Newcastle and kept them out of trouble so it was nothing new to me.

We worked out which bills we could actually pay and which bills we would ask for time to pay. I went with him the next day to the Bank of New South Wales to ask for another overdraft. We cut the hours of the shop assistant for a while and had a sale of some out-of-date unsold items and difficult-to-sell items. I sent letters to farmers who hadn't paid big bills with a warning, a final payment date and a threat to put the matter in the hands of our solicitor.

It all worked surprisingly well. The sale was a success, the bank was more than willing about the overdraft, most people we contacted started to pay their bills and the pharmaceutical creditors gave us an extra month, grateful that we had at least informed them of our difficulties. Harry never got into such difficulties again and regularly had sales to boost his various shop earnings. I was pleased to help him and it brought us close for a while, though only for a while. I realised he liked being in complete control, he wasn't one for sharing his business with his wife, though later he did go into a partnership with a man named Bill Fallon. I was disappointed, I would have loved to have been more active in his business but it was not to be.

The war dragged on. The deprivations and rationing were worse than ever going into 1945. The war in the Pacific became more brutal, with Japanese kamikaze (suicide) planes attacking American ships in huge numbers and shocking the world. The Australian soldiers were heroes, holding back the Japanese in New Guinea and saving Port Moresby, thus giving the Americans a base to launch more attacks.

I only remember fragments of other events in the last war years; it was a jumble of survival and mundane living, fighting with Harry, war news and having and raising babies. I had another baby boy, Geoffrey, in July 1945 again much to Harry's disappointment, and Iris had another daughter, Margaret. The family had grown too big for the back of the shop and we moved to a small house in Geddes Street opposite the convent and adjacent to the public school. We bought the house cheaply but it had more bedrooms and was more comfortable than the flat. It was a relief to have a bigger kitchen and a large back verandah and even a backyard with a garage. By that stage our beautiful son Bill was five and going to school.

Some fragments of family life . . .

. . . Bill, at three years old at an afternoon tea, feeling Mrs Hunt's leg (she was the wife of a big property owner) and asking what she had under them — he had never seen stockings because they were impossible to buy during the War — and asking how far up they went. This caused a burst of laughter from all the women.

... There were no baby's cots available in the war, only canvas bassinets. No prams either so we were constantly mending old prams for our babies or making them. There were no toys or tricycles and Margaret Hooke, the dentist's wife, made a train engine out of an old jam tin and wooden wheels for her son Roger. I thought that very clever.

... There was a baby health clinic in the carriage of a train that stood at Warialda Station for a few days every now and again. Baby food strainers could only be bought with an order from the clinic sister.

... There were no baby ribbons for booties, no cigarettes, no chocolates, no rice or coconut or dried fruit. We made camouflage nets for the Army and Navy.

... Anyone going to Sydney was helped out by other women with clothes, jewellery and so on. Dorothy Lanagan had a little enameled broach, I had a beauty case, Iris lent a silk dressing gown, someone else lent a suitcase. It was always a team effort.

The War brought us together in Warialda and smoothed over personal troubles, frictions or suspicions. It was bigger than all of us, engulfing us, and, for sheer survival's sake, made us harmonious. I worried that when it was over life would be harder.

36 · The end of the War and soldier settlers

We celebrated the end of the War in Europe in May 1945, but our real end of war was on 15 August when a long ringing of the bell at the school opposite the chemist shop sounded the end of hostilities with Japan and the War in the Pacific. We had heard about the atomic bombs, about Hiroshima and Nagasaki, and now we knew about the Japanese surrender and that our men and women were coming home at last. It is a moment I have never forgotten.

People came out onto the street and yelled and shouted, but it was a subdued, quiet affair compared to the crowds in Sydney and Melbourne. We were more relieved than anything else. Maybe rationing would end now?

Later, we heard the commentary on ABC radio describing the wild crowd scenes in Martin Place in Sydney. It seemed unreal.

When the men started coming back from Malaya, New Guinea and England civic welcomes were held. None of us realised what these men had been through, what they'd seen and done, but we did notice that those who had been in battle were never the same. We learnt very quickly not to ask questions as many of the returned soldiers did not want to discuss their experiences.

In Warialda, as in many towns in New South Wales, the government continued the returned-solder-settlement plan from the First World War. Returned soldiers could buy or lease cheaply two thousand acres of crown or crown-purchased land if they were certified as qualified and remained in residence for five years. This was seen as a reward for service to their country.

Remote rural areas set aside for such settlement were guaranteed a population expansion, which in turn was meant to increase infrastructure in the area.

Soldiers who were successful in gaining a block of land had the opportunity to start a farming life. There was a lot of soldier settlement around the Warialda district but sadly all of them eventually failed. The two thousand acres was not enough land and often too uncultivated to sustain the number of wheat fields and sheep needed to make them profitable. The soldiers had little money to spare for equipment and no resources to get through droughts. They were mostly inexperienced although they received assistance from government officials and advice from locals. Even experienced graziers in the area struggled. It was just too hard for novice farmers to make a living, with too little land and no financial backup.

On the other hand, things started to look up for our family after the War, mainly through Harry's industriousness and the fact that we were now part of the landscape in Warialda, proudly integrated into the society.

37 · After the surrender — civil war at home

After the War, life for our family in Warialda settled down: me raising the children and Harry getting on with his business. There was no longer the distraction of the fear of invasion, lists of dead soldiers or Red Cross fund-raising.

However, sharing a life with Harry was never peaceful. I suppose it was because we were not in love anymore, though I wanted a home and so did he. The trouble was we didn't really know one another and it had all been too fast. I belonged to the homely. I wanted a family and the patter of little feet. He didn't really, although he paid lip service to it. All he really wanted was a glamorous wife who was always available. It became clear very quickly that we were not suited to one another. We pulled in different ways.

One year we were to go to Sydney and Bill got the measles. Harry wondered why I was so angry when he took Rita Sandy, the young woman who worked in the pharmacy instead. This was to be the pattern of his life from then on. He never outgrew his youthful need for pretty young girls. This was new to me, it wasn't how my father behaved — he was loyal even to a woman he didn't love because she was his wife. How naïve I was.

Harry never grew emotionally into our marriage, even though he'd taken on the responsibility of children. He would come home and say, "I'm going to a dance tonight, would you like to come?", knowing perfectly well I was well and truly anchored at home with the children.

He was a prisoner of his childhood with the Plymouth Brethren and the time he broke from them. He was insightful enough to see through the dictums of the sect when he was young. He was a clever man, intelligent, amusing, energetic and innovative, but he wasn't emotionally equipped to be a lover or a husband. I was prepared to be a loyal wife — for life — I was grateful for a home, security and to be married to a man who was a chemist but I was beginning to realise the cost.

Later on in life, Harry became very wealthy and everyone assumed I married him for his money but that was not so. He had no money when I married him, although I do admit I was proud of his profession. I married him in the hope of a loving, secure family, which I felt I had missed out on in childhood.

Harry stopped looking at me as soon as I started having children. Maybe I was losing my looks — a grey streak had appeared through the middle of my thick hair. I had thick straight hair all my life and my stepmother had been desperate to make it curly. I had to dye my hair for the rest of my days. I put on weight when I had children but I soon lost that.

Oh, I knew our marriage was safe — Harry would never divorce me — he just wanted time and flings with pretty young things, but I had made a bad mistake. Me, who prided myself on my insight into people . . . me, who tried to advise my sister Cynthia not to marry her man . . . me, the girl to whom boys had flocked like bees around a honeypot when I was seventeen. I picked a man who gave me everything but the thing I craved most: affection and emotional support.

The trouble was that I had married because I was bored. I had wanted children and a fuller life. I wanted purpose. I married too hastily at a time when divorce or separation was a scandal. I should have been more in love than I was, we should have waited longer. I should have gotten to know Harry more. I see this now. Then I was in a hurry, as was Harry. Neither of us was ready for a long marriage to each other.

I found his growing lack of interest in me depressing and unfair. I wanted to rail against it and rail against him for blaming me for having boy babies, not girls, for blaming me for wanting to look after our children instead of going out with him at night. I wanted to rail against him for not being what husbands should be, supportive and loving. I felt helpless and alone, used and disrespected, just like I did as a child. The old feelings were back. When I got angry I let fly at him with all my might. We had terrible rows. I was never one to hold back my feelings. Harry could never handle that; he was gentle by nature but his indifference to me made my blood boil. I was expected to take it all and say nothing, which was against my nature.

Harry was a very poor sleeper and he couldn't sleep in a bed with me all night even before the first child arrived. We had twin beds behind the shop right from the start but he insisted on a separate room when we moved from the back of the shop to the house opposite the convent. He had his own room for the rest of our marriage. It disappointed me. I needed affection. I got very little. Lovemaking between us wasn't often — mainly when

I wanted to get pregnant. After my last child was born it stopped altogether although he was pleased at last to have a baby girl.

I used to think, "Doesn't Harry ever think I am a woman whose body has needs just like his? That I crave his affection and like sex. He is the least affectionate man I have ever met. And he is my husband!"

Yet, he was always a good provider. We were never short of money after the War. He was ambitious. He wasn't satisfied with just being a chemist; he yearned to be a doctor but could not enter the faculty of medicine without the Leaving Certificate pass in chemistry, so he decided to do fifth-year high school matriculation at Inverell High School. He went to Inverell once a week and passed the exam at the end of the year and then still couldn't go to university. After the War, Sydney University only took a quota and those who had served in the armed forces were favoured ahead of civilians. He couldn't get into university although he would have made an excellent doctor.

He was always an imaginative and innovative worker. He developed and printed films and photos and made picture frames and bought a machine to charge batteries for people . . . while I washed nappies and made baby clothes.

During the War, he had become the unofficial vet of the town (which never had a qualified vet) and treated many sick animals with the skill and help of a Mr Stewart, a famous veterinarian in Sydney whom he knew. Harry rang him for free advice when he was in doubt. Harry was allowed to have a licensed revolver to destroy sick animals. He used his commonsense with farmers. When he looked at sick animals on their properties he would often say to the farmer, "What do you think the problem is?" More often than not the farmer had a pretty good idea and Harry would agree. Then Harry would ring his professional vet in Sydney, get confirmation about what the farmer had said, and then work out the treatment. Farmers thought he was a genius.

One of the big graziers was especially grateful to Harry. He came to Harry with the problem of footrot in his sheep. It threatened the whole flock and the survival of his property. This time Harry didn't ring the vet in Sydney but figured out a solution through his training as a chemist. A cheap chemical he sold in the shop, Condy's crystals, was effective in getting rid of tinea in humans. Why not footrot in sheep? It was a fungus just like tinea after all, wasn't it? He riskily told the farmer to use large amounts of Condy's crystals and other disinfectants to douse his sheep's feet, as well as to wash out all sheep pens, yards and sheds. The grazier followed Harry's instructions to the letter and the footrot completely disappeared! He was forever grateful to Harry for saving his sheep and told anyone who would listen about it.

After the War Harry was instrumental in getting tennis courts built in Warialda and he also began the work to get a fire station built. He was a town council all on his own.

He was also instrumental in getting an x-ray machine for the hospital and even did the initial x-rays for Arthur. He taught him and the staff how to use the machine. One farmer brought to the pharmacy a valuable sheepdog that had broken its leg. He wanted Harry to x-ray it to confirm the break before doing anything. Harry realised the cost of the x-ray would be too much and take too long to develop, so he drove to the hospital with the dog and borrowed an x-ray of a human broken arm. He brought it back and showed the farmer. The farmer was convinced and they put the dog's leg in plaster.

As the chemist shop began to make money in the postwar boom, Harry became more confident in his business ability. He decided to lease the White Way café in Hope Street and run it as a second business. It went well until the "Great White Way Ice-Cream Disaster" of '48. The café always had big caskets of ice-cream which came up from Sydney surrounded by dry ice and were placed in a large refrigeration plant in the café. One summer, when the fridges were full, the electricity in the shop broke down over one weekend.

By Monday morning the ice cream had melted, broken through the cardboard caskets and spread all over the café floor. It was white melted ice cream as far as the eye could see. Like snow. Harry was devastated, as was the staff. Not only had the ice cream melted but it had also entered the electrical wiring system and every crevice in the shop. It took three days to clean up the sticky, smelly mess and the shop never recovered. Harry abandoned cafés forever.

In a doctor's appointment with Dr Wheatley around that time I brought up the subject of Harry — that I was unhappy, thinking what a mistake I had made, and thinking of leaving him. Arthur understood but said it was best to stick with him, that the "pretty girls" meant nothing and he would always be a good provider. "You'll get what you want from your children and his money. He loves you as much as he loves anybody." I'm not sure Arthur understood my need for affection in marriage. Iris never talked about the intimacies of their marriage to me, such subjects were off limits. I don't even know how much loving attention she received.

Then Arthur said something startling that I never forgot and which was to resonate with me much later in life. He said, "You know, Jean, your depression isn't necessarily anything to do with your marriage. You're coping as well as anyone with the realities of marriage. Almost everyone is disappointed in some way in marriage, even me. And I'm sure, Iris."

I didn't have time to think about what he said then because I was very busy raising our children, cooking meals, looking after our home and interacting with the other women of Warialda. The internal "marriage", such as it was, was on the backburner. It hurt but I had to cope.

In our first days in the flat behind the pharmacy Harry had found me on my knees scrubbing the floor. He said, "No wife of mine should be on her knees scrubbing the floor." "Who else is going to do it?" I asked. "When we have enough money," he replied, "we'll have a maid."

True to his word, after the War we hired a part-time maid, Clarice, to help me with the housework and look after the children. Our family had never had maids so it was all new to me and rather thrilling. Clarice also worked for Iris Wheatley and her family so we shared stories.

Clarice was a rough-edged, hard-working Warialda girl who had a way of talking I'd never heard before. She was a great help in the house but often abrupt and dismissive.

If left to feed my children late in the day (for what we called "tea" in those days) and she wanted to get home she would say to them, "Come on, stuff it all down your necks, I want to get away early."

Instead of grilling the steaks she would say, "I'm drilling the steaks." She talked about doing everything "nice and luverly".

At the Wheatleys' she'd answer the phone and if she didn't know where Arthur was she'd say, "Doctor's up the back" or "No, Doctor is busy trying to light the fumigator [which was the chip bath heater]."

At her wedding, when she was eight months pregnant, her father rose up with a glass in his hand to make a speech and said, "I don't know nothin' about public speakin' but charge your glasses and get stuck into it."

She'd come into the house early in the morning and lean over my bed and whisper, "Aunty Lou's home." This was some saying from her family I think. She was a memorable character, but not a great maid.

We never really knew much about Clarice's life. She would sometimes allow a little information out, like the time she went crabbing with her brother, not saying he was her stepbrother. She told us nothing openly. Who knew how many brothers and sisters she had? No one asked.

Once she played a casual game of cards with us (bridge). She took up her cards, concentrated on them for a while and said loudly, "Should I open? Only seven losers and one club."

She was not liked by my children. Eventually she became too tough with them for her to work for us anymore and she left and had children of her own. She was a character, and I've never forgotten her.

Life passed by pretty quickly over the next three years. Harry's chemist shop and other enterprises bloomed. We went on holidays with the Wheatleys to Yamba where my son Stephen, then four years old, was accused of stealing money left on a bedside table. He thought it was there for anyone to take. Our children became great friends with Iris's two children, Robyn and Margaret.

We played tennis on many of the surrounding properties and became friends with various country families, the Bundocks, the Browns, the Pilditches, the Owens and McMasters. We socialised at bridge parties and dinners and kept going to the various country balls, when possible.

Sometimes a circus came to town and it was frightening to hear the lions roaring in their cages. George Sorely brought his travelling and very vulgar show to entertain us and Pauline Lanagan's shrill screams of laughter urged him on to greater vulgarity. I wonder what Lance thought. He lived a long life to over ninety-five years of age in Inverell.

Harry and Arthur drew closer and went on many fishing trips to distant rivers together. Arthur bought a canoe so they could paddle up and down the river and set lines at night. One of Arthur's everyday sayings was, "I'd sooner have a big fish." We women never went on these trips, which took all weekend, with most of the activity at night. Sleeping in a tent, looking after the children and waiting for the men, was not our idea of fun.

38 · Strains in the family

By 1948 our children were growing into little personalities. My son Bill burnt our back garage down accidentally while playing with matches. What a blaze that was! Luckily there was very little inside it. It was a big event at the time as there wasn't a fire brigade and the shed simply burnt itself to the ground. Bill said later that he thought he'd put it out. He excelled at school, especially in sport. This made up for a lot, like being careless with matches. Despite warnings he got into plenty of trouble.

My second boy Stephen and Iris's daughter Robyn once stole some tools from outside the butcher shop (across a big back paddock next to our house) and brought them home, very pleased with themselves. When I saw the tools, I scolded them and sent them to take them back to the butcher.

They set off with the tools, but returned unusually quickly. "Did you return them?" I asked doubtfully. Stephen nodded yes, but Robyn said, "Threw them down the big hole, Aunty Jean, threw them down the big hole." Stephen shook his head. Iris was there at the time and she faced Stephen squarely and asked him, "What did you do with the tools, Stephen?" Embarrassed, he said, "Threw them down the well, Aunty Iris." "Why did you do that?" "Because there were big cows in the paddock."

We knew how terrified the children were of cows so we understood why Stephen had thrown the tools down the well but there was hell to pay for Stephen and we had to replace the tools. I was starting to realise the moral dilemmas one faced bringing up children.

Dr Wheatley always invited religious fanatics and doorknockers into his home where he grilled them on their theories of the existence of God. Almost all of them were glad to get away from him and none of them ever convinced him of God's existence. He said he was trying to find someone who could convince him.

Mormon gospel students came to the town to spread the word of God and, out of the blue, Iris invited them to a dinner, which we all attended. One student asked, "Do you mind if I say Grace?" Arthur, always the doubting agnostic, said, "Hit out all you can, go on have a crack at it." The same

Iris Wheatley and Jean at Moree races, 1951.

student said to him later, "Don't you feel the hand of God helping you in operations?" Arthur replied, "No, I don't. What I hear is the voice of my teachers of surgery."

Another of Arthur's sayings used to be, "Never tell anybody you like chokos." He told us once that a patient refused to pay him his overdue fee once "because he'd had a locum in" when he was treated.

One of the biggest events in Warialda in those years was the funeral of the general store's Colin Pyrke's young son Jimmy. Colin Pyrke was a good man but his blustery manner made many a person think before saying anything to him. He wanted to run the town as well as his family — he was the bossy type and hard to understand. All his intentions were good but he was often misunderstood. He tried to make his family think his way — he wanted them to be world-class tennis players and in the summer, rose at 6 am to coach them. He sent them to the best private schools and paid for tennis lessons but to no avail.

Sadly, his youngest son Jimmy was killed driving a sports car given to him by his father for his twenty-first birthday. He crashed into a bridge after not taking a corner between Warialda and Moree. The coroner broke Col's heart when he said, "I don't blame you for giving Jimmy an expensive sports car — but I do blame you for not seeing that the tyres were worn."

Jimmy had often driven to Inverell for a milkshake — just for an outing; he was so bored in Warialda. He had the biggest funeral anyone had ever seen in Warialda. My kids played "funerals" with their toy cars for months afterwards. Colin Pyrke's daughter eloped with a dubious character and his eldest son married a Catholic, which just wasn't done when you were a firm Church of England follower. His wife ran the general store's manchester section of ready-made clothes and material and was always trying to get us into debt buying these goodies. Fortunately, she didn't have very good taste and we were never much tempted.

Through all this I was becoming more miserable in my marriage. I tried hard to pretend it was working. We had three lovely kids, a house, holidays and enough money by now, but I felt an inner depression pulling me down. I became emotionally volatile and argumentative and probably unpleasant to live with. I was always arguing with Harry, trying to make him see my dilemma. There was no down time with Harry, no philosophical talks, no wonderful moments together. It was all busy humdrum and, in a way, pretence. For me, our marriage had irretrievably broken down. I suffered in silence. Harry didn't seem to notice.

In the middle of 1948 he announced that he was going to sell the Warialda pharmacy and buy a new chemist shop in Moree, sixty miles away. He wanted to expand he said, get a bigger pharmacy with more potential to make money for the family. The trouble was that he never asked my opinion — he just announced what he was doing as though it was none of my or the family's business. I protested but was ignored. I knew he was ambitious and I didn't want to appear as a killjoy to that ambition.

It was hard to leave all my friends in Warialda. I had been there for eleven years, eleven happy years and thought I had at last found a life for myself, an identity. I loved the people there. I had many friends who I kept for years afterwards. I loved the town itself, the creek with its rickety wooden bridge, Hope Street with its old buildings and lovely War Memorial Hall and the beautiful old courthouse and bank buildings.

I loved its setting at the bottom of a hill with the slopes and tablelands stretching away to the east. I loved its weather, its cold winters and frosts, the beautiful red and pale-yellow leaves of autumn, the robust wild flowers of spring, even the deadly heat of its summer. Warialda is a town that never lets you go once it captures you. It is special. My children will attest to that. It was the best that an Australian country town could offer. I would have stayed there the rest of my life. That's what I had expected but I should have known that it wouldn't suit Harry's nature. Arthur Wheatley told me he'd only give him four years in Moree before he moved on. He was right but I didn't know it then.

39 · Forbidden romance

The family moved in 1948. Harry sold the pharmacy to the Field family who stayed there for many years just as I had wanted. We bought a solid-looking house at 56 Chester Street, Moree, with a huge garden, a toilet in the backyard and a double garage. It was a step up.

My second son Stephen started school there in 1949 (amid floods of tears) and Bill continued, first in third then in fourth class. Geoffrey was still at home. Moree was flat and hot without the charm of Warialda and certainly not the weather.

It had a large Aboriginal population and Aboriginal camps, something alien to me. I was shocked that the open-air picture theatre was segregated (Aboriginal people were to sit in the front section only) and that Aboriginal people weren't allowed at all into the closed-in main cinema or into the hotels. It was the same with the beautiful bore baths. Aboriginal people were allowed into the children's pool of the main baths but not to the closed-in hot bore baths or the main pool, these were for whites only and segregated also into men and women sections.

Moree is built over Australia's great artesian basin where there is an almost endless supply of artesian hot water held in a massive basin under the earth. This basin covers almost a quarter of Australia but is accessible in only a few areas. Moree is one of them. The water is mineral spring water, very salty and is helpful for various ailments and for the health of old people, who often bathed naked there. The baths are still there although now there is no segregation.

I suppose I accepted the segregation then, as everyone did, accepting the prejudice that Aboriginal people were somehow dirtier and more ignorant than Europeans. I'm ashamed of that now and Moree has since changed but those days must have been particularly harsh for the Kamilaroi people. I wish I had been better educated about them. Educated in the history of the area and the Aboriginal people in general and our obligations to them. We all lived in fear in those days, fear and prejudice. We were ignorant, I was ignorant; it was hard not to be. I'm ashamed of it now, for there was never anything to fear, but I was one of the prejudiced.

It was around this time that I met a man called "Boy" McArthur. That's not his real name as I have to protect him. He came from a property somewhere between Moree and Warialda, I was never quite sure where, he always seemed to be getting stuck there in the muddy black soil. He was a grazier, tall, thin, mildly handsome and unassuming. There was something of the bushie about him, like my father. His real name was Hugh, but everyone called him Boy. I met him at a bachelors' and spinsters' ball in Moree.

He was, like me, in his late thirties or early forties. I had known him in Warialda but this time he asked me straightaway for a dance. I accepted, thinking nothing of it. Harry was probably off dancing with some young thing. It was a waltz and Boy danced beautifully. As soon as I danced with him everything changed. I had never danced with such a good dancer before. The way he held me, his rhythmic body movements and dance steps made me feel completely at home with him. I thought at the time, "This man is the other half of me." He was so charming and gracious and sincere. It's ridiculous to say one can fall in love during a dance but that's exactly what happened. I think he felt the same thing.

At the end of the dance I was in love, more completely than any time in my life. I didn't understand it. I had hardly looked at him. He had hardly spoken yet I had never had someone so attentive to me. And so polite. After the dance, we couldn't take our eyes off each other. It was the gentleness of the way he held me and his beautiful dancing that affected me. As well as his deep, gentle voice. He spoke openly, not at all flirtatiously, and I was affected before I knew it. I was ripe for any gentleness and affection from anyone, and in need of tenderness. And Boy was an exceptional man.

He had booked Iris to dance a later dance with him and I asked her immediately if I could have that dance. I actually offered her a pound note for it. She was shocked and amused but, being Iris, she took the money. "You can have him, what a bargain," she said. "I'll pretend I'm sick. But be careful, Jean, he's not married. You know how silly unmarried men can be."

I knew he wasn't married. It made no difference. The dance came and I could see that he was pleased I was replacing Iris. This time he mentioned that he knew I was Harry's wife and had children. I didn't care what he knew; I flirted outrageously, though discreetly. After all, I thought, Harry was cavorting with girls in his shop as fast as he could. I was a little shocked at myself; I had always wanted to be a loyal, model wife and mother.

He contrived to see me as much as possible after that. I said he should drop into the house for a cup of tea mid-morning. He did. He then suggested that my son Bill spend some time on his property as a holiday. He did.

I was head over heels in love. We had a brief affair. Although I thought I was circumspect and careful Harry sensed it, was furious and felt betrayed. He knew it was serious. It threatened our marriage, his wellbeing and reputation.

Boy asked me to leave Harry, divorce him and to come with my children and live on his property with him. I thought about it long and hard. He was the love of my life I thought but I also knew a divorce and separation would be emotionally destructive and endanger the wellbeing of my children. If I'd been without children there would have been no question, but I took an oath then that my children came first. As Arthur said, Harry would always provide and a loveless marriage was better than a divorce that meant my children lost their father. I knew Harry would never leave me and only had dalliances with the shop girls, that he wasn't capable of any great affair.

Boy accepted my decision with good grace. He knew how close our souls were, it was never a frivolous proposal. We lost touch quickly after our break-up and he married much later. I knew he was hurt but he knew what the problems were when we started. Harry was never certain what happened between Boy and me but he knew I had been swept away.

He never forgave me for the affair, but I had never met anyone who suited me so well. I did not feel superior about it, or callous, or even terribly guilty, it had just happened and I wasn't going to pretend it hadn't. I hadn't wanted to hurt anyone. I had ruined my loyal wife image of myself and in Harry's mind but I had to live with that. I had been a liar and had secrets as a child and perhaps that was my nature, to be deceptive? Cynthia always said I was wicked. I didn't feel wicked though, mainly because of Harry's behaviour. I felt that what I had done was a necessary balance for myself. However, I kept my mouth shut about those thoughts. Harry and I never spoke of it again; we staggered on with our marriage and left Boy behind.

I recommitted to Harry and I told him so. He accepted that, given his own escapades, it was all he could do, but it was now an uneasy alliance. He was never fully trustful of me again and I can't blame him. Wives are expected to stay faithful in marriage but that generally only happens when husbands are faithful in return. Doesn't it?

I never felt that I fell in love with Boy solely as a reaction to Harry's behaviour or for revenge anyway, I thought it was more the effect of Boy's personality on me. In truth, looking back, I was deprived and I commited adultery to ease that deprivation. This is regarded as a sin even in the Methodist church. At the time I convinced myself that I was justified. I didn't count on the long-term effects on our marriage or that Harry could never forgive. I'm sorry he was hurt. Despite his dalliances, which never really stopped, he never let me forget this act of betrayal.

40 · Living and partly living — a hard-won partial happiness

I fell pregnant again, definitely to Harry, and had another child, this time a girl, Dianne. The girl Harry always wanted, at last! It had taken ten years. I insisted on going to Warialda to have the baby delivered by Dr Wheatley. Harry showered me with presents and attention this time. It was not that Harry and I had a very active sex life, we did not sleep together, had separate bedrooms and were never openly or privately affectionate. I was the one who still had to count the days, take my temperature and then urge Harry to make love on the one day I was fertile. It was never easy. I don't know why I wanted four children, maybe because that's how many my birth mother had, maybe because I always wanted a large family. I think it was also maternal instinct with no deep thought behind it. I loved having children and I realised deep down that, with Harry as a husband, obsessed as he was with making money and getting ahead, the family would be my solace and personal achievement.

I met Ah Fung, my father's former cook at the Dolgelly hotel, running a local market garden. He remembered me as a baby in Boomi. It was wonderful to see him again, even though he was now an old man. He had a beautiful market garden not far from our house in Chester Street and while we were in Moree I bought produce from him regularly.

The election of Robert Menzies and his new liberal party to federal government in 1949 meant the end of petrol rationing although we still had butter rationing in the country, mainly because of droughts. Most food and clothes rationing had stopped within two years of the War ending though lots of other items were still hard to get.

Moree might have been just another country town but it was a big town and, unlike Warialda, you couldn't ever get to know the majority of the townspeople let alone the surrounding graziers and farmers. Friendships were harder to make, as it wasn't a close-knit society like Warialda and not nearly as social. I was no longer part of the "in" crowd. I never enjoyed Moree the way I did Warialda.

The Mehi River that flows through Moree looked like a dirty brown creek when we first moved there but it flooded comprehensively in 1951, isolating the town and entering our backyard. The flooding also came from the Gwydir River, which passed through the northern part of Moree and met the Mehi. Luckily our house was built on a high brick foundation or the house itself would have been flooded.

Our garden was destroyed and the flood entered our backyard toilet and garage. We had warning of the flood and we even saw it coming down the street, flowing relentlessly. It was about two-feet high in our backyard and the children had a great time paddling about in a tin baby's tub or splashing in it. We even saw a snake swimming through the muddy water under a floating door.

We were told this was a minor flood, that there was a much worse one in 1946. That was good to know but it didn't help us when we came to cleaning up the yard and cellar of the house once the flood had subsided. No one tells you how much slime and silt a river flood leaves behind, covering everything. It was months before we had cleaned off the effects of that flood from our backyard.

Although it was a big town, Moree wasn't much more advanced than Warialda in 1949. Milk was still delivered by horse and cart, with the milkman usually pouring the required amount into a tin billycan left on the front porch. The milkman was Parker of Parker's Dairy. I was fascinated by the large tin container he used, with its silver cover opened by thumb pressure on a lever, and its spout so beautifully neat and effective. Milk pouring into milk is a soothing sight to me. Parker's horse knew the journey so well that it would walk by itself and stop in front of each house where milk was sold. He would call to the horse "walk on" and the horse would pull the cart to the next house and stop to wait for him. The milkman rarely needed to get on the cart.

There was a little platform at the back of the cart with the reins over the top and a small tap on the milk vat. Sometimes I would bring out a jug to fill; sometimes he would bring his can to the front door.

Horse and cart also delivered bread although it wasn't far to visit the bakery and buy bread. The baker would come to the back door with the bread in a huge basket covered with white linen. He would flip back either side of the basked to show either white or brown bread. I think the brown bread was really just coloured brown, it wasn't wholemeal or rye, like today's bread choices.

We still used a chip heater for the bathroom and a wood stove for the kitchen and all water was tank water. Harry chopped our wood in the backyard. One day the head flew off the axe and smashed into his forehead and skull. It was a deep wound and he ran inside covered in blood from head to toe, much to my horror. We rushed him to hospital where he recovered but he retained a large scar across his cranium. After that we hired a handyman to chop the wood.

There was a grocery shop very near to us where I did most of my shopping and of course the Chinese market gardens where vegetables and fruit were plentiful and cheap. For some reason, I associate a jingle on the radio with that period of my life, because it involved a mother and her child and because I, too, was always sending my children down to the grocers to buy food.

"Mother, may I go out to play?"
"Of course, you can my pet.
But first of all go to the grocery store
There's something I want you to get."
"I know exactly what it is,
Trick me if you can
It's something we keep in the pantry
In the big blue can . . . "
"Sydney flour is our flour
We use it every day.
For scones and cakes that mother bakes
You'll find that it's okay, okay?
And after you have tried it
You'll join with us and say (you'll say),
Sydney Flour is our flour
We use it every day."

This commercial jingle and others, plus the radio serials that we listened to avidly, were the fabric of female lives, at least in the country, in those days. They were important to domestic life, which is all we had. Later on, we listened to *When a Girl Marries* and *Dr Paul*, both morning radio serials designed for women.

Harry and I hired Olive Rose, who was from Warialda and famous for her horse riding to come and help look after the children and with the cooking and cleaning. She lived in with us and her only condition was that she had time off to ride in most of the country horse shows. This was fine with us and Olive was to stay with us, off and on, for about seven years. She was a good worker and wonderful with the kids. Unfortunately, she was also a heavy drinker and often came home drunk; something that eventually tried my patience. Still, I was always grateful to her for being such a hard worker. When she first arrived Geoffrey and Stephen, unable to pronounce "Olive" called her Aunty Ooo-hoo.

Olive's attending most of the shows had an unexpected advantage. There was a butter shortage in Moree around 1950 because of drought so we were using a very unpalatable margarine instead. Olive went to the Royal Easter Show in Sydney and returned with a box of butter. Apparently it was readily available in Sydney but not in the country. That seemed unfair to us then, and still does. Who produces the butter after all?

It was in Moree that my children began to mature. Bill did well enough at school while Stephen settled in quickly. Geoffrey eventually started kindergarten in 1951. Bill was the quintessential country kid, with a shanghai in his back pocket and a bag full of marbles in his side pocket. I was told he was the best marble player at the school. He said he wasn't. He was good at cricket and football and went rabbiting by himself. He had some old rabbit

Jean (left) and friend Gwen Brown (wife of a grazier) in Jean's backyard at Moree, 1949.

traps and rode his bike to a rabbit warren just outside north Moree and set traps for rabbits. When he caught them, he sold their skins to a buyer in Moree for one shilling a hide. He told me later that he stopped doing it when a trap accidentally trapped a possum and wounded her mortally and killed her tiny baby. He said he didn't have the stomach for trapping after that.

Bill was a kind of "Just William" character and he loved *Just William* books that were so popular then. He fascinated me.

I put all my energy into my children. I read them endless stories as my father had done with us, including the Uncle Remus stories of Br'er Rabbit, like my father had read us. I also read of lot of stories that related to country life, *Spear and Stockwhip, My Friend Flicka, Snugglepot and Cuddlepie, Blinky Bill, Peter and Company, The Magic Pudding* as well as many Enid Blyton books. I can still hear my son Geoffrey saying every night before I read to them, "Clear your throat, Mum, clear your throat."

Harry's parents came up one Christmas to Moree and spent a week or so living with us. I suppose there were no Plymouth Brethren in Moree to spy on them. They were immensely proud of Harry and all that he'd achieved but still condescending towards me. I wondered if they realised how that made me feel?

My feelings of depression grew in Moree. Those same old feelings of having a powerful suppressed anger or rage at the world and my stepmother. Rage at Harry for not being the husband I thought he should be. These feelings were kept in balance by the needs of my children, keeping house and having Olive as a helper. But they got stronger and took a toll on me. Lines formed on my once clear face and I started to look old.

When we'd been there two years a frock shop called Kydie Gowns, opposite Harry's pharmacy in the main street, became available very cheaply. Harry was always interested in a business bargain and knew that I would be interested. He thought we might be able to make it run at a profit. I'd always been interested in women's clothes and although I lacked experience I was confident I could cater to the women of Moree. I had Olive at home to care for the children and by then three of them were at school. Harry liked the idea so he went ahead and bought it. Suddenly I was running a dress shop.

I loved working, selecting and buying the dresses from Sydney and Brisbane and talking to local women about them. I loved being in charge of a shop; it gave me a sense of importance and wellbeing, like when I was a midwife. I was good with money and we made a small profit. The children liked dropping in there on their way home from school. I found I had the taste of ordinary women, so buying and selling them dresses they liked was a pleasure for me.

I suggested to Harry that we hold a Kydie Gowns fashion parade to boost sales in the shop. He thought it was a great idea. We chose the Moree baths as the venue — they were more than happy to have an activity there in the winter-time. Harry thought we should invite some Sydney models to model the dresses as well as local girls. He said he would pay for them if necessary as he could afford it. We invited two Sydney models, Jeanette Elphick and Louise Croppa.

Jeanette Elphick.

Jeanette Elphick later became the Hollywood film star Victoria Shaw and was not only gorgeously slender and beautiful she was also friendly, helpful and supportive. I grew to love her. She came up to Moree, then a long trip from Sydney, for not very much money, to help us with our small dress shop — not many top models would have done that. Louise Croppa stayed at our house, much to Harry's delight, to save money and was equally supportive, though she never understood how the bath chip heater worked.

The fashion parade was a big success. Moree had never seen anything like it: beautiful models modeling ordinary dresses from our shop. The effect on the shop was electric and sales boomed. I was thrilled with the whole event and grateful that Harry had the faith in me to do it. He told me he never doubted me. That made it worthwhile.

Harry carried the whole thing further. He put a reserve chemist in his shop, Charlie Wienberg, packed all the unsold and excess or out-of-date frocks in his car and took them to surrounding towns like Walgett and Mungundi where he hired girls to sell them in the street. It was surprisingly successful.

Harry was driven when it came to making extra money. He had a morbid fear of being poor again. It drove his imagination and boldness in business. I admired that in Harry and I was grateful we had a nice house and a business to support us. He was an admirable man. We just didn't connect. We had no idea of each other's inner workings, no sympathy for each other's problems.

In the end, Moree was not a lot of fun for me. It should have been with the frock shop, Harry doing so well and the children going to school. For me it was a time of anguish and loneliness though I rarely showed it. I missed the social life of Warialda. I missed the loyalty and knockabout humour of Iris and her friends. I missed the closeness of a loving husband. Moree is situated right in the middle of rich black soil country and the properties around there were mostly huge and owned by large pastoral companies. There was an impersonal and commercial brashness about the town that made me feel uncomfortable.

I regularly attended the Methodist church as a comfort as I liked the minister. In a remote way, I fell in love with him. Our children went to Sunday school there and an unusual memory is a Sunday school teacher ringing to tell me that she'd asked all the children in the class to make one wish for Christmas and that six-year-old Stephen had said that he wished "there'd be no more wars". Stephen told me later he said it because he never wanted to fight in a war himself.

I remember Sundays in Moree with affection because we always had a large family dinner (lunch nowadays). We usually had roast lamb or beef and vegetables with fruit salad and my homemade ice cream for dessert. In those days roast chicken was a luxury and only eaten rarely, rather like today's turkeys and there was no ice cream in packets.

I especially remember that at 12.45 pm each Sunday, on almost every commercial radio station, the Aeroplane Jelly song was played. It was another domestic icon, like the Sydney Flour song. It was only a commercial for a jelly company but for us in the country it signified a way of life and had for many years. It was so admired and sung, so much a part of all our lives, of my life, that I have to include it here:

> I like Aeroplane Jelly
> Aeroplane Jelly for me
> I like it for dinner,
> I like it for tea,
> A little each day
> Is a good recipe
> The quality's high
> As the name will imply,
> And it's made from pure fruits
> One more good reason why
> I like Aeroplane Jelly
> Aeroplane Jelly for me.

It was sung by a child with a high-pitched appealing voice and it echoed around every Australian household at Sunday dinner, a must in those days. There was a joke in circulation that the singer was actually the jockey Athol Mulley when he was a child, the humour being that Athol Mulley was a tough, weather-beaten, untrustworthy-looking bloke. The real singer was a five-year-old Joy King.

Another funny story about this song was told in Warialda by some returned airmen who'd been in the RAF during the war. A popular English singer and pianist was entertaining a hall full of mostly Australian airmen with song after song and his boast was, "I can sing and play *any* song that you all know. I'll bet you can't name a popular song that I can't play and sing." One airman immediately piped up "What about the Aeroplane Jelly song?" "Never heard of it. It's not a popular song," replied the singer. The crowd roared, "Yes it is!" "Sing it then," said the singer. And the whole hall sang "I like Aeroplane Jelly" to the astonished Englishman, who then claimed it wasn't a song but an advertising ditty. "It's a song!" cried the Australians, so the Englishman then sang it with them.

I still can't hear that song and not feel the mixture of pain and hard-won partial happiness that was my experience of Moree.

Moree seemed full of music then. The children loved music on the radio, Gene Autry singing *Rudolph the Red-Nosed Reindeer*, Frank Sinatra singing *Four-Leafed Clover* or Bing Crosby singing *Don't Fence Me In*, Hank Williams singing *Hey Good Lookin'* or *Cold, Cold Heart*, and Eileen Baron singing *If I Knew You Were Comin' I'd've Baked a Cake, Hired a Band*.

Stephen heard and learnt a song recorded by American singer Eddy Arnold, *My Daddy Is Only a Picture* and sang it to anyone who would listen. He was commended at school for singing it in front of the class. I was reminded of Cynthia when she was young. Imagine the effect of a five-year-old boy singing the following song to adults, just after the War. I don't think my child was aware of the effect. People were in tears when he sang it to adults dining at our house.

> My Daddy's only a picture
> In a frame that hangs on the wall.
> And when I talk to my daddy
> He never talks at all.
>
> I tell him all my secrets
> And all my little plans

And by the way he smiles at me
I know that he understands.

The angels took daddy to heaven
When I was only three
But I know he wouldn't have left us
If he knew how lonesome we'd be.

I try to cheer up my mommy
When the tears roll down her face.
My Daddy's only a picture
But I'm trying to take his place.

The Moree baths played pop music on their loudspeaker and the songs of The Weavers, *Goodnight Irene* and *On Top of Old Smokey*, still ring in my ears from my times swimming there.

It was that time when I first took anti-depressants and sleeping tablets. I didn't understand why I found it hard to cope with everyday life except to blame it on my "sad sack" nature and marriage. I knew that I had a problem that kept me "sad", a big problem that wasn't going away.

Harry was loyal in one way: he was a good provider. However, he continued to dally with pretty shop girls, behaviour that was distressing and insulting. I thought, "Why am I still married to a man with whom I've had four children, who I don't love and who doesn't love me?" It wasn't comforting to take Arthur Wheatley's advice either and find satisfaction in my children and our nice home. I talked to a doctor in Moree about it, but we never got to the bottom of anything. Sometimes a depression would last for weeks, sometimes just a day. There was no way I could talk to Harry about it. Harry and I should have split up, but it wasn't an option. Divorce was unheard of, and neither of us wanted it.

Around this time my youngest sister Eva married Cecil, a huge six-foot man. The marriage only lasted a year or so as he turned out to be violent. They divorced and Eva went to live with Annie in Burwood. Eva never recovered from the break-up of her marriage. She stayed with us occasionally but I was never close to her. She had stayed the closest of any of us to my stepmother.

I made a mistake with one of my children in 1952. When Bill was twelve I urged Harry to let me send him to boarding school in Sydney. I wanted to give him every chance in life of a good education, something my own

Jean (far left) at a dinner at Max's hotel at Moree, 1952.

family had missed. Sydney was a long way away and Bill didn't want to go. He had made a lot of friends in Moree and loved it there. But I insisted and his father duly took Bill to Sydney to start first-year high school as a boarder at Scots College, the school a lot of Warialda boys attended.

I didn't realise that Bill, who loved family life, took this to mean he wasn't loved at home and that we wanted to get rid of him. From being an amiable loving son at home he turned into a rebel at Scots. He didn't want to be there and he let the teachers and other boys know it. Unfortunately, it took us a long time to realise what happened. After three years we took him out of Scots, but by then we were living back in Newcastle.

41 · Movement, turmoil and misery

In 1953, as hungry for more business success as ever, Harry wanted to move back to Sydney. He'd always wanted to get back to where he came from. He'd found a bargain chemist shop in Bondi and thought we'd be better off closer to Bill's school. We moved, first to a flat in Dover Heights as a stopgap and then to a beautiful house in Balmoral, which wasn't as exclusive then as it is now. The move was terribly disruptive for the children, having to change schools often, and difficult for me moving our furniture so much. I did my best to make it work. So did the kids.

However, we were in Sydney less than two years, from early 1953 to the end of 1954, before Harry found a chemist shop in Newcastle and a partner, Bill Fallon. Bill would be the mainstay in the shop and give Harry the freedom to run sales and make money. Wallace and Fallon. We moved again, first to Soldiers Point on Port Stephens in a temporary house for a few months, then to a large house in poor surroundings in Merewether, Newcastle. Again the children suffered from changing schools. Despondently, I was back in Newcastle, something I'd tried to avoid.

My depressions started to get deeper as we moved around the countryside. I had been brought up in two houses and here we were, changing not only houses but towns and cities every two or three years.

Harry and I had an intermittent sex life — only not with each other or within sight of each other. We had separate bedrooms and never slept together again. I was no saint and neither was he. I was discreet and, for the most part, so was he. I had made a promise to stay committed to him as he did to me, and we both intended to keep that commitment for the sake of our children.

Harry's partner Bill Fallon was a staunch Catholic and was only thirty years old. He had been a rear gunner in RAF bombers during the War (although he'd tried to be a pilot) and was trying to get started as a pharmacist. He was concerned that Harry and I had separate rooms and had no sex life. As a Catholic he believed in a moral life — he was shocked by Harry's sometimes ruthless business attitudes. This didn't stop him, however, from a having a brief fling with me. We were absolutely secretive and it only happened when Harry was away. It's funny how the devout often stray. I felt I was just helping him develop; he was so awkward with women, such a little boy. It was never serious. Harry never found out about it and it was of no importance or threat. He was desperate for a wife. He had a curiously handsome, pockmarked face from some serious youthful acne. I spent a lot of time trying to introduce Bill Fallon to eligible women but in the end he made up his own mind and married a nurse in New Guinea. He went to work there as a pilot some years later. Unfortunately, he died in New Guinea from a heart attack in his early forties. He was a lovely man and I was very upset for his wife and two children.

In 1957 we moved from 36 Macquarie Street, Merewether to 28 Alexander Street, Hamilton, also in Newcastle and just around the corner from where my dear Uncle Ernie had lived. He had died in 1953. His wife Ruby Sharp still lived there and she looked after one of my sons for two weeks when I had to go into hospital in Warialda to have a hysterectomy by Dr Wheatley.

The children, except for Dianne, were starting to go to boarding schools and I was at home alone a lot. My depressions were getting worse. Harry and I were having terrible fights despite our commitment and we were no closer to understanding one another.

It was then that Harry had an open affair with the cosmetics girl at his chemist shop. Nora X. Nora was very beautiful, in her late twenties, and seemed to buy all Harry's promises of a wealthy life together. Harry left me and lived with her in a flat at Bar Beach for about five months. The children were horrified. There wasn't much I could do except wait for Nora to come to her senses, which she did quickly enough. Harry was no Cary Grant and his money was limited. After five months she saw the light, left him and he came home, tail between his legs. I was silly enough to forgive him but I had no choice. It was a childish escapade that was wounding.

With Bill Fallon keeping the chemist shop together, Harry became an agent for a diet pill called Tafon ("no fat" spelt backwards). He left Newcastle to travel Queensland and sold the tablets — which, in fact, were ineffective — in large numbers to a gullible public. It was clever of Harry to see the possibilities in being the sole agent for the pills and to hire someone like Jack Davey, a radio star of the time, to promote it. Part of it, I assumed, was to get away from me. He clearly felt tied down at home.

My son Bill had now left Scots College and was attending Newcastle Boys' High School. He left in fifth year after a trial exam which resulted in him being asked to go back to fourth year. Later, Stephen and Geoffrey were each at different boarding schools when Bill became a sort of teenage rebel. He ran away to Condoblin with Brian Casey, a school friend. Harry was away during this crisis and I had to get in my Morris Minor and drive to Condoblin to find out what had happened to Bill. He was working in a sawmill in Condoblin and I spoke to the police there. They persuaded me that Bill was all right and they were keeping an eye on him. They told me that Brian Casey was droving somewhere and not to worry about them as they weren't doing anything illegal. They urged me to go back to Newcastle and stop worrying. So I did, without actually seeing Bill. He did come home soon afterwards. Brian Casey ended up becoming a great friend of the family and later came to live with us. Harry returned to Newcastle and took Bill to Queensland with him to try and resolve his education problems.

After that Harry gave up buying pharmacies altogether and started buying hotels. He sold the pharmacy in Newcastle and bought a hotel in Surfers Paradise. He thought there was more money to be made in buying and selling hotels and working as a publican than being a chemist. His famous joke later was: "Hotels are easier than pharmacies to run because there's only one line to sell (alcohol) and all you have to do is tell the customers when they can start and when they have to stop. Chemist shops sometimes have one hundred different lines that have to be replaced when sold and you often have to talk customers into buying something."

We stayed for a holiday in Surfers Paradise in the summer of 1957 to '58.

In late 1958 Harry sold the Yalta private hotel (accommodation only) in Surfers Paradise and bought the freehold of a hotel, plus a few shops within the hotel building, at Longreach. He was then working in a pharmacy in Surfers Paradise and he apprenticed our son Bill to him. A lessee ran the Longreach Hotel so he was free to apply for a manager's job running Menzies Pharmacy, the larger of two pharmacies then in Mount Isa. Bill went with him to Mount Isa as his apprentice and enrolled in a first-year pharmacy correspondence course in Brisbane. The rest of the family stayed with me in Newcastle.

Harry and Bill were in Mount Isa for just over one year when Harry obtained an alternative apprenticeship for Bill in a pharmacy at Wynnum in Brisbane where he attended the pharmacy course at university. Harry sold the Longreach hotel and bought the lease of the Tourist Hotel at Port Macquarie. He ran this hotel himself.

In 1961 we had to sell our house in Hamilton and move to Port Macquarie. We lived in the hotel until we moved first to Wollongong and then to Fairfield, Sydney, in 1963 after Harry bought and sold further hotels in a sort of business frenzy.

My stepmother Annie died in Sydney in 1968. She was still living in Burwood with Eva. She was very close to ninety years old, but we were never certain of her age. I went to the funeral with as many of my family as could be mustered but I still felt angry with her so there wasn't much grief from me. Eva was devastated as she was very close to her in her final years, as was Cynthia, who regarded her as her "best friend". I was the still-alienated one, the one who blamed her for everything difficult in my life. My brother Tom who had sheltered her and given her money mourned her and never understood my attitude.

"You never understood Mum's personality," Cynthia told me at the wake. "She was brought up a strict Methodist. That's all she had."

"She never told us the truth," I reiterated. "All that piety didn't hide her personality from me. Sorry. She treated us step-kids badly."

"She didn't. And don't speak about Mum like that," Cynthia retorted. "That's your version. She wanted us to help with the household chores? Yes. Wasn't that reasonable? When did she treat you badly? When?"

"All the time when I was little. She beat me when no one was looking. You were lucky, you didn't have to look after the babies or hang out the washing or do the messages all the time. I was the 'nurse girl'. You were always sewing or knitting inside. You were her little willing slave, weren't you?"

"Sarcasm is the lowest from of wit, Jean. I tried to help with the family as much as I could. We all did. Even Winnie and Eva did when they were old enough."

Winnie, standing nearby, suddenly joined in.

"I never had a problem with Mum. None of us did. I never understood why you went off with that guy on the motorbike when Mum forbade you to do it. Of course she got upset. You deliberately provoked her."

"Oh, all right, Mum is a saint and I'm a bad girl."

"We just don't understand," said Cynthia. "She was a good mum to us. You were tough on her."

"With good reason," I replied. Then to Winnie: "She was your real mother so you were treated well. She never loved me or showed me any love. I was

Annie Sharp at about eighty years of age, visiting the Blue Mountains. (Photo courtesy Carol Ray)

just Wilhelmina's brat to her. Cynthia, Bill, Tom and I, we were all just Will's brats!"

"I was never aware of any difference."

"Of course you weren't. You were too little."

"She was good to me," cut in Cynthia again.

"She wasn't, Cynthia, you just want to think she was."

"We never understood you," said Winnie.

"No, you didn't, because you weren't treated like me! You all wanted to be goodie goodies and go to heaven. None of you want to see the truth."

And they didn't. My other siblings, Tom and Bill, never complained either, even though they too had been adversely affected by our upbringing. Their compliance and silence never impressed me, just made me sad for them. None of them really escaped what I thought was the emotional and spiritual poverty of our childhoods. They were poor and struggled for most of their lives yet Tom kept giving Annie money. He sometimes rebelled though and jokingly once said under his breath that Eva and Annie were both "too heavenly minded to be any earthly good".

"The silence of the Sharps," I thought. "That's what's caused all the pain. The silence of the bloody Sharps! It's amazing how much damage that wretched, working-class, immovable, pious, self-denying 'silence' can do."

Dr Arthur Wheatley died in 1965. He was only sixty years old but died of a sudden heart attack while driving his car in Harbord in Sydney. The family had moved from Warialda to Sydney after he sold his practice because of his worsening health. Iris eventually settled in Mosman with the two girls. He was never forgotten in Warialda, where he is still honoured. His influence and words of wisdom remained with me all my life.

By this stage, while my boys were happy to live in a pub in Fairfield, my daughter Dianne and I insisted on a permanent home and convinced Harry to buy a house at Collaroy, a northern suburb of Sydney. It didn't stop Harry's peripatetic habits with businesses and relief work at country chemist shops but it gave us a permanent base.

Harry sold the pub in Fairfield and bought another one at Guilford. He sold that and bought one at Waitara, and then sold that and bought The Oxford at Drummoyne. He sold that hotel to buy the hotel-motel in Gateshead, a suburb near Newcastle, in the 1970s. When we had the Gateshead business we had a house at Eleebana. I helped out in the motel office and Collaroy was too far away. He needed me in the office and for a while we emotionally reconciled as we worked together.

Bill graduated in pharmacy from Queensland University; Stephen in arts from Sydney University and Geoffrey went into hotels with his father to learn the liquor trade. Dianne, much to my horror, didn't want to go to university but went to secretarial school and trained as a secretary. Bill worked as a pharmacist Stephen went into film and television.

Buying and selling hotels proved very successful for Harry. He always made a profit and at that time there was no capital gains tax. He eventually sold the Gateshead business and bought a bottle shop at Balmoral Beach (essentially for Geoffrey to run and eventually own). Later he bought the General Gordon Hotel in Sydenham for Dianne to run. She later sold it and bought a cheese shop in Gordon. All this time Harry still travelled the country relieving rural chemists. It was a way of life he loved, always on the move. Harry and I were unofficially separated by now, still married and often sharing the same house and meals but leading separate lives.

The family either lived in the house at Collaroy, which had a sea view, or travelled overseas. Dianne lived in New York for seven years, Stephen in England for two and Geoffrey travelled all over Europe. Dianne and I went to England in 1966 together, then she went to Perugia in Italy with her father in 1967. Harry had a bedroom at Collaroy but spent as much time as he could away. Communication between us was uneasy. Christmases with the family were strained. We pretended goodwill for the children. We had very little to do with each other and only spoke directly to one another when we needed to discuss the children's welfare, maintenance for the house, outstanding bills and so on. It was difficult for us both but we tried to do our duty.

My younger full brother Bill died from cancer in 1971. He was only fifty-nine years old. In hospital he was never told what his illness was, but I think he knew. He was a gentle soul and was married with a lovely daughter, Carol.

In 1974 my dear sister Cynthia died of a heart attack. She and Jim had only just moved into the new home they'd built in Shoal Bay at Port Stephens north of Newcastle. She was sixty-eight years old. She had so much wanted a garden of her own but she only enjoyed her new house for a few weeks. I went to Newcastle for the funeral at Beresfield and was horrified when Jim refused to give any of us the family photographs that Cynthia had, or any of her belongings. It was as if she didn't belong to us any more, only to him. He was possessive of her to the last.

This was a stressful event for me. I'd known Cynthia for sixty-four years, all my life, from when she was a bullying six-year-old and I was a toddler. I never knew what happened to her on that ill-fated trip to Queensland when she was fifteen, why she so suddenly turned from a confident, dynamic girl into a trembling little mouse who never recovered. She never fully explained, not believably, perhaps because she didn't know herself. Whatever it was, the secret died with her. She was by far the most intelligent person in our family and of all our family's lives I thought hers was the saddest.

It was sad that she died without time to enjoy the house that had taken her and Jim so long to finance and build, and at a time when they had a bit of money to spare. Yet I accepted her early death more readily than I expected to. I thought, "Oh well, that was her life and times" as if she had brought it all on herself and her death didn't matter much to anyone. Probably not even to Jim, I thought callously, even though I knew that was untrue. I was deliberately unsympathetic because Jim had never endeared himself to us. He barely shared her. I suppose I felt she'd been taken from us a long time ago and that made our grieving difficult. Grieving for what? A lost sister? She had been lost to us since he met her. I had had the barest access to her for forty years and now we couldn't even have some of her family belongings or photographs to keep. Jim said later there were no photographs. There was no wake either. Jim left the crematorium straight after the funeral and drove home alone.

It was all, thus, a bit cheerless. Our family hardly spoke, even to each other. As usual we remained silent about our feelings.

"That was the way we've been brought up," I said to my brother Tom as we left. "Never complain, never explain. Accept your lot. Jim can do what he likes to our Cynthia. We suffer in silence. God forbid that anyone speak up on her or our behalf. Or offend tight-lipped Jim! We're the same as we always were."

"Not you, you're not the same," said Tom, "that's why I'm proud of ya."

It was a difficult thirty-one years from 1953 to 1984 and I don't think, dear reader, that you want to hear any more details about bringing up my children, exams, broken teenage romances (one my son Bill's ex girlfriends, Sheila Hardie, actually came to live with us), university, trips overseas, illnesses, operations, the death of my dear older brother Tom in 1983 at seventy-five, running hotels, learning to play bridge, making friends in Collaroy, and generally settling into old age.

Through all this movement and turmoil I tried to emotionally support my children as best I could and Harry did his best to help them financially and practically. I kept in touch weekly with my half-sister Winnie and to a certain extent Eva and my brother Gilbert. Winnie and I rang each other on Sunday mornings (she lived in Swansea, just south of Newcastle) and completed the *Times* cryptic crossword in the *Sunday Herald* together. My old boyfriend from Mayfield, Bill Claridge, rang me whenever he could, even when he was in his eighties. So occasionally did Vic Poole. Neither of them wanted any more than just to keep in contact. I was flattered.

Jean's brother Bill in his twenties (Photo courtesy Carol Ray)

Jean's sister Cynthia in 1961 aged 55. (Photo courtesy Dale Worth)

Jean's brother Tom at his wedding, late 1936. (Photo courtesy Dale Worth)

Jean in the 1970s at Collaroy, Sydney.

However, during this time my relationship with Harry completely broke down. We became entirely alienated. Of course, it hadn't been a happy household for years, not since the early days in Warialda, but now I would dread the times when he came to stay at Collaroy or Eleebana. We always seemed to fight. We both accepted that we act as unified parents to our children when they were present, but we had nothing to do with each other otherwise. He was away relieving a pharmacy in the country whenever he could and even when he came to stay I hardly saw him. We were polite but distant, although I cooked meals for him occasionally and he gave me an allowance. It was never very friendly and sometimes became unbearable. We still upset each other.

One night at Collaroy he became so drunkenly agitated that he chased me around the house, I locked the door of my bedroom and he tried to bash the door down. I escaped through the window and hid with the neighbours till he calmed down. One of my sons found him crying at my door, saying he was having a nervous breakdown. Things weren't that happy for Harry — the mess of our marriage tormented him too. As he aged he took to heavily drinking whisky. Neither of us talked about our feelings to each other, it was beyond that. We needed counseling and psychiatric help but it was not a possibility at that time.

I found out an odd thing later. Harry told the children that getting married and having a family was the making of him, that he was nothing until he had family responsibilities. It was a pity he didn't tell me that or value me more openly. Yet I knew that, emotionally, I was too strong for him and perhaps I could have been emotionally gentler myself. Over the years I screamed at him, threw plates at him in the kitchen (and missed) and lashed out verbally. One is never completely free of blame.

My general despair worsened as I ploughed through my early seventies. I took a great deal of medication as well as sleeping tablets. I drank too much. I often went into psychiatric clinics for weeks at a time. In my sixties, my son Stephen asked me to start writing down all I could remember about my life, as it might both help me and be of interest to others. I tried to do this until my eighties. That is where all this writing began. I must admit it did start to make things clearer in my mind.

Harry died in October 1984 from the deterioration, and complications, of his pancreas. I was seventy-four he was seventy-five. His death was brought on by stress and heavy consumption of whisky. He'd been warned by his doctors not to drink. It was a sad way to die. He was working with Dianne at the General Gordon Hotel in Sydenham at the time. He was in St Vincent's hospital for a week before he died, mostly in an induced coma because of the pain. The children went to be with him but I couldn't. I went there when he was close to death and stood at the doorway for a long time looking at him lying so still, just as I had looked at my father's body at Wentworth Falls so many years before. I eventually went in closer but he seemed agitated with my presence so I left. As I did I had such a confusion of emotions that I didn't know what I felt. We had been at war too long. It was the most difficult, most regretful moment of my life.

While I stood at the doorway I remembered back to Warialda in 1938 when he had proposed to me with so much ardour. The emotional chaos of our marriage wasn't particularly his fault or mine. It was mostly that we weren't suited and weren't capable of discussing it rationally. I believe Harry should never have married. My original love for him had died long ago and I found myself in the hospital looking at a man who was almost a stranger even though we'd been together for forty-five years and he was the father of my children. I didn't feel proud of myself at that moment, it was a failed marriage on many levels and I'd always hoped for a happy one. It wasn't all bad though. We had stuck it out, we never divorced and I think the children benefitted from that when they were young, despite our fights. It was an emotional release and relief for me when he eventually died. I always respected the way Harry provided for his family. That was important. Financially he'd left me relatively secure, the children were all financially independent, I had access to the old age pension and I owned the house at Collaroy. I'd come to terms with my long marriage. I wasn't bitter about Harry, he was who he was, I was disappointed in myself for my original decision. I'd been right about him in one sense, as a loyal provider, but I'd misread him emotionally. That was all in the past now. I should have been happier.

My life wasn't miserable or difficult. I mostly lived alone with my cats in the house at Collaroy, and my children were all busy with relationships, work and families. I played bridge four or five times a week with good friends. I was an enthusiastic reader of books from the local library (had been all my life) and I did a mature students' course in literature at the University of Newcastle. I enjoyed a small flutter on horse races, a legacy from my time with the sign-writing boys in Newcastle and at the Warialda picnic races. I watched the races on television, unheard of in my day, which always made

Jean visiting her father's house, in 1989. Tom Sharp built the house in 1904–05. Jean lived there briefly as a child.

my Saturdays. I often had my friends and children to dinner and sometimes they came to stay for a while. Eventually there were four grandchildren. In one sense, I was a normal widow of a businessman.

Yet none of this stopped my depressions . . . the way they strongly attacked me when I was alone and lonely. No amount of bridge parties or close friends, relations or even charity work could halt those demons. I had plenty of psychiatric help and plenty of medication but the unresolved torment continued.

I became suicidal . . . drinking too much and taking so many sleeping pills that I was unable, sometimes, to walk to my bedroom from the living room. Embarrassingly, my sons often found me collapsed on the floor in the hallway, semi-conscious from sleeping pills and alcohol. I didn't know what was happening to me. I told myself that I had achieved things in my life, I wasn't worthless, my children valued me. I'd stayed married to Harry for them. I was pleased that I would be able to leave my children some money. More than had been done for me, although I never ceased loving my father. Love and kindness, you can't beat them. None of this was enough.

I had proved myself with the dress shop in Moree. I thought, I can cope

. . . I have a lot of friends . . . permanent friends. I had built a life and it wasn't going to fall down. It never had before. I wish I could have married the love of my life but it wasn't ever to be . . . and in any case he may have changed too . . . lovers have a habit of doing that. Are relationships ever perfect? I had those two encounters later in my life but they meant nothing. I wish people would get some of these "affairs" into perspective. I don't regret either of them. I needed them; they kept me sane. No one was badly hurt or lost anything. Harry never knew or, I think, cared. Harry himself had continued his infatuations and dalliances but by then I had long since stopped being concerned.

Working this all out in my mind helped but didn't stop the depressions. They were getting worse and worse. Fortunately, although I didn't know it, a change was on the way.

42 · The tarot reader

One Christmas, when I was in my very late seventies, my daughter Dianne, now back from New York where she had worked as a secretary, gave me a present, a visit to a tarot card reader and astrologer. She thought this particular reader might be able to help me understand my depressions. I went to see her.

He name was Jo and she was an American, about thirty-five, and living in a minute flat with a panoramic view of Neutral Bay. Dianne had told her nothing about my history, but had given her my date of birth.

She laid out the cards in front of me and said she could see already that I was born in the country and that my mother had died when I was young. She also said I had had a difficult marriage and my husband was dead.

That was impressive. We talked.

She said I had a problem that had tormented me for years but that the problem wasn't my marriage or my husband. I was reminded of what Dr Wheatley had said years ago in Warialda.

The problem she said was, of course, my mother.

"Yes," I said, "my stepmother."

"No," she said, "not your stepmother, your real mother."

I was surprised. My birth mother? A problem? No. Surely not. How? She was a martyr, a saint, long dead.

Jo went on to say that my birth mother had made a choice in the Moree hospital in 1912, an adult choice that was to deeply affect my life. She said my childish conception of the past and of my mother's actions — that I was tragically robbed of my heroic mother and brutally given to an unfeeling stepmother — was psychologically misleading.

She tried to put the past into perspective for me. She said that my birth mother might have unconsciously wanted to die, despite being a strong woman, because she found life very hard to cope with in the country. It was very primitive in those days. She had to cope with the hardships as well as look after her husband and children. Whatever, she said, my mother had the choice at childbirth to stay in hospital and recover or risk everything and go home. She went home against advice and chose to risk her life. Foolish when she had three children at home, a new baby and a husband who had urged her to stay in hospital.

Jo surmised that my mother was waiting for my forgiveness for abandoning me, that she knew she had made a mistake, that she had let me and her other children down. She said that my stepmother Annie had come into my life, past a normal marrying age, ignorant of family life and desperate to have her own family. She hadn't known how to raise me or my siblings except as she remembered her family had been raised. Yet she had stayed and persevered, with the man who had chosen her sister as his wife. She was aware she could never replace her sister in his affections. That had been very hard for her.

This made me think more impartially about Annie. Perhaps Jo was right. I had always thought of my mother as a heroine, a tragic victim of circumstances and Annie as a manipulating, grasping stepmother. For the first time in my life I allowed myself to see things slightly differently.

Under Jo's guidance I stood in Annie's shoes for a moment and realised how ignorant she was, how uneducated, how dependent on the traditions of the Methodist church and the way of life for women at that time. Her sister — my mother — was the eldest child in the family and the most successful — a headmistress. Looking after her four children was an unexpected burden and as an unmarried woman in her thirties she didn't have much time to have her own children. Annie had no choice but to take on the burden of her sister's children. In those days she was obligated, whether she liked it or not. She knew nothing about mothering or being a wife and had to learn fast. No wonder she stuck to her religious principles and upbringing, she had little else to guide her.

Jo went on to say that Annie probably had experienced very little open emotion as a child, being from such a large family in those times, and she was thus unable to show emotion herself. She wouldn't have been able to understand my feelings of rebellion.

I was impressed. This was a new way of thinking for me.

We were all victims, Jo said, if we allow ourselves to be. Everyone has a problem with his or her parents. It's one of life's repeating dilemmas. She made me feel proud of myself that I got out of it all, survived and found a life for myself but it would have been better if I had understood earlier what was happening to me, and maybe easier for me if I'd understood my stepmother's actions objectively. Marrying Harry was my way out of the dilemma but he, too, had problems of childhood. He hated being poor and fought those demons, but I wasn't to blame for his demons. Harry had to deal with them and, despite my resentment, he, too, never abandoned me even if he was emotionally unsupportive. He could have taken off to Queensland forever or overseas and disappeared — a lot of men have — but he didn't. He never abandoned our children, he stuck by them and made sure they could all make a decent living. He had been a good husband and father in that sense, I agreed. My son Geoffrey put these grateful words on his grave: "He cared for his family."

Despite the hardship and the lack of a loving husband, Jo said, my stepmother did raise me, fed me, clothed me, and kept me healthy — she did her duty. She didn't leave me to fate; she tried, in her own way, to stick by me, even though her life wasn't easy. It was her own upbringing that stifled her. And it wasn't just Annie herself that affected me . . . it was the relative poverty of our family and the apparent indifference of my father that had hurt me. That hurt had stayed with me, buried but not dead, for seventy years.

Jo said it was time I came to terms with the past and dealt with my resentments in a more adult fashion, not from the point of view of an eleven-year-old. My life at home in Mayfield had been as good as it could have been.

It was a long and powerful session. I went home with a lot to think about.

Back at home, I began to think things through. Annie was a convenience for my father and she knew it. She reacted to looking after three of her sister's children by making them "helpers" to her as she coped with her own three young children. She hadn't seen what she did to them or how much they needed her love too, just like her own children. She simply tried to build a life for herself in the same way she'd been brought up and which was justified by her religion. She was never deeply thoughtful. I saw all that now; I couldn't then. She had been, in fact, a rather unknowable figure for me as a child.

It was only after the tarot card reading that I talked gently to her, in my imagination, in my bedroom, for the first time in my life. I had tried to never think about her and I had been somewhat mean to her over many years. She hardly was ever invited to our house and I gave her very little money even though I knew she was poor. I expected Winnie and her own children to look after her although I knew Tom was generous to her. She came to Newcastle once and to Warialda once with my young half-sister Eva. I stayed angry with her all those years and I knew she never understood why. She spent all her time praying and reading the Bible with Eva who joined the Children of God religious group and became sexually involved with one of its leaders, Fred X. As a fourteen-year-old schoolboy my son Stephen told me he was ashamed that they were in such a state after he visited Grandma Sharp one Sunday. She was living in a large rented bedsitter with Eva in Lucas Road, Burwood, in very poor conditions. He thought we could have helped them. I refused to be sympathetic even then. I had been cruel.

It might have been too late but I decided to ask for her forgiveness for my behaviour. I had been wrong to blame her for so much. I didn't forgive her for the beatings and harsh treatment I received from her as a child or for not telling me about my mother but I tried to understand why she acted that way and why she'd needed to favour her own children. I could see more clearly how overwhelmed by her circumstances she was, how lacking in education and why she'd hung on to the rules of her own upbringing and religion to survive. As an eleven-year-old the treatment I received from her seemed grossly unfair but now, as an older woman with my own children, I could at least see her point of view. I felt sorry for her. She'd had a hard life, harder than mine. I rang my sister Winnie about it. She said that she never understood my attitude to the family, and that they'd all tried to help Mum with money and had valued her.

Alone in my bedroom I imagined saying to my stepmother that I understood her better now and wanted to apologise for my lack of understanding. She was long dead but I knew it was important for me to apologise to her, if only for myself. I've always found apologising hard, in fact, I have rarely apologised to anyone in my life. I forgave my birth mother for dying and leaving me, though I had never really blamed her. For those who do not believe in the afterlife this might seem futile but I knew that it was necessary . . . not for them, for me. If there *was* an afterlife they would hear, if there *wasn't* then at least I had recognised my errors of thinking.

I felt a weight lift from my shoulders. It was a relief that my depressions hadn't been about my marriage but were about my suppressed rage at not being told about my birth mother. It was tangible. The long-held hurt slowly weakened as I began to understand and stopped condemning Annie. That surprised me.

This mightn't have been just because of the tarot reader. I had sought psychological help and had been in and out of clinics for years. Katherine, my psychiatrist, had a powerful effect on me, counseling me to accept the things I could not change, to accept other people as they were, accept the past, the family silence, the symptoms of ageing and my marriage . . . let it go . . . give up the struggle. Live in the moment, she advised, live one day at time, one moment at a time. Be willing to take guidance, she advised.

Well, I was more than ready to take Jo's guidance.

During the months that followed, my depression lifted. At first, I didn't believe it. I thought it was temporary, but the release proved permanent. I knew then that the root cause of my despair and insecurity was not my marriage but my childhood in Mayfield and my inability, as Jo said, to break away from my childish view about what I thought happened to me. I still felt alone, vulnerable and sad about that childhood but now, at least, I wasn't going to die in a deep depression.

In fact, I was about to "celebrate" my childhood in Mayfield.

43 · Return to Bull Street

One weekend in 1989 my daughter Dianne and I spent two nights at a motel in Singleton in the Hunter Valley as a relief from the city. On our way home, I casually mentioned to Dianne that as we were travelling through Mayfield on our way home we should make a detour so she could see the home where I spent my primary school years from ages six to eleven.

We turned off Maitland Road at Hanbury Street, Mayfield, and after a few mistakes arrived at that sturdy little home in Bull Street, now the Industrial Highway. There it stood, a plain stone-coloured (once green) little house quite on its own. The old Lysaght Welfare centre was on its left and it looked out over Stewart and Lloyd's as if seeing through it and down to the Hunter River. I don't know how old the house was but I told Dianne it sheltered me from 1916 to 1921 — I don't know when it was first built. It still stood proudly and starkly there and I felt proud of it for the first time in my life. I had always been ashamed of it.

I told Dianne it had no bathroom and no sitting room, only three bedrooms and a kitchen with a few wooden chairs and a deal table and a dresser. When we lived there we didn't bother about numbers on houses, you lived next door to somebody else. We lived next door to the Lempkes on one side ("Where are you Harold?") and Mrs Nelmes on the other ("No, Mervyn can't come in today because Winnie hits him"). After that were the Gullivers and next to them lived the Russells. Old Mrs Russell who always dressed in black and had a strange daughter who was "Miss Russell" to us kids. The Russells' house is now Simpson's Cottage and is a National Trust house. Only the western side of Bull Street had houses on it down our end in those days. We faced the BHP golf course and a Chinese market garden and a few dairy farms down to Ingall Street and after that there was only a swamp until the BHP.

The old house was now on a non-stop big truck highway. Dianne drove her car up the driveway and pulled up beside the house. I cheekily hustled out of the car and walked right around to the back of the house, all pebble-decked now — the black sandy soil I knew covered over. The house was now a government office of some kind. As I looked around at the rear I became aware of a small but voluble man with a large dog shouting at my daughter Dianne at the front of the house. I went to defend her. He turned to me and asked angrily who I was and what I was doing there.

I said I used to live here once and he said, "No you must be mistaken. I'm sure you never lived here." He went back over the tenants in his mind out loud and our family wasn't one of them. However, I stuck to my guns and he eventually quietened down and started to think. He asked what year I was talking about? It seems he was thinking only as far back as 1926 and I was able to say I went further back to 1916 to 1921. He then changed his tone completely. He believed me but put me through the third degree before he completely trusted me.

Did I know Mrs Richard who had a small shop in Vine Street? Yes. Who had the other shop? I knew. And, finally, he thought to ask me what my name was. I said Jean Sharp and he said did I know Tom Sharp. Yes, he's my father. And Tommy Sharp? I was Tommy's sister. His face crinkled up in a huge grin.

"I knew them all," he said. "You are right. You did live here."

He was an old Welshman by the name of Jack Pitt who was the caretaker of our now government-owned house on Bull Street. He lived just around the corner in Avon Street.

He became more excited. "Come around to my house and I'll show you some old photos," he said. "Do you remember it was called Pommy Town? Do you remember Gwillan Allen?"

I did remember and I did know Gwillan Allen, of course. They were the first Pommies I had met. They used to live at 23 Avon Street. All the Welshmen I knew — Di Anstey, Bill Arthur, Sid Merchant, Bill Tozer — were mentioned. I couldn't remember the Oatens he mentioned, although I had heard of them. But I did remember "Bouncer" Bill Claridge, of course, who was my boyfriend for a while (told me I was pretty and who still rang me up), and Jack Hunt the Welsh boy I had been in love with but never spoke to. All the Welsh names came back to me — no wonder my star of stars was Cary Grant in *An Affair to Remember* because he was a Welshman and fascinated me. My first contact with another culture was with these Welsh. Such lovely voices and different expressions: "Yes indeed to goodness" and "I sat down and cried bitter". My memories of them were strong.

"We lived in this old house which had a huge backyard," I told him, "and it belonged to my grandfather who actually owned all the houses around there, ours, Nelmes', a vacant block, then Gullivers' house. He also owned the land behind them, which ran halfway to Crebert Street. How he came to own it all I never knew. Certainly, we never shared in the wealth. And when he died there wasn't much left."

Avon Street, I informed my daughter, was born when Lysaght purchased Grandad's land to build houses for their workers.

We went into the first house in Avon Street, number 23, Jack's house, whose backyard cut off our garden, which must have broken Dad's heart at the time. They were well built brick houses with bathrooms and with the sewer on, unlike ours. The Allens were the first Welsh people in this house, but the only occupant since then I realised was this man, Jack Pitt.

I remembered at that moment a man named Bob Miller, one of the foremen of Lysaght who moved into Gullivers' house, saying to my father, "You come along w'me on Sundee, Tom, and I'll show you over t'works."

Photo after photo came out from Jack Pitt — mostly men in football teams — he didn't mention any women except a Mrs Richards, a lady who was very pretty and dark with a creamy complexion. I remembered her myself. I remembered the workmen in these football teams were the workmen my father steered Cynthia and me away from in the 1920s.

Jack Pitt showed us through his home and introduced us to his wife, Wyn, who was busily cooking Sunday dinner. He showed us more photographs.

He asked if I'd like to go out to his garden and see the pump my father had first put in. My heart stood still. I was going to place my hands on our old pump with its black head and long black handle. We used to pump deliciously cold water on the hottest day. Like everyone we also had water tanks. But alas there was only the pipe sticking out of the ground.

"But where is the black head and long curved handle?" I asked.

The image of it was so strongly stamped in the brain of my childhood self that I could almost see it in front of me.

"Somebody stole them when I was away," he said.

I was heartbroken. It would have been wonderful to see it again. In memory I saw our cow Nellie being leg-roped and milked and the quince and guava trees and Dad's garden and his tomatoes and onions and his neat tool shed and a stack of *Bulletins,* and me a brat of a kid with no sense.

I had lived in Newcastle with my husband for many years and had been past Mayfield a hundred times in my later adult life but I had always been too frightened of bad memories to visit our old house. Now I realised someone was still alive who had known us and remembered our family with admiration.

Talking to Jack Pitt that day I felt proud and happy to have lived there, to have had Tom Sharp as my father and Tommy and Cynthia as my siblings. I hadn't been back there for about seventy years but it seemed like yesterday. The big difference was how I felt.

Thank God for that good little Welshman who gave me the opportunity to realise I had nothing to be ashamed of.

44 · So . . .

The trauma of my life has been, as I've detailed throughout this memoir, that as a child I wasn't told that my birth mother had died and that the person I called "Mum" and treated as my mother, who I thought treated me like a "slave", was my aunt. My family says I should have known, that it was never a family secret, that Cynthia knew, that Tommy vaguely knew, that even my younger brother Bill had been told by Grandma, and that it was not such a big deal.

But it *was* a big deal, for me. I didn't know. I never knew. It was too big an emotional exercise for the members of my family who felt they could not break the "silence of the Sharps" and discuss my mother's death with me. To tell me I was mistaken to call Annie "mum". It was too complex an operation . . . too difficult for any family member to deal with my confused reaction or deal with the angry reaction of the rest of the family for bringing the subject up.

Cynthia should have told me. It's true that it might never have occurred to her. Why would it? She struggled enough in her own life. No need to spoil my illusions. She hardly recollected it herself. She was only six at the time and it had traumatised her.

Why didn't Dad tell me? I knew I was his favourite but still he never thought to tell me or explain till later. He implied he thought I knew, that somehow I remembered and it was too painful to bring up. I don't know . . . it was odd that in all that time he never mentioned her name.

I suppose everyone in our family was unhappy in some way that prevented them speaking. By the time I was old enough to be told about my mother, it was far too late for Cynthia and Tom, too suppressed in their minds. And it was a taboo subject for my parents.

I forgave Cynthia because she was my sister and I couldn't blame my father because he lived in the fog of a lost marriage and was always nice to me. So I blamed Annie for everything. And I lived that blame for the rest of my life. This, coupled with our family's disheartening apathy, absence of ambition or fight and my feelings of not being loved, all suppressed for years, had caused my depression. As Jo said, I never escaped my child-self. I felt so differently now. I saw it clearly and without resentment.

* * *

I have been, in lots of ways, an ordinary woman with ordinary faults and strengths but my intentions have always been honorable, although yes, I've been good and bad, like everyone. Most people don't admit to any "sordid" details in their life, but we all have secrets we'd rather others didn't know about. I may have been considered attractive when I was young, I may have loved many men and been loved by many, I may have had a failed marriage and an alienated husband, I may have betrayed him and he me, I may have annoyed many friends or hurt some, but I was always honest and hopeful. Maybe not always brutally honest but then who can afford to be that when people can get unnecessarily hurt? No one likes relentless honesty; we would rather live with a few illusions.

The most important things in my life were my children. I was always maternal, even as a child, and I wanted to make something of my life with my children. When they came I was passionate about them and their welfare, I lived for them and they benefitted from that. I was proud of them all. They were my best work.

I also built a life that was comfortable without help from my original family. I was loyal to all of my friends and siblings. I kept friendly contact with my old lovers, even from when I was sixteen. I lived and loved as best I could. I didn't achieve anything exceptional for society and never was going to but I contributed to life here as passionately as I could, within my limitations. I was a midwife. I was a loving and supportive mother of four. I worked in the Red Cross for the war effort. I was a wife to the best of my ability even if the marriage failed. I was a steadfast friend to many. Isn't that something to achieve?

How do you make a victory out of an ordinary life? Do we need to see life in terms of victory or defeat? I think I've learnt that all victories are transitory and all failures are, well, just an opinion and certainly not fatal. Perhaps life is always a matter of struggle, for survival, for experience, for love, rather than a summation of achievements. There is no *Newcastle* or *Sydney Morning Herald* obituary for me, nor should there be.

I feel grateful that I have lived Australia's history in my over eighty years of life, like a kind of pioneer. Born in the outback, living in Wallsend during its coal-mining era, living through the First World War as a child, living through the life of the BHP steelworks in Mayfield, through the life of Lysaght, the Crown Street Hospital in Sydney in the thirties, the Harbour Bridge opening, the Great Depression, the Second World War, life in a country town during that war and the prosperity and struggle after the War. Bringing up a family in various cities and towns in New South Wales, including Newcastle, in the fifties and sixties during a troubled marriage.

Despite everything, I always felt I was a loving part of this world. I don't die disgruntled or unhappy; I die worn out and satisfied, like my sweet grandmother. I gave the world and my family all I had to give, there was no more left in me. I survived. I die without the mental depressions I once suffered. I die, as much as one can, at peace with the world. I hope the world is at peace with me.

Jean's mother Wilhelmina Susan Sharp (née Hibberd) as a very young woman. Jean never saw this photo. (Courtesy Darelyn Dawson, granddaughter of Margaretta, Wilhelmina's sister)

Epilogue

"The silence of the Sharps" and the hurt behind that phrase was voiced to me by my mother as soon as I was old enough to understand. It has taken most of my life and her writing for this memoir for me to fully appreciate why that "silence" affected her life so strongly.

Throughout my life, and the lives of my two brothers and sister, Mum told us stories about her childhood in Mayfield during the First World War, about her father, her difficult stepmother, her often unkind older sister. We never met our grandfather but we all met Grandma Sharp, who appeared to us kids as rather frail and withdrawn, even sad; we met Cynthia too, who was extremely intelligent if self deprecating, but so uneasy with us it was hard to imagine her as a bully.

I sat in kitchens all over New South Wales and listened to Mum's stories for years and years without fully understanding them or knowing why they were so important to her. She said she felt sad all the time. As we children grew up her "sadness" grew worse, she went into clinics for months at a time and sought permanent therapy. She became a heavy drinker and consumer of sleeping tablets. I'd often come home to Collaroy and find her semi-conscious on the floor in the hallway, unable to get to her bedroom. Once I had to lift her up in my arms like a child and carry her to her room.

I believe the unconditional love she sought in life ultimately came from her children. There never was "silence" in our house and never a lack of motherly affection. Or love for her. She was as loving a mother as you could get. I realise now how important this love was to her and why. I wish I'd known then.

She was both sympathetic to and proud of her children, loyal to her wealth of friends, emotionally and financially generous all her life, despite her pain and anger. Two of her former Mayfield boyfriends came to her memorial service in Sydney. Her sister Winnie asked to be buried with her in her grave in Byron Bay and named her fourth child Cheryl Jean. She was unaware of the strong effect she had on people. She lived through difficult times, especially for women, but she never gave up fighting for herself, her children or trying to understand her past. At the end of her life she was exhausted, she had no more to give. What she didn't give us in life she willed to us children in death. She would have been both thrilled and embarrassed to see this memoir in print. It would have made her struggles more worthwhile as she had loved books, bookshops and libraries all her life. She knew the memoir wouldn't be completed in her lifetime (or maybe never) but she wrote it anyway.

Whatever her story it is part of us all, my brothers Bill and Geoff, my sister Dianne, our dad, myself and of course Mum's own siblings Cynthia, Tom, Bill, Winnie, Eva and Gilbert (with their spouses and children), who lived it with her.

She died in November 1995 in Byron Bay, New South Wales. She had moved there only six months before to be near my brother Bill. She was eighty-five.

Stephen Wallace

Index

Note: bolded and italicised page numbers refer to photographs.

Adams, Miss (at Winns), 92
Aeroplane Jelly song, 195
Ah Fong, 3, 189
Albion Hotel, Hannell Street, Wickham, 38
Allen, Gwillan, 219
Annesley Court, 50
Anstey, Di, 219
Arnold, John (dentist), 137
Arnott 'Holme', 50
Arnott, William, 50
Arnott, Long Bill, 50
Arnotts factory, Cooks Hill, **59**
Arthur, Bill, 219
Ash Island, 52
Avon Street, Mayfield, 44
Ayton, John, 121

Balmoral, 199
barber shop, Newcastle, 162
Battle of Britain aircraft names, 153
Battle of the Coral Sea, 166
Baz, Jo, 145
Baz, Normie, 147
BHP steelworks, Mayfield, 19–**21**, **34**
Binegar, NSW, 124
Bingara, NSW, 129, 138
Blackfriars, Sydney, 79
Blake, Sexton (author), 28, 87
Bon Ton (shop), 95
Boomi, NSW, 4, **5**, 6, **211**
Boundary Road, Plattsburg, 13, **15**
Braye, Cragg and Cohen (lawyers), 81
Breckenridge (family), 57
Brown, John, 79
Brown, Amy, 157
Brown, Jack, 170
Brown, Gwen, **192**
Brown's (paper shop), Mayfield, 46
Browns (family), 180
Bryant, Walter, 90
Bull Street house, Mayfield, 18, 20–22, **49**, 55, 218
Bundocks (family), 180
Burgess, Tessie, 157

Cameron, Lockie (Lachlan), 150
Cameron, Mrs Hazel, 150
Carrol, Lewis: *Oxford to London 1884* (poem), 27
Casey, Brian, 201

Casino, Mrs, 55
Cazneaux sisters, 81
Champness, Miss Olive, 65, 67
Charleville, Queensland, 64
Chinese market gardens, 47, 55
Church of England ball, 147
Clarice (maid), 179
Claridge, Bill, 97, 206
Clarke Agnes (matron), 103, 110
Cleal (family, Noel, Les), 132
Colonial Sugar Refinery Company Ltd, The, 33
Cox's dairy farm, **53**, 57
Cooks Hill Intermediate High School, 30
Cookseys (family), 50
Cooper, James Fenimore (author), 28
Cootamundra hospital, 112, **114**
Crebert Street, Mayfield, 25, 44, 55, 220
Crebert, Harold C., 41
Croppa Creek, NSW, 125
Croppa, Louise, 194
Crown Street Women's Hospital, 100–11, **102**, **105**, 121

Dalgarno, Matron, 152
Darcy, Les, 29
Darwin bombing, 161
David, C., 112–14
David Jones' and Farmer's catalogues, 148
de Groot, Captain, 106–7
Dinsmore, Elsie (author), 49–50
Ditchfield, Mr, 139
Dolgelly, NSW, 4–6, 74
Dudley public school, 25
Duncan's, Miss (shop), 95
Dunkirk, 153–5
Dunstan, Norma, 156
Durham (family), 57
Durkin, Jim (saddler), 145

East Sydney slums, **109**
Eastwood Methodist church, 141
electric trams, 45
Elphick, Jeanette, **194**
Emden sinking (German cruiser), 31
Exclusive Plymouth Brethren, 137, 141, 175

Fallon, Bill, 171, 199–200

Gallus, Erma, 127

227

Game, Sir Philip (Governor), 107
Gane, Harry, 29, 48
georgette hat, 95
Giles, Mr (chemist), 46
Gleason (family), 55
Goldman, Bill, 150
Goninans, 35, 50, 57
Gosford, NSW, 6, 8–11
Gournama, NSW, 125
Grant, Cary, 200
Gravesend, NSW, 124, 132, 134, 137, 156
Greenbah, 79
Gullivers (family), 55, 220
Gunyerwarildi, NSW, 125
Gwydir River, 190

Hadleigh, NSW, 124
Hanbury Street, Mayfield, 2, 39, 42–4, 218
Hardie, Sheila, 206
Harrison, Dr Selwyn, 105
Hawthorn, Lillian, 82
Healey, Reverend Father, 131
Henry, Mrs, 25
Hibberd, Maggie, 37, 71, **73**, 79, 99
Hickson, Brian, 170
Holloway, F. G. (dentist), 99
Hong Yuens, 145
Hooke, Margaret, 157, **169**
Hooke, Mr (dentist), 157
Horton, Miss, 82
Hunt (family)
    Jack, 63, 82
    Margaret, 82
    Mrs, 171
    Rosalyn, 82
Hunter Girls' High, 81, 92
Hunter Street, Newcastle, **94**

Ingall Street, Mayfield, 25, 54, 55, 57, 61, 218
Inverell, ii, 124–5, 129

Jellet, Dr Henry (author: *A Practice of Gynaecology* or *A Short Practice of Midwifery*), 133, 137–8, 145, 147–8, 177, 180, 183
Julie frock (dress), 95

Kamilaroi (Gamilaraay), 143
Kandos, 151
Keats, John quote from *La Belle Dame Sans Merci*, 27
Kellys Gully, NSW, 126
Kerr Street, Mayfield, 55, 57
Khayyam, Omar (*Never blows so red the rose,* poem), 123
Kratz, Louis, 129
Kuhn, Kitty, 55
Kydie Gowns, 193

Lanagan, Athol, 157, 170
Lanagan, Lance, 157
Lanagan, Pauline, 145, 157, 180
Lane and Trewartha (grocery shop), 57
Lang, Jack, 95
Latham, Mr, 57
Lauder, Gilbert, 64
Lee, Nelson (author), 28
Lempke, Mrs, 29, 55, 68–9
Lempke, Mr, 52, 55
Loy, Meta, 157
Lysaght, John, 61
Lysaght ironworks, **53**, 61–3, **62**

MacIntosh, Angus, 128
Mackays (family), 125
Mactiers (family), 157
Maitland Road, Mayfield, 44
Mary Street, Islington, 58
Matron's Ball, 147
Mayes, Bishop, 134
Mayfield
    foreshore, **53**
    map, **22**
    public school (now East Mayfield public), 25–6, 30, 42
    terminus, **45**
    see also Hanbury Street, Maitland Road
McArthur, General, 159–61
McGregor, Alexander (butcher shop), 44, 57
McGregor (family), 57
    Mrs Jean, 132
    Mr W. D., 132
    Senior, Mr and Mrs A., 132
McMasters (family), 125, 180
McNaughton, Charlie, 38
Mehi River, 189
Mellick, Olga, 147
Merchant, Sid, 219
Merewether, NSW, 199–200
Merriwa, NSW, 112
Methodist church, Mayfield, 50
midget submarine attack on Sydney 1942, 161
Midkin sheep station, 123
Miller, Bob, 61
Miller's Signs, 94
Minmi, NSW, 14
Minter family, 57
Mo (McCackie), 163

mock weddings, Mayfield public school, 26
Moore, Roger, 145
Moree, NSW, *7*, 185
Moriaty, Frank, 170
Mormons, 181
Morrison (family), 35, 50, 57
Moss, Alice, 17
Mrs Hunter's fruit shop, 46
Mullaley (family), 57
Mungundi, 2, 3, 194
Munro, Mavis, 103, 105, 115, 121
Musk, Mrs (mother), 156
Musk, Teddy, 156
My Daddy is only a Picture (Eddy Arnold), 196

Nellie Stewart gold bangles, 35
Nelmes, Mervyn, 218
Nelmes, Mrs, 55, 220
Nelson, Morry, 170
Newcastle Beach, 1, 68
Newcastle Central School, 81
Newcastle Morning Herald and Miners Advocate, The, 31
Norgard (family
    Nellie, 35, 46, 55
    old Mrs, 55
    Peter, 55

Oatens (family), 219
Owens (family), 180

Page, Miss (Mrs Wells), 147
Pallamalawa, NSW, 124
Paragon Café, Kistofferson's café, Beaumont Street, Hamilton, 85-6, 90
Parker's dairy, 190
Parkes, Misses (drapery shop), 44, 59
Parks, Maizie, 14, 16
Patey's Lane, 94
Pearl Harbour attack, 159-61
Peate (family)
    Tesse, 157
    Molly, 157
    Tom, 170
penicillin discovery, 167
Phillips, Nat, 163
Pilditches (family), 180
Pitt, Jack, 219-21
Plattsburg High School First Year 1922, *16*
Plattsburg, NSW, 13, *15*
Plattsburg Primary School Class 4 1916, *16*
Please give me a penny sir? (song), 9
Pommy invasion, 61-3
Pommy Town, *49*, 219

Poole, Vic, 98
Powell, the Reverend William, 125, 130-1, 134
Pritchard, Mrs, 55
Pyrke (family)
    Colin, 145, 170, 183
    Mr Colin, 126
    Jimmy (death), 183

Quinlan, butcher, 145

Ray, Carol, vii
Raymond Terrace, 52
Reading, Matron, 152
Red Cross, 155-6
Rhodes, Cecil, 197
Richard, Mrs, 219-20
Robertson, Mr Headmaster Mayfield public school, 25
Rose, Olive, 191-2
Rosie (imaginary friend), 46
Rossetti, Christina: *At Home* (poem), 65
Roy Rene, 163
Royal Hotel, Hope Street, 134
Rundle (family), 57
Russell, Miss, 29
Russell, Mrs, 55

S.A.O. biscuits, 50
Sandy, Rita, 175
Schofield (family), 57
Sharp (family)
    Anne (aunt/stepmother), 9, 13, **73**, 197, 202, **203**, 214-5
    Bertha (aunt), 13
    Bertram (uncle), 13, 38
    Bill (brother), 12, 31, 39, 81, 115, 205, **207**, 222
    Cynthia (sister), 3, **5**, 6, 8-10, 26-8, 40-1, 64, 90-9, 118-19, 162-5, 202, 205-6, **207**, 222
    Donald Wilhelm *see* Bill
    Ernest (uncle), 13, 18-23, 38, 115, 155
    Eva Edgecomb (sister), 39, 197, 216
    Gilbert, 81, 206
    Harriet (aunt), 38
    Jack (Ernie's son), 155
    Janet (aunt), 1, 86
    Janet (grandmother), 12-13, 58, 74, 78-9, 80, 86
    Maude (aunt), married name Lauder, 13
    Mary (aunt), 13
    Oliver (uncle), 13, 38
    Rita, 118
    Ruby (Ernie's wife), 155, 200
    Stuart Granville (brother), 12, 29-30

Thomas (grandfather), 4, 85, 115
Tom (brother), 3, 5-6, 37, 87-9, 206, *207*, 215
Tom (father), *4-5*, 13, 51-4
Tom (father's death), 114, 117-8
Wilhelmina (née Hibberd), 68-79, *80*
Winifred (Winnie) Ayton (sister), vii, 10, 12, 23, 25, 28, 31, 39, 64-5, 68, 70, 81, 85, 115, 119, 121, *122*, 139, 162, 202-3, 206, 215-16, 218, 225-6
Shaw, Sister Edna, 101, *102*, 103, 110
Simpson, Charles (Collector of Customs), 55
Small, Cheryl Jean, vii
Smith, Mrs, 131
Smith, the Right Reverend P. A., 131, 134
Snape, Chaddie, 145
Sorely, George, 180
Spanish Flu, 38
Stanley, Harold (Jim), 119
steam trams, 42, *43*
Stephenson (family)
Stephenson, Mona, 157
Stephenson, Nell, 157
Stevenson, Thell, *133*
Stove, Bob, 25, 42
Strike Me Lucky (film), 163
Sydney Flour song, 191
Sydney Harbour Bridge opening, 105, *106*

Tafon, 213
tarot reader Jo, 213
Taylor, Bill, 52
Taylor, P. G. (married to Pauline Lanagan's sister), 157
terraced houses, Newcastle Beach, 40
Tobruk, 153
Towns, Theo, 52
Tozer, Bill, 219
Trewartha, old Mr, 57
Trewarthas (family), 35, 50, 57

Vaisey's shoe store, 46
Vine Street house, Mayfield, 81

Wallace (family)
Dianne, 189, 200, 204-5, 210, 213, 218, 226
Geoffery, *169*, 171, 185, 192-3, 201, 205, 215
Harry (Henry) 134, *141*, *144*, 210
Howard (Harry's father), 137
Stephen (birth etc.) *169*, 170, 180-1, 185, 192, 195-6, 201, 204-5, 209
William (Bill), 153, *154*, *160*, *169*, 181, 192-3, 197-8, 201, 204
Wallsend, NSW, 13, *14*
Wallsend-Plattsburg public school, 15-16

Waratah, Newcastle, 2, 25, 36-7, 42, 44, 49-56, 88-9
Council Chambers, 36, *37*
Hill (Braye Park), 52
Park (Braye Park), 52
Public School original school, *26*
Waratah House (Simpson's Folly), *53*, 55, *56*
Warialda, 125, *126*, 143-9
District Hospital, 122
Church of England, 134
Hope Street, *133*, 135, *147*
Pharmacy, *147*
Presbyterian church, 126, 131
Warialda Creek, 125, 128, 134, 143, 151, 167, 184, 189
Weinberg, Charlie, 194
Weinthal (family)
Ethel, 132
Fred, 157, 170
Mr J., 122
Ray, 157
Wentworth Falls, NSW, 117
Westclox, 58
Whaley, Lady, 110
Wheatley (family)
Dr Arthur, 125-132, *133*, *135*, 136-184, 204
Grandma, 134
Iris, née Goldman, *ii*, 128, 132, *133*, 151-2, 170, *182*
Margaret (birth etc.), 171
Robyn (birth etc.), 170
When I survey the Wondrous Cross (hymn), 63
Whiteman, Nurse, 39
White, Mrs of Gosford, 8, 12, 79
White Way café, 145
White Way Disaster 1948, 178
Wickham school, 81
Willy's Knight, 125
Wilson, Wendy, 168
Windeyer's property, 54
Winn (family), 57
Winn, Isaac, 50
Winns (store), 35, 50, 57, 94
Wiseman, Thora, 31
Witherspoon's (grocer shop), Mayfield, 44, 57
World War 1, 15, 31-2
Worth, Dale, vii
Wyndham, Tom, 99

Yagobi, NSW, 124
Yalta Private Hotel, 201

(Left to right) Iris Wheatley, Stephen Wallace and Jean Wallace, 1995.

About the author

Jean Wallace (née Sharp) was born in Boomi, NSW, in 1910 but spent her childhood in Mayfield, Newcastle. She worked as an obstetrics nurse in Sydney and country NSW before marrying and raising four children. Always interested in writing and books she spent the last years of her life in Collaroy, Sydney. She died in 1995.

About the editor

Stephen Wallace, Jean's second son, is a filmmaker whose films include *The Love Letters from Teralba Road*, *Stir*, *Blood Oath*, *For Love Alone* and *Turtle Beach* as well as television features *Mail Order Bride*, *Women of the Sun*, *Captives of Care*, *Olive* and others. He formed his own theatre company, Impulse Theatre, and has directed 17 full length plays, mainly for schools. He received an AM for services to the Australian film industry in 2005. He is married to Fiona Verge and has two children, Lucinda and Guy.

Make Your Mark is a comprehensive, soulful, generous guide to creating a better you, from a personal AND a business perspective. Jessica has provided glorious diagrams, and generous, thoughtful step-by-step exercises. As you close the pages, having worked through the "markercises", I can personally attest to the fact you will be ready to take on the world with purpose and clarity.

EMMA MACTAGGART
Author, publisher, speaker, and founder of The Child Writes Fund, The Lighthouse Toowoomba and International Read to Me! Day

If you have ever wondered what is possible in life and how to really have it all, then read this book. Jessica makes it easy, with step-by-step instructions and philosophies that are much more than just hype. I wish I had this book years ago – it might have saved me many hours of fumbling around figuring some of these things out!

ADELE ANTHONY
Founder, director and principal lawyer of Your Legacy Lawyer

A refreshingly practical step-by-step guide to rediscovering and redefining your self-worth, love, strengths and gifts. The way *Make Your Mark* is written is an insightful way to partner with the reader. It feels as though Jessica is beside you gently taking you through the exercises. The reflections were real, personable, relatable and powerful.

ALYCE KANE
Financial services

Make Your Mark is a timely and important reminder of what it takes to make a difference in the world, whether this is for a big vision or for something that is personally important. The book is written in a way that is like sitting down with Jessica and talking directly with her: she shares personal insights, stories, humour, strategic points to think about and, most importantly, encouragement to dream BIG. Jessica reminds us that making a mark is a journey of discovery, regardless of where we are on the pathway. This is a book you, the reader, will also savour over time.

KATHY REES
Director of Only About Quality, and author of *Courageous Auditing: Beyond Compliance – Towards Being a Catalyst for Change*

Insightful and down to earth, *Make your Mark* provides useful tools and guidance to unleash the inner legend in all of us. Written from the heart, Jess takes the reader on a journey, drawing on practical examples and her own personal experiences to motivate and inspire.

SARAH WHYTE
Head of Brand